Penguin Critical Studies

# Shakespeare's History Plays: Richard II to Henry V

Dr Moseley was educated at Queens' College, Cambridge. He teaches Medieval and Renaissance literature in the University of Cambridge, and in the remissions of this activity confides his thoughts to his word-processor, a machine which has the double virtue of not answering back and garbling them only on occasion.

For Penguin he has written major studies of Chaucer's *Knight's* and *Pardoner's Tales*, a critical study of Shakespeare's *Richard III*, and is engaged on an edition of Milton's *Shorter Poems*. He has also edited and translated, for Penguin Classics, *The Travels of Sir John Mandeville*, an author for whom he retains his early enthusiasm and whom he feels to be too little known and enjoyed. He is also the author of *An Century of Emblemes*, published by Scolar Press.

*Penguin Critical Studies*
Advisory Editor:
Bryan Loughrey

# Shakespeare's History Plays

# Richard II to Henry V

# The Making of a King

**C. W. R. D. Moseley**

**Penguin Books**

PENGUIN BOOKS

Published by the Penguin Group
Penguin Books Ltd, 27 Wrights Lane, London W8 5TZ, England
Viking Penguin, a division of Penguin Books USA Inc.
375 Hudson Street, New York, New York 10014, USA
Penguin Books Australia Ltd, Ringwood, Victoria, Australia
Penguin Books Canada Ltd, 2801 John Street, Markham, Ontario, Canada L3R 1B4
Penguin Books (NZ) Ltd, 182–190 Wairau Road, Auckland 10, New Zealand

Penguin Books Ltd, Registered Offices: Harmondsworth, Middlesex, England

First published 1988
10 9 8 7 6 5 4 3 2

Printed in England by Clays Ltd, St Ives plc
Filmset in Monophoto Times

Le théâtre est un point d'optique. Tout ce qui existe dans le monde, dans l'histoire, dans la vie, dans l'homme, tout doit et peut s'y réfléchir, mais sous la baguette magique de l'art. L'art feuillette les siècles, feuillette la nature, interroge les chroniques, s'étudie à reproduire la réalité des faits, surtout celle des mœurs et des caractères, bien moins léguée au doute et à la contradiction que les faits, restaure ce que les annalistes ont tronqué, harmonise ce qu'ils ont dépouillé, devine leurs omissions et les répare, comble leurs lacunes par des imaginations qui aient la couleur du temps, groupe ce qu'ils ont laissé épars, rétablit le jeu des fils de la Providence sous les marionnettes humaines, revêt le tout d'une forme poétique et naturelle à la fois, et lui donne cette vie de vérité et de saillie qui enfante l'illusion, ce prestige de réalité qui passionne le spectateur, et le poète le premier, car le poète est de bonne foi. Ainsi le but de l'art est presque divin: ressusciter, s'il fait de l'histoire, créer, s'il fait de la poésie.

Victor Hugo, Preface to *Cromwell* (1827)

# Contents

# Foreword

There are too many books on Shakespeare, and too many people spend their time reading them rather than his plays. This book must therefore, in all courtesy, begin by apologizing for its existence.

In many years of teaching, I have been struck by two recurrent problems that face the student just beginning the study of this myriad-minded man. The first is that to get properly to grips with him a good deal of background is necessary, and the long march in through the foothills can exhaust the student before he even glimpses the peaks. For, like it or not, the past is not the same country as the one we live in, and we need maps. I felt there was a need for a book of manageable size which would gather in one place at an accessible level the essential background knowledge about the thought, the values and the theatre of Shakespeare's times. Secondly, the four plays that Shakespeare wrote about the consequences of the deposition of Richard II – which I shall call for convenience the Ricardian plays, to distinguish them from the history plays that cover the later fifteenth century – need looking at, not necessarily together, but at least in the context of Renaissance concepts of history, the history play, and the practical problems of English politics.

I have therefore written this book in two parts. In Part I, I have tried to provide some contexts for what is inevitably our *reading* of the history plays, so that perhaps we may guess at the impact they may have had on their contemporaries. I shall suggest, by implication, a way of approaching Elizabethan drama that may be generally useful. Part II is a consideration of what I think are some major issues in the Ricardian plays. (There are those who will feel they can go straight to it and start reading there.) I hope that it will be seen as an 'enabling' book, whose job is to send students back to the reading of a good annotated edition to face their own problems and responses; it emphatically does not attempt to provide a final view.

It is therefore written to be discarded; when it has, I hope, sent its readers back to Shakespeare, perhaps with an enhanced enjoyment and understanding of what are beautiful and moving and hugely enjoyable works of art, it can go back to its primeval dust.

Quotations and references are to the New Penguin Shakespeare editions.

# Acknowledgements

A list of my debts to predecessors in this field would be longer than the book itself: they have reaped the corn, and I come after, gleaning. But I have great personal debts to those long-suffering friends who read the manuscript and made invaluable comments as it grew. Many of my pupils in Cambridge, with exemplary patience, have had bits of the material tried out on them. Mr J. W. Humphreys of St John's College, Cambridge, was of particular help when I was working on *Henry V*. I am particularly grateful to Dr Stephen Coote, the best of editors, and to Miss A. J. D. Moseley, of the University of St Andrews; they made many acute comments and valuable criticisms while the book was being written, and I have only myself to blame for the ineptnesses that remain.

Reach, Cambridgeshire                                              C.W.R.D.M.
Lammas, 1987

# Part I  A Context for the Histories

# 1. Introduction

It is doubtful whether there could be a more unsatisfactory way of approaching Shakespeare and his plays than the one suffered by generations of English-speaking people. Almost universally, our first experience of the man's work is in the classroom, where – often under the shadow of impending examinations – the once fair body is dismembered into forty-minute chunks of dreamy afternoons. It is hardly surprising that the vast majority of his compulsory readers never willingly open a text or go to see a play after they escape from the educational system.

The study of the plays as printed texts can be extremely interesting and rewarding, and indeed is utterly necessary, but what has happened to the plays as academic material could not be further from Shakespeare's intentions when he wrote them. He seems, from one or two remarks and characters, to have had no love for school and to have regarded schoolmasters and academics as harmless drudges of comic self-importance. Shakespeare was a working dramatist in a very competitive world; he was writing highly topical plays to catch a particular market, and if he did not pull in an audience, the theatrical company in which he had a substantial financial share did not eat that week. What he and his fellows were selling was not a printed book but a heard and seen experience. As a result, he was far more concerned with the design of a very complex system of communication, as a tool to make the audience respond as he wished, than with a merely verbal text.

The very word 'text' raises problems to begin with. A book containing a poem or a novel may seem to be the same sort of object as a book containing a play, and we use the shorthand word 'text' to cover them all. But there are obvious dissimilarities. The novel presents the solitary reader with a complete armoury of the material the author has designed to convey what he wants to talk about; it can be read slowly or quickly, it can be put down while one gets a drink or whatever, or one can flip back a few pages to refresh one's memory. The only clues to meaning lie in the words on the page. But the play is a shared experience, taking place in a special building (in Shakespeare's day with very clear and important symbolic overtones) and it goes at the speed the actors and director decide rather than at the individual viewer's. There is no flicking back here. Moreover, our reception of any play is greatly affected by personal animal responses to the appearance, personalities and voices of the actors taking part, and by the control of those elements by the director's choice of pace, emphasis and even scenery. In everyday life much of our communication is in any case non-verbal – by inflection, tone, gesture, facial expression – and these factors obviously operate on the stage as well. In Shakespeare's case, we know that he – though apparently not a great actor himself – was deeply interested in the craft and was clearly on hand in the theatre to tell people how he wanted things played. Take a crucial example: at the end of *Lear* there are two mutually exclusive ways of playing Lear's death. He can be seen as dying in the belief that Cordelia is alive, thus on an ironic upbeat, or he can be seen as dying in utter despair. The words will carry both senses (*King Lear*, V.iii.303–9). But Shakespeare chose only one, and told his company which it was. He is not around, unfortunately, to tell us. So when we speak of a 'text' in drama, we ought to do so with a mental reservation, recognizing that we have a very complex interaction of sign systems to cope with. Especially, we ought to recognize that the printed words are merely one notation of one element in something which works not only by sound but also by vision; indeed, the dramatic spectacle is a speaking picture – a favourite Renaissance catchphrase – and the way pictures work will obviously be relevant to the way plays do. Some of these different languages – of vision, sound, movement and so on – we may be able, by scholarship, common sense and comparison with other works, to recover; some of the most important – what it felt like actually to be a Renaissance man, for instance – are unknowable.

The problem with any great art, especially perhaps the classic drama of the past, is that it works in all periods and can be significant in many different cultures where its original techniques and assumptions are not shared. One has only to look at the way in which the drama of classical Greece, originally tightly linked to a communal religious festival quite irrelevant to us now and using many techniques of which we can know little or nothing, has fertilized the minds, imaginations and art of Western men over something like two millennia. It can emotionally pulverize a completely unscholarly audience today. Moreover, ideas and concepts that have developed since a work of art was made – sometimes partly as a *result* of that work of art – can usefully and powerfully affect the way we look at it; and, conversely, the way we see it affecting us. So, for example, if people want to play *Hamlet* as a comic romp or as a Freudian exploration of sexuality, or Falstaff as the sort of uncle we all think we'd like to have (all approaches that depend on insights into human nature formulated since the plays were written), all well and good; the only proviso is that we recognize that we are bringing to the plays our own preconceptions, which may well not be Shakespeare's. But, on the other hand, many have believed over the centuries that Shakespeare is one of the greatest geniuses the world has ever seen, whose penetration and understanding of the human condition is of extraordinary profundity. I would like to think that in studying Shakespeare, as perhaps not in watching him now, we are making an attempt to open ourselves so as to get to grips with that unparalleled mind for what he has got to tell us rather than for what we can foist on him. But before we can do that, we need to learn his language. We also need to recognize that he was a man who existed in moving time like ourselves, and that his assumptions and conventions are not ours. They too are part of his language. He cannot fairly be read if we pretend he is other than he is: a man of the Renaissance, in the peculiar late form it took in England.

# 2. The Revolution of the Orbs

## A The Model and its Consequences

As I look up from writing this and glance out of the window, I see a
world which no Renaissance man could have seen. I have assumptions,
of which I am not conscious, about its nature and structure which are
the consequence of my education and upbringing at a particular point in
the development or decline of Western civilization. Renaissance men
certainly contributed to the world view a late twentieth-century middle-
aged academic might have, but they could not share my post-Newtonian,
post-Einstein views of its physical nature and structure. Nor, despite the
fact that our language and speech contain fossils of their way of looking
at things, could they have shared my view of man and his society. They
inhabited, in fact, a planet that in a real sense was different, circling a
different sun. We find their footprints on the sands of time, but must not
imagine we have nearly found Man Friday.

Before we go any further, we must examine what model of the world
they used. It is worth stressing that it was a model, and that it fitted the
facts, and how they were perceived, as they knew them at the time – just
as ours does. But all models, ours included, are temporary and provisional, and none can be in any absolute sense 'true'. And while some
things are proved to be false by subsequent thought and discoveries,
many ideas, values and systems – and models – fall into disuse not
because they are proved 'wrong' but because they are victims of the
great god fashion. Chronological snobbery, for the serious student, is
thus completely out of place. It is entirely possible that in some ways our
fathers got the business of making sense of the world right where we are
getting it disastrously wrong. We may be able to learn something of real
truth and value from the Renaissance model of the universe which no
cosmologist would now accept as physically accurate.

I have just used the word 'disastrously'. It is a fossil. We all think we
know what it means – something pretty terrible, and it has meant that for
a long time (the Second Murderer so uses it in *Macbeth*). But the word
in fact is a good starting-point for our discussion of the world-model[1]

1. As will be seen below, the model is undergoing profound changes in our own period, and
so we ought strictly to talk of more than one model. But one has to start somewhere.

of the Renaissance. In *Antony and Cleopatra* (II.vii) the First Servant says, 'To be called into a huge sphere, and not to be seen to move in it, are the holes where eyes should be, which pitifully disaster the cheeks'; which is virtually incomprehensible to us. Here 'disaster', coming from the Latin *astrum*, 'star', means literally to 'de-star', i.e. 'remove the stars from'; again, meaningless. And what is the sphere doing there? Behind this short speech lies a vision of the universe, by which men lived and died for centuries, that survives now only in the flotsam and jetsam of language and the footnotes of academic texts.

## i *Ptolemy's system*

Medieval and Renaissance men developed their model of the universe from the work of the second-century scientist, Ptolemy. There is no need to go into all its complex mathematical details; the fundamental point is that Ptolemy broke with earlier Greek models of the universe (some of which suggested a sun-centred or heliocentric universe) because they did not square with the observations of the movements of the planets (which sometimes seem to go backwards) and the constellations. He put the earth at the centre, and in his time his system was able brilliantly to account for more of the observed facts[2] than any other. What he proposed was a series of concentric spheres revolving round a stationary and spherical[3] world composed of earth, water, air and fire – the four elements of which, according to Aristotle, all matter was made. This was enclosed by the invisible sphere of fire immediately below the sphere of the visibly changing moon. All this region – the 'sublunary' world – was subject to change and decay. But above this mutable and contingent region, outside the sphere of the moon, lay the series of concentric spheres occupied by the planets ('wandering stars', in Greek) in the order Mercury, Venus, the sun (or Sol), Mars, Jupiter and Saturn.[4]

2. We must remember that the ancients had no telescopes, that the Arabic system of number (including the invention of the zero) had still to be invented (it was not used widely in Europe until the sixteenth century), and that they had no algebra – another Arabic invention, as the name suggests. Anyone who is still not convinced of the brilliance of the ancient mathematicians could try doing a multiplication sum in Roman numerals (which is impossible), and then look at what became the basic textbook of mathematics for the Middle Ages, Boethius's *De Arithmetica*.

3. The idea that medieval and Renaissance men believed in a flat earth is a nineteenth-century slander.

4. Uranus was only discovered in 1781 (by Herschel), Neptune in 1846 and Pluto in 1930.

Outside the sphere of Saturn moved the sphere of the fixed stars – what we see as constellations – and finally the Primum Mobile, or 'first movable' sphere, which was directly acted upon by the Will of the First Mover, setting it in motion. All the rest of the spheres revolved at decreasing speeds until the stationary earth was reached. The mathematics of the system were worked out in great detail, and the whole universe obeyed, apparently, mathematical rules and logic. Mathematics was seen by the ancients as the key to an understanding of the created universe, and was closely linked – as it still is – to music. The mathematical relationships between the moving spheres expressed themselves, therefore, as musical tones and notes – the music of the spheres – which, however, could not be heard on earth because they expressed perfection, and all below the sphere of the moon was by definition imperfect and subject to the changes resulting from the instability of the mixtures of the opposing elements.

We need to notice one crucial difference between our own model and this one. If we look up into the heavens (that word is another fossil) we unconsciously assume a universe that is to all intents and purposes infinite, utterly beyond what our minds can grasp; but our ancestors could not know that experience, for their universe was finite. While its size was seen as vast – Ptolemy calculates that in comparison with the distance between the centre and the sphere of the fixed stars the earth has no more dimension than a mathematical point – it is basically a comfortable universe; man even has companions in it, beings of a spiritual nature who, like him, have various functions and tasks. The Greeks called them daemons; the later Jewish thinkers identified these with angels (the word means 'messengers') and by the early Middle Ages the idea that the universe was full of invisible friends – and foes – was commonplace.

In its basics, this is the model used in late Antiquity. Its details were much elaborated and re-interpreted in the light of Christian understanding of the moral and spiritual nature of creation; the revised version lasted in the West for over a thousand years.

## ii *Ordo*

St Augustine, who died in 430 as the barbarians were breaking down the gates of his city, was neither the first nor the last to affect the understanding of the late antique model. But his life and thought have left so indelible a mark on Western thought down to the present that we must look at those of his ideas that affect the way others saw the universe they inhabited. The key concept has its roots in Plato (and his followers like Plotinus, who deeply influenced Augustine's mind); Augustine calls it *ordo*. This is usually translated as 'order', but could equally well mean 'rank', 'station' – even 'hierarchy'.

Hierarchy is certainly involved in his idea. He offers us a view that sees *everything* in the universe as having its being through the love of God in a particular place, in a particular relationship to other things, with a particular purpose to fulfil – to change the metaphor to one much explored in the Renaissance, it is as if everything had a place on a ladder or chain reaching up to God. God is, like the Aristotelian One, or the Platonic Nous, the originator of everything, loving it into existence. Love literally makes the world go round. He has designed his universe so as to give the dignity of agents to a large number of his creatures: all have a job to do for Him, and He works through them. Virtue – whether we are talking about a stone or an angel – consists, basically, in discharging the obligations of the *ordo* to which the discharger belongs, in fulfilling them by being what God wanted. Thus a stone makes, by just being, a very good stone; it will make a very poor tree – if the mind can perform such a somersault – and different stones will be suitable for different purposes. A man is not an animal, and is unvirtuous if he loses his humanity to the point where he behaves as one; and men themselves are different, so that he who has been called by God to be a ruler has obligations, responsibilities and pleasures that are not open to one who is a hewer of wood and drawer of water – who has his own. The angels likewise have their virtuous place in the hierarchy, as do the circling spheres of Heaven; if they do not stay in their places in the great and complex dance, chaos is come again.

The Augustinian idea and its concept of hierarchy is vastly and intricately elaborated in the Middle Ages. The Ptolemaic system itself becomes a metaphor; it remains, as it always was, a physical description of the universe, but it also comes to express a moral and spiritual relationship and status. For the further from the centre a creature is placed, the nearer physically and by nature of its being it is to the beatific Vision of God. At the bottom, so to speak, the pit of the spherical universe, lie those who have utterly rejected the God who created them and on whom they are still utterly dependent: the devil and all his angels. Here is where the universe nearly turns itself inside out, into contradiction, non-being, for this is as far away as they can get from the searing uncreated light of the love of God that forces them to know as they are known. In rejecting it, they damn themselves and bolt the doors of Hell behind them on the inside.[5] Above this pit is the world, a place of moral choice and endeavour, where men are capable of falling into gross sin but also of glimpsing the unspeakable joy of the love of God. Above the world, beyond the corrupting reach of the Fall of man (see below, pp.15ff.) in the spheres of the planets, are angels, each with their own job to do. Some are guardians of the individual spheres, some attend the Throne of Light. All of them give back according to their capacity the love that loved them into being.

### iii *Angels and planets*

Quite clearly, attempts were made to explain how the pagan crew of gods might fit into this system. At the end of the fifth century, Fulgentius of Ruspe had systematically tried to explain them symbolically. They were, he suggested, angels who had been appointed to look after particular areas of the universe – some, for example, looking after the spheres of the planets whose names they took (or vice versa – it makes no matter), and who, because of the great power they wielded, had been mistakenly worshipped as gods by mankind, most of whom had not had the benefit of the revelation God had vouchsafed to the Jews. Even the unsavoury stories about them – Jupiter's undignified amours or his appalling treatment of his father, for instance, can be seen as symbolic of truths about human life. (This is a position taken up again by the fourteenth-century Italian poet Boccaccio.) Thus the gods of Olympus easily turn into servants of the Most High,[6] yet keep their proprietary function – Venus looks after integration, procreation, sexual love and *copia* (plenty, fruitfulness), Mars after separation, strife and struggle, and so on. Saturn, deposed as king of the gods by Jupiter, retains his power as bringer of old age and disease that afflict all – *senectus ipsa morbus*, as

5. It should be remembered that despite the critical discussion in the Renaissance of the concept of a physical place for Hell, and a corresponding relocation of it in the mind, the idea never disappears entirely. Hell is thus both a state and a place.

6. This notion is flat contrary to the other view current in late Antiquity and the Renaissance – for example, in Justin Martyr, Tertullian or Origen, in Lancelot Andrewes, or in Milton's 'Ode on the Morning of Christ's Nativity' or *Paradise Lost* (I.735ff.) – that the gods were fallen angels: devils, in fact. But it is their planetary nature and function that is relevant at the moment. That apparently contradictory ideas of the gods of Olympus could comfortably be held at the same time is demonstrated, for instance, by Chaucer: in *Troilus and Criseyde* he sees Venus as a cosmic principle of love (III.1–49) and the group of gods to which she belongs as 'rascaille' (V.1849ff.).

Seneca said. But notice that, although Jupiter has a high and honoured place, the king of the planets is now Phoebus Apollo, god of the sun, of the mind and wisdom, the physical image of the divine Love and Wisdom that, according to the Wisdom of Solomon (xi.21) in the Apocrypha of the Bible, 'ordered all things in measure and number and weight'. The planets circle the earth in their unending, ordered dance, singing as they go (as Lorenzo tells Jessica in *The Merchant of Venice*, V.i), and transmitting to it according to their natures the powers God has given them. This 'influence' (whence our term for the originally inexplicable disease, influenza) is thought of as a physical substance passing through the air and causing, in the earth, the metal appropriate to its planets of origin to grow,[7] and effects on human beings, their societies, their animals and so on. (It is this idea that lies at the root of astrology.) The power of the planets is an expression of their superior place in the grand hierarchy of creation, and it is a moral and physical power and a position in space at the same time. Milton gives us, in Satan's first view of earth in *Paradise Lost*, a beautiful summary of these ideas:

> *O earth, how like to heaven, if not preferred*
> *More justly, seat worthier of gods, as built*
> *With second thoughts, reforming what was old!*
> *For what god after better worse would build?*
> *Terrestrial heaven, danced around by other heavens*
> *That shine, yet bear their bright officious lamps,*
> *Light above light, for thee alone, as seems,*
> *In thee concentring all their precious beams*
> *Of sacred influence: as God in heaven*
> *Is centre, yet extends to all, so thou*
> *Centring receivest from all those orbs; in thee,*
> *Not in themselves, all their known virtue appears*
> *Productive in herb, plant, and nobler birth*
> *Of creatures animate with gradual life*
> *Of growth, sense, reason, all summed up in man.*

(IX.99–113)

*officious* performing their allotted task.

One figure in this pantheon has briefly to be looked at separately: the moon, Diana, the planet whose appearance is never the same two days together, the patroness of the changeable sea, beneath whose sphere all is subject to change. By the Middle Ages the moon had become identified

7. Gold for the sun, of course; silver for the moon, copper for Venus, lead for Saturn, mercury for Mercury, iron for Mars and tin for Jupiter.

with the late antique figure of Fortune, the force that seemed irrationally to control the affairs of the world irrespective of deserts or natural justice. Fortune was often personified as a queen, blindfolded, as Fluellen in *Henry V* remembers (III.vi.29–37), standing upon an unstable ball and turning a wheel in her hands. On that wheel the great of the Earth rose and fell, whatever their merits: the noble with the despicable, the strong with the weak. This amoral figure and the concept she embodied became one of the major ideas in popular medieval and Renaissance thought, fundamental to the very nature of existence on earth. Humanity was universally vulnerable to her power, and responses to that power occupy no small part of the drama of Shakespeare and his contemporaries.

## iv *Chain of being: macrocosm and microcosm*

Within this broad outline each class has a hierarchy, again subdivided. The basic elements of earth, air, fire and water of their nature form a hierarchy, with fire – the purest and lightest element – at the physical and metaphorical summit. Inanimate things like stones have different qualities and properties; at the top of that particular group is the diamond, just as at the head of the metals is the incorruptible gold. Then animate objects: those with one soul – just the capacity to live, the vegetable soul, like the plants; those with two – the capacity to live and to feel, the sensible soul, like the animals; then man, who has three souls – vegetable, sensible, and with the capacity to reason, the rational soul. In his possession of a rational soul, which functions both by logical reasoning and by intuitive understanding, man is the link between the creatures that have material bodies and those (like angels) that live by intellect and intuition; he is the lynchpin of the universe, binding its two great provinces of matter and spirit together. When he fell in Eden, everything below him was affected as inevitably as an object hanging at the bottom of a rope ladder will fall if the ladder fails halfway up.

At the top of this hierarchy, or, as it is sometimes called, Chain of Being, are the angels (nine orders of them were later recognized), each with a different job to do and a different and secret joy in doing it that only God and that angel can share. Some angels (who have the special name of 'Intelligences') are given the job of looking after a planet's sphere; they 'keep within their sphere'.[8] Every link in the chain is vital to all the others.

8. This need not conflict with an understanding of a heavenly body as a physical object, any more than saying that a man is composed of £7.30-worth of chemicals tells you what a man is.

The principle of God working indirectly through the minute differentiation of his creatures and of their function is worked out in great detail. Each minor class is again differentiated. The oak is king, so to speak, of trees; the birds, insects, fish and animals all have their hierarchies, each member having peculiar properties and talents which are not duplicated elsewhere. Men, of course, have a complex social organization which is hierarchical too. The planets themselves observe a due precedence and order, with their chief, the sun, throned in the centre of them, flanked by three below and three above. It will be clear that this model of the universe is an extremely complex one, and that the artificial gap we have made since the seventeenth century between physical and moral nature would be incomprehensible to those who believed it.

The concept of the Chain of Being implies that what happens anywhere in the system has consequences for everything else. (We have, perhaps too belatedly, recognized this physical and moral truth about our world's fragile ecology; we even use the same metaphor when we talk about food-chains.) Sometimes these effects will be negligible: a tile refusing to fulfil its unique role and stay in place on a roof may be inconvenient but is not likely to make the sky fall on our heads. Sometimes, however, the effects will be really serious. A particularly unpropitious 'constellation' – that is, the position of the planets with regard to one another – will affect the earth, either in terms of natural happenings like earthquakes, or in an individual's fortune, or in the full-scale politics of men. (A generation like our own, when many people who should know better swallow the completely bogus science of what used to be called 'judicial' astrology, can perhaps understand the cast of mind that accepted this notion.) Conversely, human action, which is based on moral choice, has effects right across the created universe. For example, Macbeth's murder of Duncan is a double breach in the human order, for he has not only killed, but killed his king; as a result, an owl kills a falcon (that is, a common bird of night kills a noble bird of day), Duncan's horses deny their nature and eat not only flesh but each other, and disorder in the heavens is expressed in a terrible storm. Similarly, Lear's refusal to fulfil his allotted task of being king leads directly to the disruption of order in the state (to tyranny, chaos, war and invasion), to the disruption of social and family order, and to madness in his own mind. The tempest on the heath is both a symptom of and is caused by Lear's original action.

For a very important idea was that man in his make-up mirrored the very structure of the universe – he was the 'microcosm' or little world, reflecting (and affecting) the 'macrocosm' or great world. Hence the cosmic parallels to Macbeth's or Lear's actions; but also, within man himself, a conviction that even his well-being was dependent upon order. Reason was captain of his soul, and ruled his passions and feelings. If the position was reversed, he fell into grave error of thought and conduct, even into the ultimate disorder of madness. His bodily health was dependent upon a just balance of the four bodily fluids, known as 'humours', that medical theory recognized; if one predominated (another fossil word, echoing concepts of hierarchy), the patient was sick until that offending humour was purged by medicine or bloodletting. Even his body itself, with its separate specialized members cohering in one man under the control of the head, was an image of hierarchy, of the State itself – the 'body politic' – and each part of it was related to and was acted upon by particular planets and particular constellations. 'Taurus? that's sides and heart,' cries Sir Andrew, with his customary inaccuracy, to Sir Toby in *Twelfth Night* (I.iii).

We need to recognize that our fathers' belief in systems like these is not just of academic interest. It affects how they acted and what they did to each other. Their books, paintings, buildings and politics – and medicine – cannot be understood without taking this into consideration.

## v *Correspondences*

The multiplication of sub-hierarchies in this world view had profound consequences for the language we speak today. The key area is in the range of imagery and correlatives that is opened up; when we say, 'She's a jewel', we are using an idea of hierarchy, for we are implying not only that she is precious but that she stands in relation to other women as a jewel does to other stones. Each hierarchy can 'correspond' to the others in several ways. The correspondence can have magico-medical effects (in theory, anyway), for, as Chaucer's Doctor is reported as saying, gold in medicine is good for the heart; the heart, as the seat of the rational or highest soul, is the most important organ of the body; gold is the most important metal, therefore ... The purity and hardness of a diamond, worn as a jewel, can make the wearer pure and victorious, and guard him against the impurity of poisons. Or the correspondence can be metaphorical, emblematic or heraldic: a king is a lion (king of beasts), an oak under which lesser men may shelter, a dolphin (Antony is so compared in *Antony and Cleopatra*, V.ii) mastering the unstable element of the sea, whose governing planet is the changing moon. In *Richard II* the fall of Richard is seen in terms of the sun being cast out of his sphere – for is not the sun the king of planets, and would not his fall be literally as cataclysmic as the sacrilegious deposition of a king, whom God has put in his position to do a particular job? (So the Yorkist badge in the Wars of the Roses of a 'sun in splendour' – the same device adopted by Louis XIV – is not just a badge but a political manifesto.) The ultimate result of this perfectly sensible way of thinking is not just the enrichment of the language by exploiting the capacity of any hierarchy to mirror the others (which it certainly does); it is to establish and support in almost every area of discourse in the Renaissance a set of moral parameters within which the question at issue can be discussed. The entirety of human experience is necessarily seen as moral, exemplary, showing forth in its very nature and being the mark of the Creator's handiwork. And this idea had biblical sanction, both from the Old Testament (Psalm 19, Authorized Version) and the New (Romans i.20). The twelfth-century poet and theologian, Alanus of Lille, put it beautifully:

> *Omnis mundi creatura,*
> *quasi liber et pictura*
> *nobis est, et speculum;*
> *Nostrae vitae, nostrae mortis,*
> *nostri status, nostrae sortis,*
> *fidele signaculum.*

(What is created, in the whole world, is for us like a book, picture or mirror; it is a faithful sign of our life, our death, our situation and our fate.)

Renaissance and medieval imagery, be it on the simplest linguistic level or the most complex dramatic one, is based on this fundamental principle. Its necessary corollary, that everything in the world (and the world itself) is metaphor, as well as what it appears on the surface, must at least in part be recognized as one of the reasons for the extraordinary linguistic and imagistic richness of Elizabethan writing. If we do not bear it in mind when approaching Shakespeare's work we shall have greater difficulties than merely failing to understand the chance remarks of the First Servant.

## vi *Free will and the Fall*

The intricate detail of this model would seem to leave little room for free will and moral choice, what with Fortune's great power, 'the influences of these planets high', the magico-medical effects of natural objects, the inertia as well as the authority of hierarchies, and so on. But in fact there is a good deal.

In making man, God gave him, as a free and unconstrained gift, a selfhood. That selfhood would never find its true being and its true rest until it found them in a loving relationship with its Creator; but to be a self at all it had to be free not to choose to love God. Love that is not freely given, where the giver is not free not to love, is not love at all: it is slavery. In *Paradise Lost* (IX), Milton makes Adam try to dissuade Eve from leaving him to work alone; Adam has the right and power to force her to stay, but recognizes that the use of authority and destruction of Eve's freedom will destroy the very thing he desires: 'Thy stay, not free, absents thee more'. So with man: knowing that man would disobey, God had to give him freedom if any relationship between them were ever to be possible.

And so from free will came the Fall. Man's peculiar position in the Chain of Being meant that all the world that was given into his charge fell with him – all the links below were affected. In man himself, reason, the mark of God in his mind, was dimmed and he no longer saw clearly. He could no longer converse with God as a man with his friend in the cool of the evening; his mind and spirit were darkened. Because of the Fall man can never of himself, by his own efforts, do anything that is not in some way unsatisfactory, corrupt, ambiguous; indeed as Kant, a much later thinker, recognized, there is something radically wrong with human nature in even the very best people which makes them powerless, in the last analysis, to help themselves. The myth of the Fall has a profound moral truth. But the rescue operation that culminated in the first Easter showed that God's grace and love was still there to be accepted and taken up – if a man was humble enough to do so; his free will was not taken away. The courtesy of God is infinite; and the love that moves the sun and other stars, that is the ultimate reality in the universe, can be embraced or rejected by each man's free choice.

This understanding of man's plight emphasizes the necessity, the inescapability, of moral effort and choice in the whole of human life. Subject to Fortune as we may be, our response is still free. We may accept and be constructive, or rail and curse. Our stars may govern our condition, as Kent says at one point in *King Lear*, but they merely deal us a hand which we play as we choose. None of us has the same hand, and some hands are worse than others; it is still the playing that matters. In *King Lear* again, one of the villains, Edmund, is made to open this question right up:

*This is the excellent foppery of the world, that when we are sick in fortune – often the surfeits of our own behaviour – we make guilty of our disasters the sun, the moon, and stars, as if we were villains on necessity, fools by heavenly compulsion, knaves, thieves, and treachers by spherical predominance, drunkards, liars, and adulterers by an enforced obedience of planetary influence; and all that we are evil in by a divine thrusting-on.*

(I.ii.118–26)

Edmund, who refuses all moral rules and restraints, who does not recognize the very concept of morality, is the one who is made to underline the absolute moral responsibility for their own actions of everyone, himself included, in the play – and outside it. (Transferring the terms from 'stars' and 'spherical predominance' to 'Oedipus complexes', 'isolation problems' and 'the capitalist system' makes the point quite clear.) And so for all; men may hide behind excuses, but the Renaissance world picture allows man absolute moral freedom. It is precisely that moral freedom that is one of the major topics of the literature and especially of the drama of the period.

What I have said will be enough to indicate that the world view of which the Ptolemaic description of the stars and planets is a major part is a beautiful and satisfying creation, a major work of men's minds, an intellectual edifice of the first order. It contains a very great deal of moral truth. It presented men with a universe that made coherent sense, a universe that was *alive*. It lasted, in essentials, for a very long time and still affects us deeply now, in ways noticed only by harmless scholars who walk backwards into the future. It is also, in some rather important respects, wrong.

## B The New Philosophy

In 1543 Nicolaus Copernicus published his *De Revolutionibus*. This brilliant mathematician demonstrated that the sun did not in fact revolve round the earth, but was at the centre of the system of the planets. We tend to look back on this event and see – rightly – a watershed in scientific thought, and then assume that the old system immediately lay in ruins; we also tend to believe that everyone was quite devastated by this. The reality is much more complex, and also more interesting. Much has been written about this topic which is quite misleading, and so it is necessary to go into it at some length.

In the first place, the vast mass of people knew little and cared less about cosmological theories. No more do they now. What had been good enough for their fathers was good enough for them. The old system had many years of life left in it in the popular (and not so popular) mind – indeed, I recall being told by a far from stupid old man in the Fens of East Anglia in 1966 that of course the sun went round the earth – one could see it doing so. (He then proceeded to give me an explanation of earthquakes identical to that given by Hotspur in *1 Henry IV*, III.i.24 ff.) In a thoroughly misguided way, the administrative apparatus of the Church decided that to attack the old system was to imply an attack on the doctrines of the Church itself – which of course it was not – and defended a lost cause until well into the seventeenth century. (We all know the story of Galileo being forced by the Inquisition to repudiate his observations about the motion of the earth.) Secondly, we need to be quite clear that Copernicus did not think he was proposing anything new. He argued that he was restoring an old doctrine to be found in two ancient pagan writers who had a special place in Renaissance Christian respect, Philolaus and Pythagoras, in whom the light of God's wisdom had shone despite their having lived without the Christian revelation (exactly the same sort of respect that had been given to Plato from the time of Augustine to the seventeenth century). His system, he maintained, enhanced the importance of the sun, and ruled out the anomaly that the most brilliant of the planets, the one which for long had been a symbol of the wisdom of God, even of Christ himself, should not be that round which everything else moved like subjects round a monarch. Copernicus maintained that it was hinted at in many authoritative texts respected by theologians – like the remarkable *Celestial Hierarchies* of an author who, until the seventeenth century, was accepted as being Dionysius the Areopagite whom St Paul converted. He was also repeating and demonstrating the truth of what had been said in the fifteenth century by no less an authority than Nicholas of Cusa: *Iam nobis manifestus est terram istam in veritate moveri* ('Now it is clear to us that the very earth is in truth moved').

Many agreed with him. John Dee, for example, the finest English mathematician of the century, perfectly understood the system, and his pupil, Leonard Digges, defended it in print. This is particularly significant, for John Dee had a huge European reputation, was much favoured by Elizabeth, and was certainly connected with the group of men and women associated with Sir Philip Sidney who were in the very forefront of philosophical, political and scientific thought. Now John Dee was a magus; that is, he practised an art – *magia* – which sought, in Francis

Bacon's phrase, 'the effecting of all things possible' and the repairing of 'the damage of our first parents', in other words, to undo the Fall, not only by practical and mechanical means but also by training oneself through rigorous personal devotion to use the musical and mathematical harmonies of the hierarchical universe. Man would labour in partnership with the angels to do God's work, and thus fulfil the destiny God gave him in Eden.[9] Shakespeare too, we may be sure, was sympathetic to the aims of people like Dee, and built the figure of Prospero in *The Tempest* on him.[10] The cosmological and magical ideas were certainly talked about in intelligent circles, and the Copernican system was accepted by many. In so far as it affected the concept of the Chain of Being at all, it seemed to refine it.[11]

So the concept of degree or *ordo* remains largely intact, something to which all men, whatever their cosmological persuasion, may refer. In *Troilus and Cressida*, Shakespeare puts a passionate statement of it into the mouth of Ulysses. It says it all, and could serve as a summary of the ideas the first part of this chapter has been discussing:

> *The heavens themselves, the planets, and this centre*
> *Observe degree, priority and place,*
> *Insisture, course, proportion, season, form,*
> *Office, and custom, in all line of order,*
> *And therefore is the glorious planet Sol*
> *In noble eminence enthroned and sphered*
> *Amidst the others; whose med'cinable eye*
> *Corrects the ill aspects of planets evil,*
> *And posts like the commandment of a king,*
> *Sans check, to good and bad. But when the planets*
> *In evil mixture to disorder wander,*
> *What plagues and what portents, what mutiny,*
> *What raging of the sea, shaking of earth,*

9. We may laugh at the magus's aims; but *magia* is where modern science starts, and modern science seeks to do the same thing. It looks rather less likely to deliver the goods. Bacon's scorn (and Ben Jonson's, in *The Alchemist*) is based not on the notion that it is silly, but that it doesn't work.

10. Prospero is not Shakespeare's only magus; Glendower hints he is one, and Hotspur is scornful (*1 Henry IV*, III.i.50ff.). Hotspur's scorn is the more discourteous if we accept, as the first audience would have done, that there really were such magi.

11. Not all the scholars accepted Copernicus's model, of course. Tycho Brahe, a fine astronomer, is a good example. He proposed an extraordinarily complex model where the Earth moved round the sun and the rest of the planets orbited round that pair. Difficult.

> *Commotion in the winds, frights, changes, horrors,*
> *Divert and crack, rend and deracinate,*
> *The unity and married calm of states*
> *Quite from their fixture! O, when degree is shaked,*
> *Which is the ladder to all high designs,*
> *The enterprise is sick. How could communities,*
> *Degrees in schools, and brotherhoods in cities,*
> *Peaceful commerce from dividable shores,*
> *The primogenitive and due of birth,*
> *Prerogative of age, crowns, sceptres, laurels,*
> *But by degree, stand in authentic place?*
> *Take but degree away, untune that string,*
> *And hark what discord follows! Each thing meets*
> *In mere oppugnancy: the bounded waters*
> *Should lift their bosoms higher than the shores,*
> *And make a sop of all this solid globe;*
> *Strength should be lord of imbecility,*
> *And the rude son should strike his father dead;*
> *Force should be right, or, rather, right and wrong –*
> *Between whose endless jar justice resides –*
> *Should lose their names, and so should justice too.*
> *Then everything includes itself in power,*
> *Power into will, will into appetite;*
> *And appetite, an universal wolf,*
> *So doubly seconded with will and power,*
> *Must make perforce an universal prey,*
> *And last eat up himself.* (I.iii.85–124)

However, this powerful speech is in a context ironic in the extreme, for the play is one which examines the break-up of these very ideas. Shakespeare, man of his time as he was, may well have felt the emotional and moral force of the old ideas, but he is also painfully aware that they do not supply all the answers – if they ever did (see below, pp. 54ff.). He is also aware that men may refuse consent to this vision of order, and gives us in *King Lear* a terrible vision of the universal wolf's career before the balance is in some way restored – but at appalling cost.

Weakening of the old ideas came from two fronts. One is a consequence of radical religious ideas. The Reformation unleashed many things, not the least interesting in England being a rabid assumption that all the inherited scholarship and learning of the past was tainted with the corruption of the Church of Rome. Bonfires of priceless books were common; one of the finest libraries of medieval Europe, the gift of Duke Humphrey of Gloucester to the University of Oxford, was systematically destroyed and burnt in the street by members of the University. The extreme Protestants saw the accumulated learning of the Middle Ages and its intellectual systems – anything dating after the Council of Chalcedon in 451 – as useless or worse, and so destroyed what they could find. There are some who would dislike the world model for no better reason than that it had developed in the centuries before the Reformation. Medieval procedures of inquiry and systems of knowledge – what we now call Scholasticism – were consigned to the rubbish heap. All this was an attempt to return, by a radical and necessary pruning of superfluous matter, to the simplicity that had informed the Church in the first centuries. But it left men, however devout, with a world to be explained and a world to be managed in the business of day-to-day living. They had to put something in the place of the intellectual systems they had destroyed. One replacement – not the most popular, though the one whose heirs we are – was radical indeed: to take nothing on trust, to reason from observation rather than authority or first principles, to schematize knowledge not according to the principles of the medieval schoolmen but according to practical necessities. People like Peter Ramus, the educational reformer, were simply not interested in the metaphysical and mystical speculation that went with much of the old learning; his *Dialectique* (1555) systematically challenged and refuted Aristotelian and Scholastic logic (see below, Chapter 11). He had his followers, not least in England. His books were translated (by William Temple and Andrew Melville) and used at Cambridge in the late sixteenth century, Dee possessed his practical treatises, and the Sidney circle knew of his ideas. Francis Bacon, who in a real sense was the founder of modern scientific method, was keenly aware of his work and used a lot of his ideas in *The Advancement of Learning* and the *Novum Organum*. The magnificent moral, mystical and cosmological edifice this chapter has been describing was necessarily going to be under threat, eventually, from this quarter.

A more immediately serious threat, however, came from another angle. Suppose a man like Edmund in *King Lear* were to deny consciously all moral restraints on his conduct, all constraints of degree; suppose he were to gain real power, and make the gaining and keeping of that power his only moral imperative. Theoretically, the whole creation would turn on him and restore a just and holy equilibrium. But there had always been examples of men who had done just that, and who had survived; some, even, had turned out to be successful rulers. As Queen Elizabeth's godson, Sir John Harington, cynically put it,

21

> *Treason doth never prosper; what's the reason?*
> *If it do prosper, none dare call it treason.*

An uncomfortable thought indeed, which eventually would lead to the unravelling of the seamless web of the old world view. It was even more disturbing when erected into an article of policy: in his little manual for autocrats, *Il Principe* (1513), Niccolò Machiavelli developed it into a theory of recommended conduct where the only good was the extension by any means of the ruler's power.

Niccolò Machiavelli (1469–1527) was a Florentine statesman, historian and philosopher, who in all probability would have been largely ignored, except by scholars, had it not been for *Il Principe*. The book is undoubtedly one result of his deep researches into Roman history (especially in the work of Livy), as well as of an analysis of recent Italian. It is an attempt to describe (and prescribe) how politics work in practice rather than how they should work in theory. The notion of a mystical order in the universe which embraces and is mirrored in the human state is not so much rejected as ignored: Machiavelli is interested in providing a manual of effective political conduct for a modern ruler anxious to secure and maintain his position. (He is writing, of course, with particular reference to his idealistic desire for a ruler who would unite a divided Italy and drive all foreigners from its territory.) Conventional morality – justice, honour, mercy, truth, all the 'king-becoming graces' – are thrown aside. The sole criterion by which a ruler should govern is usefulness, and he sees the duplicity and intrigue by which his hero Cesare Borgia had operated as admirable because they were effective. The end justifies the means.

The book caused an outraged reaction: some went so far as to claim his book was inspired by the devil, and it provoked a crop of replies that reasserted the old values. Some people, of course, only knew the original through the replies to it, but by the middle of the century translations were circulating, in manuscript at least, in most of Europe. Machiavelli's was one of those books of which everybody professes horror – and reads under the bedclothes; his very name became an English noun, the Machiavel, signifying an utterly amoral, clever villain. The policies of a number of Tudor politicians – Thomas Cromwell, Cecil, Leicester – were influenced in some degree by it, and Francis Bacon, Walter Ralegh and Christopher Marlowe all made some intelligent use of it, even if occasionally gingerly.

The horror arose not only from moral principles, but from a recognition that no system has a defence against the man who refuses consent to it. Machiavelli's ignoring of the obligations of degree, and his making the will of the prince the highest moral imperative, fascinated as well as appalled. What is also important is not just that Machiavelli's ideas are so direct a challenge to the system – which they are – but that the very holding of those ideas themselves could be seen as evidence that the world was, in fact, drawing near to its latter end. It is this that John Donne, Shakespeare's contemporary, is driving at in his *First Anniversarie: An Anatomie of the Worlde*; that such thoughts are thought is evidence of a growing darkening of Reason before the final end of history:

> . . . ⟨*Corruption*⟩ *seis'd the Angels, and then first of all,*
> *The world did in her Cradle take a fall,*
> *And turn'd her braines, and took a generall maime*
> *Wronging each joint of th'universall frame.*
> *The noblest part, man, felt it first; and than*
> *Both beasts and plants, curst in the curse of man.*
> *So did the world from the first hours decay,*
> *That evening was the beginning of the day,*
> *And now the Springs and Sommers which we see,*
> *Like sonnes of women after fiftie bee.*
> *And new Philosophy calls all in doubt,*
> *The Element of fire is quite put out;*
> *The Sun is lost, and th'earth, and no mans wit*
> *Can well direct him where to looke for it.*
> *And freely men confesse, that this world's spent,*
> *When in the Planets, and the Firmament*
> *They seeke so many new; they see that this*
> *Is crumbled out againe to his Atomis.*
> *'Tis all in peeces, all cohaerence gone!*
> *All just supply, and all Relation:*
> *Prince, Subject, Father, Sonne are things forgot,*
> *For every man alone thinkes he hath got*
> *To be a Phoenix, and that there can bee*
> *None of that kinde, of which he is, but hee.*

Donne is not alone in this gloomy view; George Goodman in *The Fall of Man* (1616) maintains that the world is already in its last days, that all is on the verge of the final break-up. Yet what is interesting is that neither Donne in the passage above nor Goodman, radical though they are, is able to get away from the ideas and terms of the Chain of Being. Its vitality as a systematic model may be doomed, but as an imaginative force it is not yet dead.

This chapter has inevitably summarized and thus distorted some very complex issues. One possible misunderstanding can, however, be cleared up. It is all too easy with hindsight to see clearly what events, people and ideas we think really do weigh in the scale of history, and to ignore the fact that they are necessarily untypical of their period. The reformers, religious or academic, did not ride on a wave of informed popular support; they exploited the levers of hierarchical power. The vast majority of the population carried on, living and partly living, desiring only to be left in peace to carry on their own concerns. Revolutions in cosmology disturbed them little; then as now, revolutions in politics meant a change of one master for another. Their ideas are not always homogeneous, articulate or even consistent – people can quite happily hold two contradictory ideas in their heads at the same time. It would be ludicrous to suppose that all – even educated – men today are agog over the latest conundrum in quantum physics; why should we assume the Elizabethans were less various than ourselves? And it is this many-headed multitude that Shakespeare is addressing, the instrument on which he plays. To his tools we must now turn.

# 3. Actors on the Scaffold

In any discussion of the plays we must be constantly aware of the background of the original medium, namely sound, vision and movement in the Elizabethan theatre. It is possible to find out a good deal about these things, though there is still much we do not know. It is, moreover, quite beyond us to understand what it was like as a contemporary to experience these elements in the theatrical techniques of Shakespeare's time; the best we can do is to ensure that our historical imagination is based on as little supposition as we can manage.

## i *The theatre building*

Much has been written on the theatre's physical form. The old idea of the Elizabethan theatres as identical copies of the yards of posting inns will not stand up; it may well be that the players, when they had to travel the shires either for extra cash or because they had to leave London when the plague reached the level where the magistrates closed the theatres, used inn yards for their performances. But I suspect that they did so because yards like those that survive at the Eagle in Cambridge or the George in Huntingdon allowed them to use some of the resources of their theatres and were physically not too unlike them. For there seems to be little doubt that by the period we are talking about – the last quarter of the sixteenth century – the theatres were purpose-built or adapted buildings, and it is virtually certain that they were not identical in design though they may well have shared common features. Some were very large, and could, according to travellers, accommodate up to 3,000 people.[1]

There was money to be made in drama. To see the theatres that were built or altered as necessarily a sign of a new respectability for drama, or even of a public-spirited concern to take it seriously, may be too charitable. When James Burbage (father of the great Richard) built his theatre

1. True, the companies could and did act elsewhere – in great houses (as the mechanicals do in *A Midsummer Night's Dream*, or the Players in *Hamlet*), on scaffold stages at fairs, against the screens in the Temple; but in most halls they would find the essential features of doors for entrances and exits, a (music) gallery above for battlement or balcony scenes – as in *Romeo and Juliet* or *Richard II* – and a large playing area.

in Shoreditch in 1576, he did so in all likelihood because the company (incorporated as Lord Leicester's Men in 1574) was doing well enough to afford a semi-permanent structure [2] to shelter its customers, who might thus be lured in future from rival troupes.

Their shape – octagonal, hexagonal or just 'in the round' – may owe something to the experience commercial operators had gained of cock-pits, or bull- and bear-baiting rings,[3] of getting the maximum number of paying spectators into the cheapest and most compact space; certainly they seem to have stacked the wooden galleries so high, with so little headroom, and packed them so full, that a modern Fire Safety Officer would have been reduced to gibbering despair. (And once you get a lot of people into a confined space for a long time, you can sell them pots of ale and pipes of tobacco, and apples and oranges to throw at the actors – one might as well make the profit one way as another.) An immediate consequence of this shape and structure was that a very large audience could have – even if only near vertically – a good view of the stage, and every person in it would be close enough to pick up silent expressions on actors' countenances. Moreover, the sheer physical closeness of players to audience made for an intimacy, a cooperation in the dramatic experience, we rarely experience today. This had profound effects on acting style, gesture and especially the language of the plays.[4]

## ii *The stage*

But the sharp end, so to speak, of the theatre is the stage, and it is here that controversy will never be stilled. (I use 'stage' here in its modern sense of the whole works; in the sixteenth-century sense the word indicates just the raised area in the theatres on which plays and spectacles were exhibited.) We do not know exactly what an Elizabethan theatre looked like – indeed, it is highly probable that not all the fifteen or so

2. Timber framing, with the members slotted and pegged together, meant that the whole structure was, if necessary, portable. James Burbage's theatre was dismantled in 1598, moved to another site on the South Bank, and rebuilt with some modification the next year as the Globe. Both at Shoreditch and on the South Bank, Burbage, like most owners, was careful to keep outside the jurisdiction of the City magistrates.

3. Burbage's company, which Shakespeare joined, had financial interests in a bear-baiting pit.

4. This is, of course, to ignore the Blackfriars theatre – which is in any case not strictly relevant to the plays this book will concentrate on as the company only started using it in 1608. This theatre was an enclosed oblong auditorium, with artificial lighting, and the opportunities this offered certainly affected the composition of Shakespeare's later plays.

London theatres working between the 1590s and the 1640s were identical, though they were probably broadly similar. We have to be extremely cautious in interpreting contemporary or near contemporary prints of theatres as reflecting the London practice because very often the prints were influenced by concepts of the theatre and of the stage that descend via the books of the Roman architect Vitruvius from the theatres of late Antiquity; these were being advocated as an ideal, and sometimes copied, by the avant-garde in Italy and France.

There is, however, some evidence of English practice. The outside appearance of the Bankside theatres can be seen in the various panoramic engravings of London that have come down to us: Norden's of 1600 is less helpful than the beautiful and justly well-known engraving published in Amsterdam in 1616 by J. C. Visscher, which shows the Globe, the Bear Garden near it, and the Swan. Wenceslaus Hollar's print of 1642, when the theatres were about to be closed by Act of Parliament, also depicts the Globe (labelling it wrongly). It was of course the second Globe, constructed after the fire that destroyed the first. The first Globe can be partly reconstructed from the surviving papers connected with the removal of the theatre from Shoreditch, and we know that the Fortune theatre (the contract for which survives) was modelled on the first Globe. The common ground shared by all these pieces of evidence is of a tall building enclosing an open stage area, which has jutting into it a substantial gabled structure.[5] Even without trying to work out what was inside, we can see how different the Elizabethan theatre was from the grand, scientifically designed stone structures of the ancient world, or the elaborate, indoor, picture-staged creations that were so soon to become fashionable. It is the latter, of course, that were the ancestors of most later theatres until the 1950s.

The Dutchman Jan de Witt, who visited London in 1595 or 1596, made a drawing (later copied by Arnoldus Buchelius) of the interior of the Swan theatre. It is not a good drawing. But it is almost the only direct visual evidence, as distinct from that inferred from the needs of the plays themselves, that we have of the appearance of an Elizabethan stage. We cannot be quite sure that de Witt or Buchelius has not subtly altered what he actually saw to fit it more neatly to his idea of the theatre, which was derived from the theatres of Antiquity; certainly he labels parts of the theatre with somewhat misleading Latin names, which

5. To judge from the prints, the orientation and size of this structure may well have ensured that the playing area was shaded from the sun during the hours of performance in the afternoons. The contract for the Fortune theatre refers to it as a 'shadow'.

suggest functions more appropriate to a Roman theatre. However, he cannot have altered the physical shape too much. He shows us the Swan with a large flat stage, raised above the level of the yard. Behind it is an elaborate structure with two functioning doors giving on to the stage, and on the next storey a sizeable gallery.[6] Two large columns support a canopy over the stage (the usual existence of this is corroborated by the contract for the Fortune theatre I just mentioned, which specifies a 'shadow' or 'cover'), and the whole structure is crowned by a 'hut', which can be seen on all the engravings mentioned above. From the hut a flag flies and a trumpet was sounded when the play was due to begin. (De Witt's trumpeter seems about to step into thin air.)

The playing area – 'stage' in its old sense – seems to have been large and rectangular. It may have been temporary, on trestles, which could be dismantled if the building was to be used for another purpose. There was certainly a good deal of space below it – the cellarage – of which many plays make use for scenes with Hell, ghosts, graves, corpses and so on. The contract for the Fortune theatre gives an idea of the size of the stage; it specifies an area 43 feet wide, extending halfway into the 55-feet-wide yard. As the length of the theatre was specified as 80 feet, this would suggest a depth of around 40 feet, and so the stage took up an enormous proportion of the open area. The de Witt drawing also suggests that a relatively huge stage was usual. This very fact points to a real difference between the way Elizabethans and we ourselves might see the stage. We have, with real gains, broken away from the nineteenth-century straitjacket of the picture stage behind a proscenium arch, but the implications of our modern terms 'thrust' or 'apron' suggest something important behind, from which the apron projects as a sort of extension. We are still accustomed to all looking in the same direction, as it were. It seems quite obvious that a stage as large as an Elizabethan one is spatially the dominant feature of the building, and watching action on it would be more like watching a boxing or wrestling match than sitting in a modern theatre. The way we see the action represented on the stage as a world into which we physically look, as observers, relies heavily on the psychological effects of the perceptual, dramatic and acting language of the

6. De Witt's gallery seems to have spectators in it, and there is a lot of evidence that, when not used in the action, seats in it would be sold to those who wanted not only to see but to be seen – just as flashy young men were able to hire stools to sit on the stage itself. Both these facts emphasize how differently our fathers conceived the distinction between theatrical action and the audience watching it.

proscenium arch enclosing a more – or less – realistic set.[7]

We must, I think, recognize that Elizabethan playwrights and actors regarded and used the tiring-house façade behind the stage in ways quite different from the ones we easily assume we would have adopted in their place. Even in our attempts to re-interpret Elizabethan drama using open stages, with thrusts or not, we are carrying with us assumptions of which we may be unaware, including the one that we only need to change our angle of vision to recapture not only what was seen but *how* it was seen. It is likely that the audience perceived less of a gap between the represented action and their own lives, and that being so close to the actors made them see the *acting*, as well as the illusion it created, as worthy of attention. (See below, pp. 45ff.)

How the yard was used is problematical. It is, to my mind, most probable that it was full of paying customers – the cheapest place, where there was no protection from the rain. But it just might have been used for entries on horseback, as in the first scene of the anonymous *Famous Victories of Henry V*; and C. Walter Hodges suggests that a cart representing a ship (on wheels, one hopes) could have been brought in and moored to the side of the stage in *Pericles*. Certainly those plays give us problems that might best be resolved in this way, and one has to admit that de Witt (or Buchelius) labels the yard the 'arena', which does suggest some sort of playing area. But the evidence is quite inconclusive.

### iii *The tiring-house façade*

The tiring-house rose, with a more or less elaborate façade, behind the stage. It was of at least two storeys, and may in some cases have had three or even four. As the name implies, it was used as somewhere for the actors to change and to store props and costumes, and from it at least two and possibly three doors opened on to the stage. There was a balcony, which de Witt's drawing shows running across the whole width of the façade. This was used extensively; it was the battlements of Flint Castle in *Richard II*, the walls of Harfleur in *Henry V*, Cleopatra's

7. In 1605 Inigo Jones introduced a proscenium stage and full scenery into England for Jonson's *Masque of Blackness*. The revolutionary effect of this was to make the dramatic action resemble a picture suddenly come to life, endowed with a time dimension; the form exploited the different signs and conventions of pictures, as well as deliberately setting out to create a total illusion – another world into which an audience could peer through a transparent fourth wall. So revolutionary was this that some of the aristocratic audience could not cope with the experience of painted perspective.

monument in *Antony and Cleopatra*, Juliet's balcony in Verona. Real controversy, however, surrounds the question of whether it did or did not thrust out to cover an 'inner stage', curtained off from the main one and used for 'discovery' scenes, like Ferdinand and Miranda playing chess in *The Tempest*, or Hermione's statue in *The Winter's Tale*, or Falstaff asleep behind the arras in *1 Henry IV*. One can see the value of such a device – it would be ideal for Henry IV's bedroom in *2 Henry IV*, or Richard II's prison – and it is possible that later, as audiences demanded more complex and stunning effects, stages were modified to include this useful facility.[8] The only evidence for it, however, is extrapolated from the texts of plays, and no contemporary description or illustration indicates one. There is the huge problem, too, that action tucked away under a balcony would have been impossible to see if you were sitting high up or at the side; and you would not be too pleased if you had paid for one of those more expensive places. Discovery scenes could be managed if the doors of the façade were wide enough to be swung back to reveal a space, and if curtains could be hung over the opening so formed. The de Witt drawing shows double doors which could do this, and there is an engraving of a 'Theatre of the World' (of which more later) in Robert Fludd's *Ars Memoriae* (Oppenheim, 1623) which shows two open arches and one obviously functional set of double doors.[9]

The space revealed need not have been very large, and when we look at the evidence found in the plays it is clear that what was presented in it was often more in the nature of a tableau than a continuation of the main action; indeed, the focus of our interest is often what the characters in the play make of what they are looking at – as, perhaps, in the way we (and Hamlet) watch Claudius watching a play (which may in turn make us think about ourselves watching a play . . . our conscience is a quarry,

8. Classical theatres had a means of 'revealing what had been hidden' in the *ekkyklema*; but this employed large central doors in the *scaenae frons*, and perhaps a wheeled trolley.

9. Fludd's evidence is problematical. His theatre may in fact be no more than the sort of magical memory theatre many Renaissance men were interested in from the earliest Venetian one of Giulio Camillo right through the sixteenth century. There is no space here to go into this in detail; briefly, one could use the form of the theatre (and real ones were built to do this) to pigeonhole information in a way that allowed its retrieval and combination – a sort of early memory bank plus computer. (The theatre could be an imagined one, of course.) One remembered one's wife's birthday was on 1 April (New Style) by imagining her sitting on the first row down on the fourth bank of seats, for example. But it is worth pointing out that Fludd would not have sanctioned this engraving of even an imaginary or ideal theatre had it not borne some relationship to the real thing; it had to be recognizable as a theatre like those in common use, or it would not work as a memory system.

too). The problem once again is our ingrained assumption that one of the summits of the playwright's and producer's skill will be the illusion of realistic action – verisimilitude; and we assume that Juliet's tomb, for example, would not work on stage without the nearest equivalent we can imagine to the 'fade' technique. But this seems not to have been the way our fathers saw things; in *2 Henry VI* (III.ii) the king tells Warwick to go and see the corpse of his murdered uncle, Humphrey of Gloucester: 'Enter his chamber, view his breathless corpse,/And comment then upon his sudden death.' A few lines later the Folio text records what is probably a prompter's note, *'Bed put forth'*, and then, *'Warwick draws the curtaine, and shews Duke Humphrey in his bed'*. The action is not realistic – Warwick has only moved a couple of yards, and the discovery is made by drawing a curtain on the stage rather than by entering a room in a palace. But what is there is naturalism of response, though often achieved by highly conventional and coded means.

## iv *The heavens*

From the tiring-house façade, at what must have been a high level, projected a canopy. Sometimes, as in the Swan, it was supported on what were obviously elaborate and massive pillars; sometimes, as the contract for the Hope in 1614 suggests and as C. Walter Hodges claims for the second Globe, it was cantilevered out with none. It was often called the 'heavens', and there is much evidence to suggest that its underside was painted elaborately with the signs of the zodiac and the circles of the planets. When Othello swears vengeance on the supposedly unchaste Desdemona (III.iii) by 'yond marble heaven', his hand is raised to point to the thing all the audience could see – the painted (marbled) representation of the delicate and harmonious machine of the Universe held together by love. The moment is utterly convincing; but it should be realized that the actor is made implicitly to refer to his role-playing in a theatre – he is covered not by the sky of Cyprus but by a painted canopy. The canopy is therefore not just a convenient way of keeping the actors' expensive clothes dry (the audience in the yard did not really matter); it is part of the props of the theatre and an important component in its symbolic economy which we shall have to consider at greater length below.

The canopy supported the hut, from which the three trumpet blasts were sounded at the beginning of each performance. The hut also had other functions; it housed the machinery for sound effects like thunder (half tree-trunks hollowed, with cannon balls to roll down them), and cannon for battle effects (it was the stopple from one of these that lodged in the thatch of the first Globe in 1613 during a performance of *Henry VIII* and burnt the place to the ground). It also housed machinery which to us seems not only clumsy but tasteless: winches for letting heavenly visitors down on to the stage. Ariel in *The Tempest* may have 'flown' by this means; Jupiter is lowered on his eagle in *Cymbeline*; the portent of three suns appears in *3 Henry VI*, and these would have been lowered from the canopy so that all could see them. (Again, it is clear it is the symbolic effect that is wanted rather than anything within the narrow confines of 'realism': the king of the gods and the most beneficent of the planets descends *visibly* from and through Heaven to reassure – jovially! – the suffering Postumus that all will be well.) It is obvious that the canopy was much more than a shelter from the rain and sun, and was part of a symbolic structure which as a whole had implications and associations that differ sharply from our own ideas about the theatre.

## v *The theatre as metaphor*

It would be foolish to maintain that Elizabethans saw the theatre as Wagner wanted his countrymen to view Bayreuth, or that they considered it as seriously as the Greeks. For the Greeks, going to the theatre had been part of a shared ritual in the context of a religious festival, where the fable of the play had openly carried reference to complex philosophical, religious, moral and political issues. One of the principal ways in which it worked was through emotional involvement; the audience obviously knew they were watching an actor – a 'hypocrite' in Greek – playing a role, but the playwright's skill engaged their emotional response to the point where real and deep feelings were experienced which, coupled with the audience's prior knowledge of the events of the traditional plot, allowed both sympathy and objective judgement. Entertainment was thus a means to a religious and philosophical end. Nevertheless, the Elizabethan view is far closer to this than it is to the idea of the theatre as mere entertainment, where originality of plot or convincingness of character is of major interest.[10] No one would argue

10. Something of this seriousness of attitude is to be seen, ironically, in the way we now look at the drama of Shakespeare and his contemporaries – as 'classic'; watching it is 'good' for us, and we take coach parties of often reluctant children to performances in some vague unexpressed hope that somehow they will be civilized by the experience – a sort of moral disinfection.

that entertainment and enjoyment did not matter to the Elizabethans – of course they did, and any play that didn't provide them did not pay the bills. But their attitude to human life and the world were different from ours, and deeply affected the way they approached the theatrical experience.

A few minutes with a concordance to the works of Shakespeare will demonstrate the importance of the life/theatre/'All the world's a stage' metaphor: drama reassumes from life the metaphor that life is a drama. Ultimately, though the actual phrase 'playing a part' in English antedates the existence of any theatre, I think this universal metaphor develops from the extremely popular religious plays of the Middle Ages (see below, pp. 52 f.), where human life in time is presented as a drama acted out against the backdrop of eternity, in a moral landscape between a (sometimes) physically represented Hell at one pole and Heaven at another. In the Elizabethan theatre the whole building becomes a metaphor: the stage can be a world between the canopy/Heaven and the cellarage/Hell, the men on it representing life in the eye of eternity. The Globe theatre's own motto was a line from the twelfth-century Bishop of Chartres, John of Salisbury: *Totus mundus agit histrionem* – 'The whole world is acting'. Where the plot was a known one – as in a history play – the audience could hardly escape the idea that their vision of events was similar to that of Divine Providence. The possibility of the theatre as moral metaphor is amply demonstrated not only by allusion and reference, but also by the very titles of books of emblems, moral pictures plus verses, intended to help one to live a virtuous life: the collection by the Dutchman Jan van der Noot was translated (partly by Spenser) in 1569 as *A Theatre for Worldlings*, while Thomas Combe, whom Shakespeare could well have known, translated Guillaume de la Perrière's collection as *The Theatre of Fine Devices* (1593; 1614). Emblems – pictures which symbolize in fairly standard ways abstract moral ideas – clearly affect staging (see pp. 38, 43f., 124, 144). The implications of this metaphor extend further; the moral judgement demanded by the watching of a play bounces back on the audience, for they too are actors and their very language never allows them to forget the fact. Sir Walter Ralegh puts it succinctly in a short poem that exploits this commonest of conceits with a wry perception of when the playing has to stop:

> *What is our life? A play of passion,*
> *Our mirth the music of division.*

> *Our mothers' wombs the tiring-houses be,*
> *Where we are dressed for this short comedy.*
> *Heaven the judicious sharp spectator is,*
> *That sits and marks still who doth act amiss.*
> *The graves that hide us from the searching sun*
> *Are like drawn curtains when the play is done.*
> *Thus march we, playing, to our latest rest,*
> *Only we die in earnest, that's no jest.*

This issue is clearly integral to the concept of character we need to assume behind Shakespeare's creations. It is also integral to the language Shakespeare develops in and for his plays, and I shall discuss it in greater detail below (Chapter 3.ix and Chapter 11).

But no building, however neatly symbolic, is going to entertain an audience for long. Having built our theatre, as it were, we now have to consider its physical resources and limitations (and the conventions attaching to them), props, styles of acting, and the systems of financing and patronage that supported it.

## vi *The resources of the building*

Despite the fairly elaborate machinery for letting things down from 'Heaven', making various sounds, and calling things up from 'Hell', the theatres of the 1590s, however ornate in style, were in no way capable of creating the complex illusion for all the senses that we expect of a modern, totally enclosed theatre, with artifical light, spots, and elaborate special effects. In the first decade of the next century, indoor theatres were built that did use artificial light and elaborate effects; Shakespeare's company had control of one – the Blackfriars, much nearer the Court and the houses of the nobility than the Globe – and it is tempting to see the changes that at this time came over both the type of plays he wrote and the way he wrote them as in some way caused by his awareness of a theatre with different resources and a much more aristocratic audience. The resources of the open stage were limited indeed, and ludicrously inadequate, sometimes, to the subject of the play – if one was looking for a realistic treatment:

> *But pardon, gentles all,*
> *The flat unraisèd spirits that hath dared*
> *On this unworthy scaffold to bring forth*
> *So great an object. Can this cockpit hold*
> *The vasty fields of France? Or may we cram*

> *Within this wooden O the very casques*
> *That did affright the air at Agincourt? ...*
> *Piece out our imperfections with your thoughts:*
> *Into a thousand parts divide one man,*
> *And make imaginary puissance.*
> *Think, when we talk of horses, that you see them,*
> *Printing their proud hoofs i'th'receiving earth;*
> *For 'tis your thoughts that now must deck our kings,*
> *Carry them here and there, jumping o'er times,*
> *Turning th'accomplishment of many years*
> *Into an hourglass ...*

> (*Henry V*, Prologue, 8ff.)

*Henry V* is a peculiarly difficult case, of course: an 'epic' play of which the numerical and spatial scale is huge, about the Elizabethans' ideal hero-king, already the subject of other plays – and thus open to odious comparison on exactly these grounds of presentation and illusion if a disgruntled spectator were so inclined. But the Prologue's apology states the obvious; no one would seriously go to the theatre to *see* the conflict of kingdoms, but to be made by the play to *imagine* them. Realistic illusion is impossible. So when, on a bright sunny afternoon, perhaps, in 1606, Macbeth says, 'Light thickens, and the crow makes wing to th' rooky wood', what we are experiencing is scenery – but scenery and setting conveyed entirely through language within a believable context of spoken interchanges in the play. The weakness of the building directly demands the strength of the language, and the peculiar richness and imaginative power of the dramatic language of writers in this period is, I think, in some measure a consequence of this necessity. The obvious point must be borne in mind, of course, that Elizabethan dramatists when they talk of the need for the audience's imaginative cooperation in the creation of an illusion were in no way complaining; they could not perceive a lack in the theatre since they had no knowledge of what later became possible, and all they were doing was writing a play in the most effective and economical way.

Other resources we take for granted were also lacking. Though a curtained stage may have been an innovation used in the theatres that began to be built in the 1600s – Ralegh's poem suggests so – the normal ones had none. The expectant, chattering audience had to be quieted not by the lowering of lights and the raising of a curtain, but by voices and a presence that demanded attention; the massive punctuation mark between scenes a later dramatist could use was not available; what went on to the stage had to come off it as visibly, so stage deaths had to be so arranged that the corpses could, within the plot of the play, be removed from sight. There was no change of scenery, either; the symbolic stage had to be a castle, a jousting field, a garden, a prison, a palace, the open country and a London street – all in one play alone. Again, what people were actually given to say has to do the job for us, and the movement from one scene to another makes not only for rapidity of action – and there is evidence that Elizabethan actors went through their performances like a train – but also forces the audience to compare and contrast adjacent scenes. I shall say more of that later, for this juxtaposition is a very important element in the design of Shakespeare's (and others') plays and a significant contributor to meaning.[11]

Yet there were some resources which we easily ignore. Despite the lack of what we would call scenery – the word is not recorded in English in its modern sense until the 1770s – it does seem that the audience's anticipation of the type of play they were to watch and the sort of response they were being asked for could be primed in one or two ways. One obvious way was by the classification of a play in its title or advertisement – as we can discern through Polonius's laughable misuse of this idea. Another was in the playhouse itself; the trestles of the stage were usually concealed by drapes, and their colour was changed to reflect the type of play:

> *The stage is hung with black; and I perceive*
> *The auditors prepared for tragedy.*
> (Induction to *A Warning for Fair Women*, anon., c. 1590)

or

> *What time the world, clad in a mourning robe,*
> *A stage made for a woful tragedy.*
> William Browne, *Britannia's Pastorals*, I.v (1613)

This practice was clearly commonplace, and it is possible that other colours were used for other types of play. Even the absence of black would in fact tell the audience what the play was *not*.

---

11. Briefly: the division into acts, and in many cases scenes, which we, working from printed texts, take for granted, originated with printed copies – in Shakespeare's case, the acts were the creation of the Folio editors of 1623. Act divisions are always imperceptible unless mechanically marked by intervals or curtains, and the effect of rapid continuous presentation of the drama is to make hay with the supposed 'classic' five-act structure imposed by the editors. It allows the play to break down in our minds into 'movements' of groups of scenes (see below, pp. 85, 113).

## vii *Convention*

What we are touching on here is a most important concept, to which this book will return many times. The use of coloured drapes as a signal is an example of that non-verbal language, that area of common assumption, to which we give the name 'convention'. Convention is simply an area of agreement between an artist and his audience, where the terms of the discussion are taken for granted, and the focus of interest lies in what will be made with those terms. Anyone who does not share that common ground, and relies only on the spoken or written words, is highly likely to get things awry. In our own day, we have conventions every bit as complex as those of earlier periods. To take one example only, the Western film as a genre tends to employ a certain type of plot, with certain set features: the shoot-out as climax, the ritualization of conflict, a moral frame where the good guys usually win over impossible odds. The convention may even extend to details, like giving the villains black hats. Of course, once the language is established a director can play with it, even invert it, in the sure knowledge that his audience's acceptance of the norm allows him this freedom to play variations on it. Convention, properly used, is a liberating rather than restricting thing. But to learn the convention one does not run to critical works on film; one watches films. It is exactly thus with the drama, poetry, painting and music of periods other than our own; the shared language can in considerable part be recovered by alert experience of many works, which is how it was developed and used in the first place. But sometimes one needs a short theoretical discussion, even classification, to get started, much as we would look at a map to understand the country we have to traverse.

In the particular context of the resources of the theatre building, we need to be aware of two areas where convention is important (obviously it will be important in acting style and language as well, and I shall return to that issue later). I have already stressed that the conventional acceptance of the symbolic force of the theatre building affects both the way a play is written and the way it is watched. It follows that positioning on stage (or over or under it) can, if so relevant, convey meaning in a non-verbal way; Richard II's descent from the balcony – the walls of Flint Castle – to meet his adversary is a symbolic abdication of his role as king, on a higher plane than his subjects. It is at that moment he is 'unkinged', in a way that, as we shall see, denies the very fabric of the universe, even though the actual abdication comes later. Movement through theatrical space may therefore be full of a meaning lost to us;

and where there is no clear evidence from the verbal text about positioning on stage, we may be sure that the author and his actors knew very well that they could not just stand anywhere, for it would all signify. The second, closely connected, area draws in another art. It was a Renaissance cliché that poetry was a speaking picture and picture a silent poem – indeed, so close are the terms that Titian writes of some of his paintings as 'poems' and Sidney composes parts of his *Arcadia* in our minds exactly as if they were paintings. The drama is a combination of the two; composed to be experienced through the eye, it is, literally, a picture, and employs the conventions of picture, such as we see commonly in Renaissance painting. But it is a picture that has come to life, and speaks and moves through time: so it employs the conventions of poetry too. There are moments – when Richard II is holding the mirror, or Falstaff is aping Henry IV – when the action on stage freezes momentarily into symbolic visual pattern, even into a reminiscence of emblem pictures;[12] there are others when our memories suddenly recall an exactly similar visual structure and we are forced to look close to the heart of the play by 'looking on this picture, and on this', as Hamlet urged his mother. One such moment is when we recognize that Henry Bolingbroke giving judgement (*Richard II*, IV.i, especially ll. 114ff.) is in a visual structure identical to the first scene of the play. Comparison in detail of those two scenes takes hours; but the visual pictures say it all in a split second. What we have here is something not far removed from the technique of the diptych or triptych painting, where the panels are complete in themselves but mean much, much more in relation to and comparison with the others. Or the recollection may be of a visual commonplace – to use the technical word, *topos* – outside the play entirely, well enough known to be confidently referred to by the author. A good example of this is in *The Tempest*, where the young lovers, Miranda and Ferdinand, are 'discovered' – that is, a curtain is drawn to reveal them – playing chess. The game of chess had for centuries been a common symbol of the 'love-battle', where victory and defeat are both sweet, played according to elaborate rules. Ferdinand and Miranda are thus signalled *visually* to be noble, restrained, in control of their passions – and very much in love. (In *Women Beware Women*, II.ii, Middleton seems to be using this

12. Shylock's holding the knife and a pair of scales with which to weigh Antonio's flesh in *The Merchant of Venice* (IV.1) emphatically (and parodically) reminds us of the emblematic figure of Justice – and just as she is blind, the point is made non-verbally that Shylock's seeking of so literal a justice is evidence of a spiritual blindness.

convention ironically.) Similarly, Richard's play with the mirror becomes very significant: a mirror is an attribute of Prudence, symbolizing self-knowledge. Visual commonplaces could be used in many ways, on and off stage; painting Queen Elizabeth with her hair loose (a signal that the lady was a virgin) and holding a few ears of corn links her firmly with the iconography of Astraea, whose attributes as Virgo Spicifera – i.e. the constellation Virgo, which is where Astraea on her retreat from the earth is supposed to have ended up – are loose hair and the ears of corn that symbolize the peace and plenty she will bring to earth (see below, pp. 43f., 62).

We must be on the alert for this tool of communication in Elizabethan drama. I cannot stress too strongly the value for the student of looking intently at the visual art of the period as a way into the signs of the drama and as a control on our reading of it.[13]

## viii *Props*

Elizabeth's ears of corn in a portrait are a prop, and lead us naturally to discuss the use of what props were available. In contrast to the sparseness of the stage and lack of scenery, there is evidence that props were often elaborate and certainly plentiful. But we must again bear in mind that even if in this respect the Elizabethan theatre is almost as versatile as our own, the use of props will not suddenly change an Elizabethan actor into a modern man; props will still be used conventionally and symbolically, even if those same props might be used differently by us.

Philip Henslowe was manager and major shareholder in the Admiral's Men, a theatrical company that was a rival to the Lord Chamberlain's (later, King's) Men which Shakespeare joined. (The actor Edward Alleyn became his son-in-law – a good move, for old Henslowe knew how to look after the pennies.) He kept a meticulous account of his financial transactions, of who was in his debt, of what he and his company possessed, of what each performance made. His diary – it is really a day-

13. There are various aids the student can use, short of buying an art gallery. Handbooks, like J. Hall's *Dictionary of Subjects and Symbols in Art* (London, 1974), and G. Ferguson, *Signs and Symbols in Christian Art* (Oxford, 1954) are a great help; so are contemporary handbooks of symbol and mythology, like Cesare Ripa's *Iconologia*, or emblem books like Alciato's *Emblematum Liber* (1531), or Geffrey Whitney's *A Choice of Emblemes* (1586), happily now available in reprints. The discussions in E. H. Gombrich's *Norm and Form* (London, 1978) and *Symbolic Images* (London, 1972) are invaluable. See also my *A Century of Emblemes*.

book – is an invaluable source of evidence for theatrical history, and from it we can get a pretty good idea of the props that were in stock, and how elaborate they were, particularly the portable ones. Henslowe's list is confirmed from Court accounts kept by the Office of the Revels, and so can be seen as pretty typical. It is a matter of some surprise how elaborate, indeed lavish, the props were.

While Henslowe's men were playing at the Rose theatre, we find they had tombs, chariots (including one to serve as the chariot of the sun, which must have been quite spectacular), mossy banks, trees (which, as the actors climb them in Dekker's *Old Fortunatus*, are unlikely to have been merely the columns of the canopy), houses made of lath and canvas, weapons, a crown, tables, chairs, stools, furry horsehair robes for 'wild men' (like Caliban), thrones, a Hell Mouth, and detached heads – not real, we may be sure. Internal evidence from the plays suggests other things as well that do not appear in this list: the putting out of Gloucester's eyes in *King Lear* requires an object actually to be palmed and then dropped – a gooseberry? It also demands that his eyes be smeared with blood – a small bladder of pig's blood held in Cornwall's sleeve? In *The Spanish Tragedy*, Hieronimo bites his own tongue out, and something bloody must be spat on to the floor. This sort of realistic detail in the fundamental unrealism of the stage is not a new thing; in late medieval plays, highly stylized as they were, there is the same sort of detailed realism. In a play of the Nativity, the midwife who attended the Blessed Virgin had a withered hand; touching the Infant Christ made it whole, and a manuscript illustration shows the withered hand hanging from the midwife's arm by a string – the illusion had been created by means of a glove. The use of props like these clearly suggests that dramatists and actors, recognizing as they did that their backdrop was symbolic and their context dependent on the audience's cooperative imagination, were nevertheless delighted to provide naturalism of detailed effect.

The lavishness of props suggests they were seen as really valuable tools, and the importance attached to them may explain the remarkable number of procession and Court scenes in Elizabethan drama. In this type of scene, not only would the stage be full of people wearing the fine clothes that, bought second-hand from the fashionable nobility, were so valuable (and powerful) a property, but the scene itself, whether static as in Court or mobile as in procession, could communicate a good deal of meaning – indeed, could be allegorical in exactly the same way as processions and tableaux in court masques could be allegorical. The use of properties of one kind or another in this sort of context is almost inescapable, and is a most valuable way of creating a symbolic spectacle. For besides their practical function, properties had their symbolic importance – the Hell Mouth in Henslowe's list cannot have been realistic in any but the most debased sense, but it was certainly symbolic. The throne of Denmark on which Claudius sits in *Hamlet* (I.ii) is already a symbol of ordered rule; but it is developed interestingly by a verbal play. 'State' can mean both state in the sense we usually understand it and also the actual throne on which a king sits. So Marcellus's remark at the end of *Hamlet* I.iv reminds us of Claudius's own unwittingly self-referential hint in his first speech in I.ii: '. . . thinking by our late dear brother's death/Our state to be disjoint and out of frame' – his hidden image of a rickety chair is suddenly seen to be very much to the point: a rotten wooden throne is a metaphor of the rottenness of the polity he has usurped by sitting on that throne. It may well have stayed on stage throughout the performance, with poetically devastating effect: the physical symbol of rottenness in the whole fabric of a kingdom focuses all the detailed demonstrations of that rottenness going on round it. In the last scene, it would be physically and visibly cleansed by the killing of Claudius while he sits on it.

The closeness of the audience meant that the effects achieved by the use of props had to be pretty good. Hence the paradox of the attitudes to acting; an actor is symbolic, he acts a role, but contemporary accounts praise good actors for doing this and at the same time for 'acting to the life'.

## ix *Acting and character: role and convention*

Acting cannot properly be discussed without bearing in mind that it is inextricably bound up with concepts of character both in life and in representational art. Those concepts in turn in this period are intimately connected with concepts of social role, its obligations, values and duties. The sense that all men are actors gives a peculiar edge to the problem. Even the praise of 'acting to the life' (a note which is sounded quite often in the early 1600s) indicates an awareness of acting as an art, and of the spectators' response as something like, 'If we did not know this was not real (which we do) we would mistake it for reality.'

Let us deal first with the ideas of character we need to bear in mind when analysing Renaissance plays. The concept of character is obviously linked to concepts of and assumptions about the theatre itself, as my brief discussion above (pp. 32f.) makes clear. What is also at issue is in essence quite simple: if Renaissance men did not think of the self in the way we do, it is highly improbable that when they came to write plays they suddenly created personalities that anticipated twentieth-century assumptions. It is a simple fact that there were certain ideas we take for granted that they *could not* have been using, because they had not, so to speak, been invented. The difference in their perception of the self is amply demonstrated in examples from all sorts of sources. Among the most telling are the design of buildings and their representation in the visual arts.

It is obvious that the sort of houses a society builds betrays assumptions about the nature of the family and of the self.[14] Unending lines of cheap back-to-back houses in a Victorian industrial town imply a view of man as an interchangeable unit of labour, whose individuation is of little interest. Modern tower blocks, or estates, equally impose restrictions on the type of life that can be lived there: man is seen as a statistic to be accommodated, a consumer like all the others, to be persuaded that certain material attributes of well-being are necessary; the physical form of the flat or house forces the family to be nuclear, near the statistical norm (or there are impossible strains on the house as a machine for living in), and has virtually killed the great and humane and immemorial benefits of the extended family – with accompanying social problems of appalling magnitude. Man can ultimately be viewed primarily as an individual, or as a unit in an economic process. Renaissance architecture and art shows us a very different idea: the houses that have survived, the treatises on good living, the pictures that calmly gaze out of time at us, all imply the essential publicness of a man's existence, and that that existence is intimately linked with a diverse community. The great houses as structures imply a degree of ceremony and formality even in the most intimate parts of one's life – at ablutions, or with one's wife – that seems strange to us; the cottages imply a closeness of contact that would be intolerable without the mental walls of structures of authority. We should find most distressing the lack of privacy – and the consequent need for ceremony and ritualized behaviour – to which medieval and Renaissance men were accustomed. All this assumes that a man defines himself by his role, that his life is governed by the obligations of that role,[15] that his

14. Some implications of this idea are examined in M. Girouard, *Life in the English Country House* (New Haven, 1978), and *Cities and People* (London, 1986).

15. Books of 'characters', like Overbury's *A Wife* (second edn, 1614), or Earle's *Microcosmographie* (1628), which are a series of short essays on 'A Downright Scholar', 'An Actor' and so on, clearly imply links between decorous physical appearance, moral behaviour and social expectations.

perception of his selfhood is formed against the background of a moral generalization of what is or is not appropriate – decorous – to an individual in his position. A king has responsibilities, temptations and joys that are not open to one of his subjects; a coal-heaver, as Aristotle is reported to have said, has some delights that are not decorous to a prince. (It is precisely this issue that Shakespeare is addressing in Henry's speech before Agincourt.) In real life each would speak differently, and have differing perspectives on the world, and different role expectations; in drama it is the simplest of all conventions that the low-life characters speak in prose, and even now we find it amusing when they attempt the artificiality of verse that on stage signals dignity and seriousness.[16] (This relationship between utterance, role and person becomes so central to Shakespeare's thinking in the Ricardian plays that it cannot easily be discussed in the present context. It will have to wait till Chapter 11 to be treated fully.)

From the cradle to the grave men acted a part, more or less consciously. It was an age when in real life men and women explicitly adopted a role, with clearly defined expectations and obligations, and asked to be judged by how well they performed it. It was an age when this objectivity about the self could extend to the actual serious rehearsal of death-bed scenes and dying speeches, when life and death could be seen as arts to be studied and ideal models were imitated. (Even as late as the 1740s, when Lord Chesterfield is writing to his natural son, we can discern this idea of the self.) In addition to her role as 'prince', Queen Elizabeth consciously adopted as a political tool a 'conceit' that she fulfilled the role and function of the virgin goddess Astraea, last of the immortals to leave the earth after the golden reign of Saturn, and whose return would herald a time of peace and justice. If we look at portraits of Elizabeth we see a representation of her physical appearance; but when we have learnt to read the picture's signals and symbols aright, we see that she is being defined not as a person simply, but as a person in a role, which is in turn defined by allusions to abstract, often moral, ideas of that role in the rest of the painting. She saw herself, indeed, as a walking symbol. In 1559, when the young queen was to enter the City of London in state, the city authorities devised a pageant, using the emblematic mode of expression so beloved of the period, to welcome her at Temple Bar. They constructed two artificial hills, one of bare earth with a dead

16. Much of the comedy of, for example, *The Knight of the Burning Pestle* or *The Shoemaker's Holiday*, or of the mechanicals in *A Midsummer Night's Dream*, depends on the perception of inverted role expectations.

tree on it, the other covered in greenery surmounted by a tree in full leaf. These were symbols of the languishing and the flourishing commonwealth, and it was the Crown's duty and privilege to encourage the commonwealth to fruit. It was a compliment to Elizabeth, since it suggested that only with her accession had things begun to look up; but it was also a veiled warning to the woman who sat on what was then the most insecure throne in Europe. They went further; between the two hills they set the representation of a dungeon, with its door being unlocked by an old man with wings and a scythe, who was thus releasing a maiden – who was not actually naked, as she might have been in the emblem books. Elizabeth recognized the emblem and its applicability to her at once: 'I too am the daughter of Time,' she exclaimed. But a modern audience can only react to this with puzzlement – why is this so clever a reply? Well, the old proverb had it that Truth is the daughter of Time, and many emblematic pictures have Time releasing her from a well or cave where she has been imprisoned by Slander and Untruth. Now Elizabeth had actually been imprisoned on a charge of treason by her sister; she had arrived at the Tower by the water entrance known as the Traitors' Gate. The whirligig of Time, however, had brought in his revenges, and Mary's death put Elizabeth unexpectedly on the throne. But with Elizabeth came the return of the reformed religion, finally ending the attempt under Mary to return to Roman Catholicism. A very Protestant City would have no doubts where Truth lay. Elizabeth's reply, in the same symbolic terms as the pageant, indicates her acceptance of the symbolic role as a control on her idea of herself. Her costly pageants, her courtiers' poetry, her progresses and her portraits – even her very clever refusal to be drawn into marriage – are all seen in terms of Astraean myth; they cunningly exploit the imagery and allusion, for the role model made a statement about the hopes of Elizabeth and her people about the relationship she hoped to establish towards the Church and the religious strife which was the bane of the late sixteenth century. We could so easily dismiss all this as a game, but it affected her personal life, the political life of the country, and the way men formulated their hopes and fears. Role models provide a political language, and some of the standards of social morality.[17]

When we approach dramatic characters, then, we need to bear these

17. Even today, when we are so sure we are wiser than our fathers, we can see the same use of visual and moral role models in the way in which American presidents and Soviet chairmen are presented to the people they rule.

ideas in mind, constantly to remind ourselves that role and its values are major determinants in the writing of a character, the way he will be dressed, attended and move on stage, the manner in which the actor will play him, and how the audience will receive him. This idea is fundamental to the history plays in this group, for Shakespeare is deeply concerned with role and person and character in them.

But as in real life a part is literally played, the terms of drama and life are interchangeable, and open up the philosophical issues about our response to acting in a peculiarly neat way. For the actor acting is also a man living, a real man suddenly acting another man who once was (or might have been) real. The illusion he creates, even if by conventional means, gives rise to feelings that are real but may not be directed to a strictly real object. Hamlet, confronted with the Player King, ex-emplifies exactly this problem. Here is the Player, on request, as a social grace, producing out of context a tragic speech. The implication of the request in the first place is that the player's art is to be enjoyed, and is not to be mistaken for reality. He appears moved by it, so that the observer sees real tears and all the signs of real feeling, and begins to sympathize with those feelings. But the actor is not moved; he is employing his art, and is pleased if it moves others – his desire is to be praised for the skill with which he does it. So the relationship between the appearance of real sorrow (the result of art) and the real thing, and the parallel between the man who appears to feel and act with no cause and Hamlet, who has cause but is unable to act or to orchestrate his feelings, become central. Hamlet sees the difficulty of coping with, knowing, genuineness of feeling – 'What's Hecuba to him, or he to Hecuba?' – and acting (in both senses) on it, while the audience is brought up sharply against the paradox of illusion, their non-illusory response to it, and the effect it has on them in real life in their own roles. For their lives do not stand still while watching a play.

The point is made stronger if we look at a rather downbeat use of this idea. With increasing frequency after the turn of the century, the word 'personating' is applied to acting. Its root meaning is linked to the Latin *persona*, 'mask', but it came to mean imitating the inner nature of people or things. In *1 Henry IV*, II.iv, Falstaff is made to 'personate' King Henry, and expresses in his charade something of the nature of his kingship (see p. 90). But when Hal plays king, we see again his long-term ends. Yet all present dismiss it as a game: Shakespeare pointedly makes Mistress Quickly (l. 388) remind us of the theatre – this is to her an imitation of the act of imitating. But Hal is saying something real that will affect them all. From this point on the relationship between the characters is changed even though none except Hal perceives it; in real time, in just this way, the audience may be affected by the whole play and yet dismiss it as mere illusion, unaware of the effect it has had on them.

The lack of physical distance between stage and audience makes the actor almost a member of the audience who is playing in a charade. For Shakespeare's audience the stage was not a remote other place, but somewhere where men of their own community might strut and fret their hour. The relevance – to use an overworked word – of the play to their own political, social and moral concerns is thus inescapable; it can hardly fail to be a discussion and reflection of them, in however remote a time and place it may be set.

The closeness to the audience has practical consequences too. Facial expressions, even as detailed as the movement of an eyebrow, will be able to be seen, and become an important part of the sign system. The sign system is of course complex, for an actor does not just speak his words; his tone, his projection of them, his gesture, his bodily attitude and, in this period at least, his clothing and props will all modify how they are received. Body language is a concept we are fairly familiar with; what is less familiar to us is the idea of it being codified and learnt as a formal grammar of movement.[18] Yet our Renaissance forebears clearly saw gesture in this way. John Bulwer's *Chironomia* and *Chirologia* (published together in 1624) are, among other things, an illustrated grammar of the gestures of the body that can convey a wide range of feelings, emotions and states. We can be sure a boy taking up the trade of acting would be required to learn all these, and learn too how to deploy them in appropriate situations. (It should be recalled that in the public theatre till the Restoration all female parts were played by boys.) Gesture, of course, extends to bodily attitude and the wearing of clothes. Ferdinand with 'his arms in this sad knot' (i.e. folded) is signifying without saying anything that he is 'inamorato', like the lover on the title page of Robert Burton's *Anatomy of Melancholy* (1651 edition), while Macduff, pulling his hat over his eyes, is signalling extreme grief – exactly how Malcolm takes it (*Macbeth*, IV.iii). (Something of this use of conventional body language survives in classical ballet.) Northumberland's entry at the beginning of *2 Henry IV* demands that he wear a coif, which tells the audience he is ill – or pretending to be. Finally, we must recall that this

18. Which, as Hamlet indicates in his speech to the Players (a nice irony there – an actor addressing actors at one further remove from reality), can be misused, or used tastelessly.

language of gesture is connected to the sort of visual pun Falstaff makes in *1 Henry IV*, II.iv, when he plays King Henry: he cannot but assume the posture, attitude and gesture that we see in prints of the queen herself in majesty.

Positioning too is important. Iago's confiding in the audience upstages what is going on behind him in a way totally comprehensible to a modern audience – and it also shows his isolation. But there are more complex examples. A formal Court scene, or judgement scene, must to make sense have been staged so that the ruler or judge was at the apex of a visual pattern symbolizing power, and in all probability sitting on a throne or judgement seat. Claudius in this position may take some people in; but a Hamlet not in colourful Court dress but the black of mourning, refusing to take his part in the visual and social pyramid on the stage, forces us to see the rottenness in this state and Claudius as a king of shreds and patches. Hamlet's visual and spatial distinction comments both on himself and the Court. Similarly, to play the first scene of *King Lear* with only the principals on stage, and as informally as if it were a visit to a family solicitor, as some modern producers do, is not only tasteless but shows a fundamental misunderstanding of Shakespeare's intentions in the play. There are only a few speaking parts, but no Renaissance dignitary was without attendants, particularly in a rather important Court scene – which is what this is. There must have been some thirty people on stage, if one allows each speaker two attendants. So the scene is visually gorgeous, and must be structured like a court where judgement and matters of political moment are to be decided – that is, with Lear on the throne, his nobles and children in ranks round him. A visual image of enormous security; yet what Lear proceeds to do is negate his royalty, pervert his justice, destroy his family, and break faith with the order of the universe of which his kingship is an integral linking part and which is symbolized in the painted heavens above him. The position of the actors makes an important moral point.

It is well to compare this scene with the very similar first scene of *Richard II*. Richard is enthroned among his peers, acting in the king's supreme judicial role of settling quarrels between his subjects. He opens the play with authoritative language delivered in regal tones. So far, so good; all the signals suggest security, justice, order. But soon it becomes clear that the quarrel actually implicates Richard's earlier action in disposing of Gloucester – the king himself is being judged. Richard fails to reconcile or even keep the lid on the antagonists, and loses control. The discourse of the scene undercuts and at the same time is itself made ironic by the suggestions of order and secure majesty in the staging (see below, p. 113).

## x *The companies and the performances*

In the last two decades of the sixteenth century, we know of several companies of players. Their organization needs brief description, for it affects the way plays were written and what could be tackled.

The companies were commercial enterprises, for whom Art was all very well – if it paid the rent. They made their money by selling dreams and illusion, and, if Alleyn (of the Admiral's Men) and Shakespeare and Burbage are anything to go by, the market was buoyant. Burbage owned a lot of real estate in London and lent out money on interest; Shakespeare, who (so legend has it) once had the lowly job of holding horses outside the theatre, retired with a coat of arms to Stratford and bought the best house in the town; and Alleyn left a fortune (partly inherited from Henslowe) to found a school. Though there do seem to have been employees, the companies were in the main free associations of individuals, each of whom bought into the company and received of the profits in proportion to his share. Originally the companies may have been groups of travelling players, moving from fair to fair and banded together for their mutual advantage; certainly the legal attitude to actors, which is exemplified by acts of Parliament that class them as vagrants and subject to the savage vagrancy laws, would be consonant with such an origin. But the uncertain legal attitude to them – for example, even late in the period the magistrates of the City of London were always trying to get them imprisoned and their theatres closed – led them to seek support from powerful people. A noble might allow them to use his name – 'Lord Strange's Men' for instance – and even wear his livery. By so doing they became technically part of his household or, to use the legal term, *familia*, and thus out of reach of the vagrancy laws. The status of actors gradually rose; Shakespeare's company became the Lord Chamberlain's Men and later, on the arrival of James I, the King's Men.

Yet even then, they were still in a precarious position. An outbreak of plague could, if deaths rose beyond a certain point, allow the magistrates to close all places of public resort except churches. A closed theatre makes no money. The London magistrates were only too pleased to shut them on any excuse, for having got them out of the City they found that the players had settled in places notorious for far less innocent pleasures, like the South Bank. The civil mind, then as now, was always looking for an opportunity to clean things up. (It is sobering to think that the sublime love poetry of *Romeo and Juliet* echoed not many yards from the notorious brothels of Southwark, that the delicacy of *The Tempest* or *The Winter's Tale* was only yards from the bear-baiting pit the same company ran – and whose bear, probably, they borrowed to chase Antigonus off stage in the latter play.) Yet if things could go badly wrong, there were also, obviously, large rewards: a Court command performance, or a performance at a big wedding (*A Midsummer Night's Dream*) might bring in a good deal of money. Thus the actors could well become the friends of the great, as Shakespeare clearly did; but that might have its own particular perils. On the eve of his rebellion the Earl of Essex arranged for the Lord Chamberlain's Men to perform *Richard II* – a move that did not go down well with the old queen, who saw herself as all too like a Richard awaiting a Bolingbroke. Political involvement could be dangerous, but, as in this case, it was not always avoidable. In the next reign, the King's Men were quietly tipped off that if they wanted to keep their ears it would not be a good idea to go ahead with a production of *Sir Thomas More*, which could well be inflammatory at a time of some unrest.

Setting aside special Court performances, plays in the public theatres took place in the afternoons. There is some evidence for seeing each playhouse as having – perhaps not exclusively – a regular clientele whose tastes, interests and concerns it understood and catered for. But even so, audiences were heterogeneous and often unruly; the appeals for sympathy to be given to the players are often quite sincere. At one end of the scale would be young men of fashion, showing off in the odious way that only young men in a group can; at the other would be citizens and their wives (or not), apprentices, and the usual swarm of pickpockets and prostitutes whose presence there the magistrates saw as good enough reason for being antagonistic to the whole idea of public theatres. Not a sympathetic audience – worse, in fact, than a schools matinée audience today. The dramatist and his actors had to get hold of it pretty fast and keep hitting it hard if control (and profit) were not to be lost. Hence the speed of performances – *Hamlet* in two hours, if we take what is said literally! – and the (to us) curious practice of following a profound and serious play with a farce, a stand-up comic, or, oddest of all, a jig performed by one of the talented clowns. Hamlet's jibes about Polonius – 'He's for a jig, or a tale of bawdry' – turns on just this, and on Polonius's inability to appreciate art (a nice

49

self-reference in the play, for *Hamlet* too would be followed by a comedy).

These contexts are not just interesting in themselves; they have a real bearing on the freedom of manoeuvre a dramatist has in composition. He has to please his audience, and get them to come and spend their money at his theatre rather than at a rival's. But he also has to cope with the restriction of what the members of his company could and could not do. Shakespeare was a working member of a company, who acted as well as wrote, and knew his fellows' capacities; it clearly had some effect on how he could plan his plays, for he had a cast before he wrote a play. Moreover, he had to find some way of using everybody – even if only in a walk-on part – or there would be squawks of indignation. He knew who was to play what when he was writing the play, and he knew that a Burbage or Kempe was a great draw and must be given a chance to do what people liked seeing him do on stage. Hence the strictly unnecessary development of Dogberry in *Much Ado About Nothing*, or, perhaps, the Christopher Sly passages in *The Taming of the Shrew*.

## xi *Moral expectations: responses to Classical theory and 'Morality'*

The last general context we must briefly consider is what were the commonly held moral expectations of drama. These are clearly not quite the same as ours – the discussion of character above has implied as much – and they will necessarily affect not only the way Shakespeare wrote his history plays but the way they would be viewed. Two elements have to be considered: the inheritance from the morality drama, and the fashionable theories about drama that were beginning to spread to England from Europe.

The rediscovery of Aristotle's *Poetics* in the late fifteenth century had a profound effect on dramatic and poetic criticism. Here was a text, by the revered figure who was often called simply 'the Philosopher', which took drama seriously, relating it theoretically to psychological and moral issues. (Aristotle's discussion specifically of tragedy is looked at below, p. 83.) It is important not just for the ideas it contained, but also for the responses it called forth. Aristotle's views demanded re-examination of Horace's on the utility of poetry and Cicero's on the functional nature of rhetoric, the art of composition and speaking. What place had these arts in civilized life and how could they be justified? Italian scholars were the first to address themselves to the problem; the first detailed commentary on the *Poetics* was that of Francisco Robortello, printed in Florence in 1548. He sees drama as primarily a form of rhetoric, a means of doing something to an audience to improve them morally. He claims that the purpose of poetry is to give delight by imitation through language, and that the imitation of a serious and dignified sequence of events in drama will not only demonstrate with what fortitude others have endured suffering, but arouse the audience's pity, fear and admiration. His justifications, therefore, are entirely moral, and he implies that a good play is one which holds examples to be imitated up for an audience's consideration.

This moral emphasis is continued in Antonio Minturno's *De Poeta* (1559). Naturally he draws on Aristotle – who at this time could not, and still be taken seriously? But he gives prime place to an idea of man's fallen state, where as a result of Adam's primal sin everything in the world is flawed, all is subject to change and decay, and nothing is to be trusted. The audience, he claims, develop an increased regard for virtue by seeing the misfortunes of others, and learn not to trust prosperity or fortune; they learn a fortitude with which to face troubles. As in Robortello, there is the implication of the audience's objective as well as imaginative response to a moral pattern.

The *Poeticae Libri Septem* of Julius Caesar Scaliger (1561) were enormously influential for more than a century. Scaliger rather tends to modify Aristotle's implication that poetry (including drama) as an imitation is a self-justifying activity peculiar to humans. He draws in Horatian and Ciceronian ideas of it as a form of rhetoric, a means of pleasurable instruction. In Book VII he rejects as inadequate Aristotle's theory of mimesis or imitation on the powerful (though not conclusive) grounds that if the definition of poetry is that it is an imitation, any imitation thereby becomes a poem. With an emphasis once more on teaching via pleasure, he concludes that the poet has a responsibility for the moral education of his audience, teaching them how to avoid bad actions and follow good. Finally, and importantly for our purpose, he sees poetry as part of a complex that includes ethics and politics, assisting the community towards harmony or happiness (*beatitudo*) through proper action, which is a consequence of being affected by good models.

Perhaps the most interesting of the Italian critics is Lodovico Castelvetro (1505–71) who published his translation and commentary on the *Poetics* in 1570. He had a considerable influence on the thought of Sir Philip Sidney. Sidney's *Defence of Poesie* (1595) altered the terms of the discussion in England for ever and a day, and it is inconceivable that Shakespeare was unaware of it – indeed, he gives lines to Theseus in *A Midsummer Night's Dream* (V.i.2ff.) which surely imply knowledge and understanding of it. Castelvetro takes an uncompromisingly aristocratic stand; for the first time ever the Ciceronian and Horatian stress on the utility of poetry is rejected, and he sees drama as pleasurable popular entertainment for the stupid common people – those who know better will read. Yet he makes one very important point: verisimilitude is the essential dramatic quality, and a play, like a poem, shows what could quite plausibly happen; it is closely related to history, which shows what did in fact happen.

The critical debate proceeds largely in these terms on its theoretical level (as distinct from the level where individual details of a dramatic construction are to be assessed). The common ground between most writers, which Sidney shares, is that drama is not only powerfully affecting but is morally charged, that watching drama is not just pleasurable but an act of moral education. There is also the clear implication that the attitude of the audience is objective and discriminatory even while they are being moved – indeed, that their very being moved is a proper object of their attention. Now in the last decades of the century, these ideas are common among Shakespeare's contemporaries: Ben Jonson and John Webster, for example, are clearly familiar with them, and it is a fair assumption that Shakespeare was too. They cannot but affect the way he wrote his plays. Once again, we find ourselves firmly directed to seeing their moral and exemplary dimension as important.

Practical traditions also affected Shakespeare, his fellows, his actors and his audiences. One was the tradition in the universities of Latin and Greek drama, either classical or based on classical models. With the heavy influence of Seneca in tragedy, and in comedy of Plautus and Terence, on its style, subjects and treatment, it never had popular appeal, but many dramatists borrow plots and occasional motifs from it. A more important influence is the interlude, originally part of a festive entertainment, often symbolic, often comic. But the really important influence derived from the Morality drama of the late Middle Ages. Briefly, the Moralities are dramas whose major aim is the moral and spiritual teaching and health of their audiences; they can be full of rough and robust humour, but it is humour in the service of a moral aim. Their formulation of issues relies heavily on the allegorical and symbolic traditions of the Middle Ages, particularly in the use of personifications like the Seven Deadly Sins (pride, anger, lechery, envy, gluttony, avarice, sloth) or the Virtues. The whole point of these figures is that they should have vivid physical attributes that express their moral nature, and the dramas in which they appear are to be amusing and yet to leave the audience with a deeper, emotionally charged, understanding of a moral issue, state or problem. *Everyman* is about the best known today, and is a good example of what I mean. We all know – intellectually – that we are going to die; the allegorical drama of this play gives a new emotional sense of what that actually might mean. The very stage on which they played, however makeshift, was symbolic of the world in which real men lived and made moral choices.

It must be remembered that until the 1580s at least these highly symbolic plays were regularly performed throughout England, and continued to be played on the continent till much later. Their influence on the drama of Shakespeare's time is often ignored, but it is in fact huge. The Porter scene in *Macbeth* (II.i), for example, cleverly uses close allusion to the play of the Harrowing of Hell, when Christ the Redeemer breaks into the Castle of Hell, in order to underline what has happened to Macbeth – and the importance of Macduff. The Porter even has verbal echoes of this well-known play. Similarly, the references to Falstaff as 'that old white-bearded Satan', to his 'dagger of lath', link him to Vice, or Riot, the tempter of Youth, in the Moralities: which makes *us* see the Boar's Head scenes in a new way (see below, pp. 93f., 143f.). Finally, we discern once again the objectivity of the audience's viewpoint – an objectivity that leaves great scope for irony – and the playing of the individual character against an expected norm.

The theatrical experience, then, is a moral and philosophical one, whatever else it is. It takes place in a symbolic building; and when the gales of laughter or the tears of sympathy have abated, the audience is presented with a moral problem to solve. And the dramatic language gives them the tools to begin to do so. What we have been discussing is ways of understanding human life, and that direction must lead us to our next topic: concepts of history. For this too is deeply involved in any discussion of Shakespeare's history plays, or anyone else's.

# 4. Sad Stories of the Death of Kings

It has often been said that the English take their history from Shakespeare and their theology from Milton. The second part of the remark is perhaps less applicable now, when both theology and Milton are temporarily out of fashion, but the first still holds some truth. Generations have grown up, particularly in this century of universal school attendance, who know only that version of late fourteenth- and fifteenth-century English history that Shakespeare gives, not with total accuracy (to say the least), in his plays. Indeed, at the end of the eighteenth century knowledge of Shakespeare's version of English history was assumed to be so widespread that for cartoonists like Gillray, Dent and Cruikshank allusion to it was a major vehicle for their political satire and commentary on the connection of the Prince Regent and the Holland House group, the events of the Regency and after. Over four centuries Shakespeare has had a huge influence on Englishmen's perception of the historical past – which must, in turn, affect the way they see themselves and their own political situation; and we need now to consider ideas and theories of kingship and of history with which Shakespeare and his audience were familiar, and which he used in his plays. We also need to look at the related issue of what he did to material he found in his sources, and the vision of England and its kings he implies in his work.

## i *Obedience and the prince*

In common experience, immortal and holy kingship may be abused by unholy and mortal man. Kings are not always good rulers, and their position – its sanctity underlined by the coronation ritual – as God's vice-gerent on earth can be abused. Some are incompetent, a few are wicked. The Middle Ages are full of examples; and full of examples, too, of revolt and rebellion against them. In theory, the sky should have fallen, and it had not done. This had long exercised men's minds, for it raised the huge issues of the subject's duty of obedience to a bad ruler and the ruler's responsibility to his people. It also, ultimately, called in question the truth of the neat and delicate fabric of the model.

*The people's duty*

Our starting-point must be the Bible, whose importance in forming the mind, shaping the history and providing a moral and spiritual terminology for Western man is simply impossible to overestimate. Its enormous authority, both as the record of God's dealings with men in history and as God's own inspired word, meant that what it said had to be taken very seriously indeed – to cite a text was often to settle the argument. But here as elsewhere, this vast collection of different sorts of books, written at different times for different purposes in different situations, is not consistent, and when we come to look at the tradition of thought that saw the king as a provisional rather than absolute authority we shall have to return to it. But for the time being I shall concentrate on the support to be derived from the Bible for the subject's duty of unqualified obedience.

King Solomon, son of David, King of Israel, was a great monarch. His wisdom, prudence and justice were already legendary very soon after his reign, and for later centuries right down to the Renaissance he is seen as one of the types of the Good King, showing in human form some of the attributes of the King of Kings Himself. Several of the 'wisdom' books of the Bible are ascribed to him, among them Ecclesiastes. This short book is written as if by a monarch, a monarch who has pursued wisdom and knowledge, and who has seen the vanity of human wishes. The writer stresses the limitedness of human knowledge and understanding, human vulnerability to chance and accident, and emphasizes that things do not always accord with what we perceive as natural justice; the wise man will seek to grasp this insight and take things as they come, knowing the limitations of his wisdom. It has, naturally enough, several political/moral pieces of advice:

> I counsel thee to keep the king's commandment, and that in regard of the oath of God.
> Be not hasty to go out of his sight: stand not in an evil thing; for he doeth whatsoever pleaseth him.
> Where the word of a king is, there is power; and who may say unto him, What doest thou?

> (viii.2–4)

Or again:

> Curse not the king, no, not in thy thought ...

> (x.20)

> Fear God, and keep his commandments: for this is the whole duty of man.
> For God shall bring every work into judgment, with every secret thing, whether it be good, or whether it be evil.

> (xii.13–14)

Equally, the writer is aware of the crucial importance of the person of the king, and the danger of weak central authority where the subjects are over-mighty and do not obey the monarch. Everyone is in for a bad time:

> Woe to thee, O land, when thy king is a child, and thy princes eat in the morning!
> Blessed art thou, O land, when thy king is the son of nobles, and thy princes eat in due season, for strength, and not for drunkenness![1]

> (x.16–17)

To this Old Testament advice can be added the historical evidence that Saul, then David, then Solomon – and others – were specifically commissioned by God to be kings; the king was the Lord's Anointed, and to oppose him was near to blasphemy, opposing God himself. The point was taken up later; the writer of the First Epistle General of St Peter[2] emphasizes, too, the duty of obedience:

> Submit yourselves to every ordinance of man for the Lord's sake: whether it be to the king, as supreme;
> Or unto governors, as unto them that are sent by him for the punishment of evil doers, and for the praise of them that do well.
> For so is the will of God, that with well doing ye may put to silence the ignorance of foolish men:
> As free, and not using your liberty for a cloak of maliciousness, but as the servants of God.
> Honour all men. Love the brotherhood. Fear God. Honour the king.
> Servants, be subject to your masters with all fear [respect]; not only to the good and gentle, but also to the froward.

> (ii.13–18)

He is here talking about the relationships between Christians within the Christian community, and also about their relationship to the secular power structures. All power structures ultimately exist on God's sufferance alone – like Pilate, they could not have that power had not one higher given it to them – and thus have a limited but valid authority

---

1. This was a text much cited – for example by Langland – during the long minority of Richard II and the regency of his terrible uncles.

2. Possibly St Peter himself, but certainly dating from well before the end of the first century AD.

which deserves obedience. Yet the writer has subtly shifted his emphasis; what is at issue is not so much the validity of rule as the moral value for the ruled of proper obedience.

We find this theologically based argument for the subject's obedience to his monarch very strongly in Tudor thought. It was of course powerfully supported by what was perceived to be the very nature of the created universe, its ordering by degree deriving from God himself. (This is as powerful an argument as it would be to say, in our terms, that an idea is independently based on theoretical and empirical evidence.) It is also supported by appeals to history, to all the democracies and aristocracies that have failed. For example, William Tyndale's *The Obedience of a Christian Man: and how Christian rulers ought to govern* (1528) uses citations from the Bible and from history to support the argument that all power is delegated from God and that no resistance should be offered to magistrates. Sir Thomas Elyot's *The Boke named the Governour* (1531)[3] defines public weal (we might call it a commonwealth) as 'a body living, compact or made of sundry estates and degrees of men, which is disposed by the order of equity and governed by the rule and moderation of reason'. At the top of a hierarchical pyramid there must be a single ruler, the prince. Monarchy is the natural form of government; the Bible makes clear – if only in the choosing and anointing of Saul and later of David – that God ordains it, and history shows it preserves order better than other systems. He suggests that kings should rule for the welfare of their subjects, but in effect the royal power – the prerogative – is theoretically unlimited; the king in his realm rules over nobles, commons and clergy (all disposed by and observing the harmony of order and degree ordained by God) like God in his universe. Indeed, Elyot's first chapter includes a very full and clear statement of the idea of degree and of the interdependence of every class with every other class, which I discussed above (Chapter 2, pp. 8–16). He goes on to argue specifically against both aristocracy and democracy, the former because, however noble the rulers may be, individuals will be 'incensed with glory, some with ambition, others with covetousness and desire of treasure or possessions. Whereby

3. The book was certainly influential. It had been reprinted seven times by 1580. Shakespeare may well have read it, since a story of Prince Hal's anger in Book II, Chapter VI seems to be one of his sources for *1* and *2 Henry IV*. He has close verbal echoes of Elyot's first chapters in passages on political theory in *Henry V* and *Troilus and Cressida*. A very large part of the book is devoted to the education in desirable qualities of the subsidiary magistrates – 'inferior governors' – through whom the prince rules, which is a consideration not far from the heart of Shakespeare's political thought in the history plays and in *Measure for Measure*.

they fall into contention.' Democracy fails, he says, because it either falls into mere tyranny or because the commons, ungoverned, 'order everything without justice, only with vengeance and cruelty, and with incomparable difficulty and unneth [hardly] by any wisdom be pacified and brought again into order'. By contrast, a well-ordered monarchy is a model of mutual benefit, like a hive of bees: exactly the image Shakespeare puts in the mouth of the Archbishop of Canterbury in the first scene of *Henry V*.

This view was by no means unusual even at the end of the century. In 1610 James I felt able to address Parliament in these words:

The State of monarchy is the supremest thing on earth; for kings are not only God's lieutenants upon earth and sit upon God's throne, but even by God Himself they are called Gods.

One recalls, indeed, the Duchess of York's remark to Bolingbroke – quite without irony – in *Richard II* (V.iii.135): 'A god on earth thou art!' (but see below, p. 168). This extreme statement might shock some people, but many more would be shocked by John Selden's view, just a little later, that 'A King is a thing men have made for their own sakes, for quietness' sake.' Even Selden, though, stresses the powers the king alone, *rex solus*, exercised as the royal prerogative, the extent of which was still very great.

The strands – utilitarian, theoretical and theological – would come together on a Sunday morning in the parish church. Article 35 of the Thirty-Nine Articles of the Church of England – which are, in effect, its agreed theological and institutional position after the upheavals of the 1540s and 1550s – enjoins the minister to read from the Second Book of Homilies, issued in 1563, to his congregation (who risked the hefty fine of one shilling if they did not attend church). The last in the book, No. 21, is 'Against Rebellion', strongly maintaining the subject's duty of obedience to the Lord's Anointed. The voice that had been speaking the Word of God was the same the parishioner heard enjoining the subject's whole duty of obedience to his divinely appointed, legally enthroned monarch, and outlining the dreadful consequences that would befall the world if obedience were refused, even to a bad king; and the man in the compulsory pew probably didn't make much distinction between the books from which the parson drew his words. No one could be ignorant, therefore, of the duty of obedience; and it was even more subtly disseminated as a received idea, beyond argument, in art, in poetry and in drama.

Article 37 of the Thirty-Nine Articles enhances the position of the monarch even further:

> ... [we give to our princes] that only prerogative, which we see to have been given always to all godly Princes in Holy Scriptures by God Himself; that is, that they should rule all estates and degrees committed to their charge by God, whether they be Ecclesiastical or Temporal, and restrain with the civil sword the stubborn and evildoers.

This in fact makes the English crown the ultimate authority in the land, and as such capable of regulating the affairs of the Church; the Church ceases to be a sort of parallel state, and becomes one of the concerns of state. This is a far cry from the power the papacy claimed for itself, to be above even kings – most vividly demonstrated in the penance, barefoot in the snow, of the Emperor Henry IV before Pope Gregory VII at Canossa in 1077. It is arrived at not just through force of circumstance; there is theory behind it.

It is often forgotten that one of the most influential books in Sixteenth-century French and English political thought is the *De Monarchia* of Dante. Writing in the fourteenth century, at a time when the Roman Church was in deep crisis and had lost much credibility as an institution, Dante draws on his huge learning, his wide reading of history, to discuss the basic issues of what government is for. (He is of course heavily dependent on St Augustine's *City of God*.) And in the end he offers a theory of government. Shortly, when we look at the duty of the prince, we shall return to Dante (p. 64); here the major point is that Dante gives to the prince the duty of regulating the Church as an institution, as acting truly as God's vice-gerent on earth – the position symbolized by the Eagle in *Paradiso* – and as accountable only to God. (He does not, of course, deny the Church's sovereign right to determine matters of moral and spiritual import.) His righteousness, because he is human, can only be a limited righteousness; nevertheless the subject has no right to question: his virtue consists in obedience and endurance. It is here, perhaps, that we should see the origins of what in England under James I became known as the 'Divine Right of Kings' and in France developed into the concept of absolute monarchy.

## The prince's person and the prince's duty

'I think the King is but a man, as I am'; ironic as it is, spoken by the disguised Henry V on the night before Agincourt, nevertheless it focuses sharply the issue of the way the man's individuality relates to the awesome office that orthodox majority opinion would have him hold. For, as I have hinted above, it was common ground to recognize that the prince had two 'bodies': the one fallible, mortal, private, the other consisting in his immortal, divinely sanctioned office, which lives on after the death of individual holders. There is no dearth of material to illustrate this – it survives, indeed, in the old French announcement of a king's death, '*Le roy est mort, vive le roy*.' Spenser, writing to Ralegh about the incomplete *Faerie Queene*, expresses it very neatly: Queen Elizabeth appears in the poem both as Belphoebe and as the Faerie Queene, 'considering she hath two persons, the one of a most royal queene or Empresse, the other of a most virtuous and beautiful lady'.[4]

As an individual in an immortal role, therefore, in the late Middle Ages and Renaissance, the type of education a ruler or prince should undergo to fit him for his almost sacred role was the subject of much discussion; for he is but a man. It is a problem that is as much with us today as it was for Plato: all states have rulers, and they need training for that job, like any other. Yet our orthodoxy is that while we expect to need training for just about everything else, even roadsweeping, we can become successful legislators and rulers simply by collecting more uninformed votes than the other person.

The private man must master the twelve private moral virtues in order to be able to compass 'that other part of polliticke vertues in his person, after that hee came to be king' (Spenser again, to Ralegh, writing of his character Prince Arthur as he planned to use him in his poem). The education of the prince is a major concern in the period and, as we shall see, an important theme of *1* and *2 Henry IV*. In real life, the young James VI and I was enabled to become the wisest fool in Christendom by being subjected to a systematic programme of princely education. John Gower's great poem *Confessio Amantis*, written originally in the unhappy reign of Richard II, was much read in the sixteenth century; in Book VII it discusses at length the education of a prince in moral, philosophical and civil arts, to enable him to be a good ruler who will hold the realm together in unity and godly love, who will do justice and love mercy. The ideal is Christian; its sanctioning example is the education the pagan Aristotle is supposed to have given Alexander the

4. Long after the idea ceased to have the serious force it had in the Renaissance, Coleridge expressed the heart of it beautifully: 'I respect the man while, and only while, the king is translucent through him: I reverence the glass case for the Saint's sake within; except for that, it is to me mere glazier's work, – putty, and glass, and wood' (*Table Talk*, 20 August 1830).

Great.[5] Sir Thomas Elyot, again, spends a large part of *The Boke named the Governour* discussing the virtues necessary in governors, the servants of the prince. The implication is that the prince himself should, within the Aristotelian ideal of 'nothing in excess', enjoy the qualities of majesty, affability, placability, humanity, benevolence, liberality, amity, justice, faith, fortitude, patience, magnanimity, constancy and temperance.[6]

That the happiness of the reign, for prince and people, is ultimately dependent on morality is a commonplace. James I expresses it in commonplace language in the sonnet prefacing his *Basilikon Doron* ('The Gifts of a King'), a little book he wrote in 1599 – the same year as *Henry V* – on the duties of a prince, for his son Prince Henry (aged five!):

> *If then ye would enioy a happie raigne,*
> *Obserue the Statutes of your heauenly King,*
> *And from his Law, make all your Lawes to spring.*
> *Since his Lieutenant here ye should remaine,*
> *Reward the iust, be stedfast, true and plaine,*
> *Represse the proud, mayntayning aye the right,*
> *Walke alwayes so, as euer in his sight . . .*

Roger Ascham, Elizabeth's tutor, likewise is concerned not only to educate his charge – which he did excellently, so that hers was one of the most accomplished minds in her kingdom – but also in his book to encourage servants of the state who mirrored the ideal virtues of the prince. Sir Thomas Hoby's translation of Baldassare Castiglione's *The Book of the Courtier* (1561) is similar; it went through four editions before 1603, which shows that there was a considerable demand for this manual of liberal and courtly education. Elyot, Ascham and Hoby recognized that power entailed responsibilities and qualities whose development could not be safely left to chance, the interest of philistine nobles who distrusted education, or the self-seeking of narrowly educated lawyers. Castiglione's views on *cortegiania* are summed up by Gabriel Harvey, the friend of Spenser, whose *Faerie Queene* also has similar political and moral concerns:

Above all things it importeth a courtier to be graceful and lovely in countenance and behaviour; fine and discreet in discourse and entertainment; skilful and expert

5. Fluellen's ludicrous linking of Henry V with Alexander is ludicrous only in the way it is done; the comparison of the ideal king, Henry V, with one of the Nine Worthies is quite serious on Shakespeare's part. The comedy avoids incredible overstatement.

6. Virtually exactly the 'king-becoming graces' Malcolm outlines to Macduff in *Macbeth*, IV.iii.90ff., quoted below, p. 116.

in letters and arms; active and gallant in every courtly exercise; nimble and speedy of body and mind; resolute, industrious and valiant in action; as profound and invincible in action as it is possible; and withal ever generously bold, wittily pleasant, and full of life in his sayings and doings.

It is in these terms that Shakespeare makes Ophelia praise Hamlet, who was 'like to have proved most royal':

> *The courtier's, soldier's, scholar's eye, tongue, sword:*
> *The expectancy and rose of the fair state,*
> *The glass of fashion and the mould of form . . .*

We shall see later that this concern is very much a part of Shakespeare's portrayal of the development into kingship of Prince Hal; and we shall see that it is the initial failure to live up to the assumptions of the nature of the prince that begins the tragedy of Richard II. What a king should not be and should not do is fully implied by John of Gaunt's rebuke to Richard (*Richard II*, II.i.93ff.).

But the king is but a man. These ideas ask a lot of a mere mortal – even though some, unbelievably, seem to have achieved it. The discussion above in Chapter 3 (pp. 41ff.) of the importance in daily life of role and ritual to define the projection of the self and give it parameters within which to work suggests one way its achievement may have been aided; one becomes the thing one acts. There is also the factor of the common consent of the governed and governor in the creation of a political myth as a means of defining and managing their relationship. I have already mentioned (p. 39) the linking of Elizabeth to Astraea – a compliment, a hope, a political statement. We are dealing with a concept of royalty that is mythic, almost sacral, on both sides; a 'divinity that doth hedge a king', of which Richard is so ironically aware, for that sweet lovely rose is betrayed by his subjects, and the garden witnesses another Fall. In the poetry as well as the painting and pageants of the time we can see this. Spenser, in the 'Aprill Aegloga' of his *Shepheardes Calender* has his character Hobbinol repeat a song by Colin Clout, who has deserted him. It is thinly disguised praise of Elizabeth: she is like Phoebe the moon,[7] her rays chasten the sun himself ('he blusht to see another Sunne below'), the muses – a neat self-reference – sing her praise, to be in attendance on her is to be in Heaven, and so on. But behind the compliment is hard

---

7. Elizabeth as the 'mortal moon' (Shakespeare, Sonnet 107) is one of the commonest visual and verbal images of the period. Diana is patroness of virginity, reflects the light of the sun, is mistress of the sea, giver of fortune – the possibilities for compliment and veiled admonition are almost endless.

sense; she is a peaceful monarch, and that is what monarchy is about. Sir Walter Ralegh also uses this convention of extreme compliment. *The Ocean's Love to Cynthia* describes the queen as a heavenly body, a mortal moon, a light-giver, and so on. Where the prince is a woman, the artificial conceits of love poetry can be a political convention; the lover's devotion extends and mirrors the subject's honour and respect. Yet there is also the irony that Elizabeth was, once, really attractive, a single woman in a Court dominated by men, whose hand in marriage, once given, would alter the political map of England and Europe. In a curious way, these poems of compliment to the monarch, the fount of all honour, are genuinely sexual too. The Two Bodies have become inseparable.

In the last scene of one of Shakespeare's last plays, *Henry VIII*, written well after the queen's death, he puts into the mouth of Archbishop Cranmer a prophecy of her virtues and powers. It is worth quoting at length, for it summarizes what we may take to be Shakespeare's positive ideas of what a monarch should be:

> *She shall be . . .*
> *A pattern to all princes living with her,*
> *And all that shall succeed. Saba* [8] *was never*
> *More covetous of wisdom and fair virtue*
> *Than this pure soul shall be. All princely graces*
> *That mould up such a mighty piece as this is,*
> *With all the virtues that attend the good,*
> *Shall still be doubled on her. Truth shall nurse her,*
> *Holy and heavenly thoughts still counsel her,*
> *She shall be loved and feared. Her own shall bless her;*
> *Her foes shake like a field of beaten corn,*
> *And hang their heads with sorrow. Good grows with her;*
> *In her days every man shall eat in safety*
> *Under his own vine what he plants, and sing*
> *The merry songs of peace to all his neighbours.*
> *God shall be truly known, and those about her*
> *From her shall read the perfect ways of honour,*
> *And by those claim their greatness, not by blood . . .*

But even in Elizabeth's day, despite the flattery,[9] there is still an

8. Sheba, whose queen visited King Solomon to see if the reputation of his wisdom was true. Shakespeare turns this passage later into praise of James I, who, supposedly, inherits Elizabeth's virtues; this does not invalidate the point that he had a free choice whether or not to write this passage, and chose in it to give a picture of ideal and godly rule.

9. So we would class it. The danger of flattery to the judgement and balance of those in authority is a constantly recurring theme in literature from the early Middle Ages onwards.

understanding that politics is the art of the possible, that human beings are inconsistent and fallible creatures, that the prince's power is not in practice unlimited. Both prince and Parliament handle this issue gingerly, avoiding a head-on clash – both have an interest in the preservation of the myth and each knows the other knows the other knows it is a myth. Myths have a way of informing, even determining, reality, and better a myth of excellence and its partial achievement than the perception of human existence, with Thersites in *Troilus and Cressida*, as nothing more than wars and lechery; for that too is self-fulfilling, as we are finding out.

The obligations of the prince are many. The Augustinian concept of *ordo* immediately puts him in a position of huge responsibility to his Maker for the people who have been given into his charge. It is not a blanket responsibility – as Henry V demonstrates to Williams before Agincourt – but it is unlike that of any of his subjects. To occupy this crucial position properly, he needs to be as far as possible a philosopher prince; as Dante stressed, as the supreme authority in his dominions he is responsible to God not only for the good management of his realm, not only for the well-being of his subjects, but also for the just and holy correction of abuses in the human hierarchical structure of the Church itself. The prince is ultimately to guarantee the conditions in which every one of his subjects can reach his highest spiritual development on earth. Like Solomon, he has a duty to seek wisdom: 'Wisdom strengtheneth the wise more than ten mighty men which are in the city' (Ecclesiastes vii.19; cf. i.12–13, ii.13, vii.25 and ix.18); and the beginning of wisdom is the fear of the Lord.

## ii *Rebellion and revolt*

What we have been looking at so far in this chapter is an ideal and a myth – an ideal of monarchy, an ideal of subjects' behaviour, which relates to an ideal picture of an ordered universe. Just as there were anomalies in the behaviour of the observable world that were significant enough to be worrying yet not extensive enough to invalidate the whole theory, so in human politics the actual coincided only approximately with the ideal. It was these perceived anomalies, in both areas, whose eventual answer led to a fundamental change in the whole theory; but it was a slow and painful process.

The political issue really comes to a head[10] over a king who fails to do

10. My image is deliberate. 'To rebel' was, in sixteenth-century terms, 'to make head', like a disorder in the blood gathering into an abscess which then bursts. See p. 14, above.

his job properly. Centuries before, feudal law recognized the king's duty to support, succour and foster his vassals, and provided a procedure whereby if either party felt the relationship no longer viable a formal rejection of feudal relationship – *diffidatio* – could be made. *Diffidationes* were exchanged between Henry III and his barons before Evesham in 1265, for example, and Worcester and Vernon in effect make one in *1 Henry IV* (V.i). But practical though this may be, it raises moral issues of some magnitude: who is to decide when, how and why a subject may withdraw allegiance?

There have always been bad kings as well as good, who abuse their power. The king is but a man. Since the twelfth century there had been a strong tradition of political inquiry and readiness to think uncomfortable thoughts. John of Salisbury, for example, in the *Policraticus*, a handbook for a ruler that he wrote for his friend Thomas à Becket in the 1150s, argues that the ruler has an obligation to his people to provide for their well-being, and that if he is incompetent, unjust or tyrannical they have a right to depose him. (He also argues, inconsistently, that perhaps it might be better to put up with him because the virtue of obedience is a moral good in itself!) At the time, of course, this was quite a hot potato, given the circumstances of Henry II's reign, and the book seems to have been well known. Two centuries later, Gower implies the same thing: the king's job is to hold his community together in mutual love and honour for their mutual fulfilment as human beings. Richard II had, in his view, failed to do this, and so he re-dedicates his book, which was 'for King Richardes sake', to Henry Bolingbroke, who was to depose him, 'for Engelondes sake'. In the sixteenth century there is a considerable and growing body of opinion which sees the relationship between prince and people as contractual – for example in the Jesuit, Robert Parsons, or, later, the deeply Protestant John Milton (see below, pp. 69ff.). Some even come to see no need for a hereditary prince at all.

This 'contractual', even republican, tradition is best seen not in a book contemporary with Shakespeare but in two written a little later by John Milton to defend Parliament's actions in deposing and killing Charles I. Milton cleverly draws on a lot of received ideas in his justification, and admirably epitomizes this strand of thought in the period we are considering. In *The Tenure of Kings and Magistrates* (1649) he argues that it has always been lawful to challenge a tyrant or wicked king, even to depose and kill him. He cites evidence from biblical, Classical and modern history, as well as from natural justice; for the king is a man, and is not any man under the law and under the judgement of God? (cf.

Ecclesiastes xii.14). He even has the audacity, as a Protestant who hated everything that smacked of Roman Catholicism, to argue from the authority claimed by the Roman Church to hold the power to make or depose kings. A year later, in *Eikonoklastes* (1650), he replies to a book describing the martyr-like behaviour of the recently beheaded Charles I; at the beginning, he cites Proverbs xxviii.15–17:

> As a roaring lion and ranging bear; so is a wicked ruler over the poor people.
> The prince that wanteth understanding is also a great oppressor; but he that hateth covetousness shall prolong his days.

He sees very definite moral restraints upon the prince's conduct, which, if ignored, destroy his title to his office. He quotes Sallust's bitter remark in *The Conspiracy of Catiline*: 'To do with impunity what one wants – that's what being a king means'; or again, 'The regal power, which in the beginning had been for the preservation of liberty and the increase of the state, turned into pride and domination.' His justification is not quite as blunt as the remark attributed to his contemporary, the parliamentarian John Bradshaw: 'Rebellion to tyrants is obedience to God'; but it is radical enough, and was so recognized by nineteenth-century radical politicians. And the context of all this is, of course, that watershed in European history and thought when a monarch had been killed, not by an assassin but by his people through process of law; and that watershed is at the summit of the slope up which the sixteenth-century discussion is climbing.

## iii *Practical politics*

The final strand in our outline discussion must be the observed facts of the way human beings, fallible and inconsistent, actually behave. It is here that we get very close to Shakespeare's (and others') concerns in drama. Despite all that has been said above about the importance of role and the way in which it defines and polarizes personality, despite the awesome mystique that surrounded the idea of kingship, as individuals kings and princes were and are fallible, inconsistent human beings, with passions like our own, who came naked into the world and must go naked out of it.[11] It is also a fact that the obligations of the role will not be discharged in the same way by any two individuals, and each will be

11. A truism that received powerful expression in the many visual treatments, from the Middle Ages onwards, of the Dance of Death. Kings, emperors, popes and cardinals join hands in the dance into the grave.

affected differently by it. In short, the area of greatest interest in actual politics, in theory and in drama, is the measure of consent given to the demands of the role by the individual ruler and subject, and the effects that has on them.

In Act II.i of *King John* – a play written between *Richard II* and *1 Henry IV* – John is fighting Philip of France, and both have what seem like moral imperatives to be at war. Suddenly, they see a way of concluding peace to their mutual advantage, and the high-minded ideals with which they came to the battlefield and for which men already lie dead are forgotten. The Bastard, Richard I's illegitimate son and therefore by his birth debarred from full participation in this hierarchical society[12] – an outsider – comments on 'commodity' (advantage):

> *That smooth-faced, gentleman, tickling commodity;*
> *Commodity, the bias of the world –*
> *The world, who of itself is peisèd well,*
> *Made to run even, upon even ground*
> *Till this advantage, this vile-drawing bias,*
> *This sway of motion, this commodity,*
> *Makes it take head from all indifferency,*
> *From all direction, purpose, course, intent –*
> *And this same bias, this commodity,*
> *This bawd, this broker, this all-changing word,*
> *Clapped on the outward eye of fickle France,*
> *Hath drawn him from his own determined aid,*
> *From a resolved and honourable war,*
> *To a most base and vile-concluded peace.*
> *And why rail I on this commodity?*
> *But for because he hath not wooed me yet ...*
> *Since kings break faith upon commodity,*
> *Gain, be my lord – for I will worship thee!*

(*King John*, II.1.573ff.)

The logical extension of this train of thought is to the ideas of Machiavelli. I have mentioned these above (pp. 22f.) in the context of the discussion of degree; they need bringing into this political context as well. Machiavelli makes advantage the sole criterion of a ruler's good, the end which justifies any means. The implication is, of course, that that particular game can have a plurality of players. The man – monarch or subject – who refuses to keep the rules and plays purely for advantage

12. Like Edmund in *King Lear* – though there the comparison stops.

fascinated the Elizabethan mind. Marlowe's picture of Mortimer in *Edward II* shows just how powerful such a man can become; yet Marlowe's play also shows that he remains a man, vulnerable to fortune at the very moment when he least expects it. Shakespeare has his fair share of machiavels too, and all get their eventual come-uppance. Yet for a long time things do seem to be going their way; their very rejection of the rules of the game helps them to win it.

Until fortune, time and mortality overtake them and they are changed in the changing times. *A Mirror for Magistrates*, written during the reign of Henry VIII and published in 1559, continues a late-classical and medieval genre of narratives of the way the famous and powerful have come to a bad end by choosing examples of men and women in English history and having them describe their falls. Shakespeare, like many of his contemporaries, knew this work well, and drew on it extensively; Clarence's dream in *Richard III*, for example, has strong verbal echoes of an important section in it. This is really the final strand in the political thought of Shakespeare's day, against which his plays must be seen: that time, death and fortune govern all, even the great, and within the hollow crown of earthly power death the antic sits grinning at the empty pomp and self-importance of struggling men.

These are not issues of merely academic importance, which the majority of Shakespeare's contemporaries could safely ignore while they got on with being Elizabethans. Elizabeth acceded to the most insecure throne in Europe. It was claimed by Philip of Spain in right of his widow; eleven years later, she had to face the revolt of the Catholic northern earls in 1569, and in 1570 Pope Pius V formally issued a Bull deposing her, releasing her subjects from their allegiance and advocating her assassination. There were several minor insurrections in her reign. Elizabeth's cousin, the Catholic Mary of Scotland, with powerful connections in France, had a good claim on the English throne (particularly since the rumour that Elizabeth was not only illegitimate, but in any case no daughter of Henry VIII had been fostered by the papacy); she had been a virtual prisoner in England since 1568, and was such a constant focus of plots against Elizabeth that she had to be executed in 1587. In 1588 Philip of Spain made his great attempt to take England by force, hoping that any landing he made would be supported by a revolt of the Catholic gentry. In 1601, Elizabeth's erstwhile favourite, the Earl of Essex, rebelled – and was executed for his pains. And it is not only events we are dealing with; ideas were in ferment too. The Jesuit Robert Parsons (1546–1610), who had a considerable influence among the

English Catholics at home and abroad, argued in his *Responsio ad Edictum Elizabethae* (1592) that the Pope's power to depose a monarch was an article of faith; two years later, in *A Conference about the Next Succession*, he adduced historical and legal arguments to prove the right of the people to alter the line of succession for just causes, especially religious ones, and revived the argument of Elizabeth's poor genealogical claim to the throne.[13] There was in fact no extended period throughout her long reign when the issues of rule and the ruler, obedience and degree, could be forgotten. As we shall see later, this helps to account for the popularity of plays about English history; Shakespeare's, particularly, are nothing if not topical. On the eve of his rebellion Essex persuaded Shakespeare's company to stage *Richard II* – a political act if ever there was one, for many (including the queen) saw striking parallels between her insecurity and Richard's.

Shakespeare's history plays and tragedies cannot be understood without some awareness of this complex background. The ideas about the state and the source of authority in it are of course conflicting, even contradictory; it is partly that conflict the plays are discussing. For Shakespeare uses all ideas; he gives perhaps the most powerful poetic expression in the whole period to the idea of degree and the subject's duty, of degree and the king's obligation, even the king's responsibility for his subjects' failure in allegiance; he is fascinated too by the notion of 'commodity'. He is aware of the limitedness of human vision and the ephemeral nature of human achievement. If he has an ultimate answer – which I doubt, for the problem does not admit of an easy one – it is not found in the happy coincidence of a legitimate monarch and his temporary success at the head of a united country in Henry V; it is in the idea of the inescapability of God's judgement and the absolute necessity of crime being paid for to the very last jot. For the brilliant reign of Henry V is followed, as the final Chorus of the play makes clear, by the disasters of that of Henry VI. The Bible's promise of punishment unto the third and fourth generation, the consequence of sin, is here fulfilled, and the crime of deposing Richard II expiated.[14]

13. These books were distributed fairly widely in England by the extreme Catholic mafia. They shocked moderate English Catholics who felt that Parsons was doing their position very little good, and possession of a copy was made high treason by Act of Parliament – which indicates how seriously ideas were taken.

14. In *Richard III*, which completes the group of four plays he wrote earlier in his career on the reigns of Henry VI and Edward IV, Shakespeare explores this issue brilliantly. Richard is the ultimate villain, whose career is possible because of all the crimes that have preceded

Nevertheless, Shakespeare can also grasp the idea of a possibly justifiable revolt. Worcester is given a very powerful and persuasive speech in *1 Henry IV* (V.i.30–71), and in *Richard II* York clearly sees a great deal of right on Bolingbroke's side (II.i.186ff.; II.ii.111ff.). Shakespeare even considers the possibility that, despite the enormous cost, God may work in human affairs through revolt, rebellion, and his beadle, war. The final resolutions of strife and discord in *The Tempest* and *Cymbeline* depend on preceding revolt and rebellion.

But the area that seems to have fascinated Shakespeare most is the person of the monarch, and to this we must return later. What does being a king do to a man, and is it possible for a man whom we might call good to be a good king? Is the sweet fruition of an earthly crown merely dust and ashes in the mouth?

## iv *The lessons of history*

There could hardly be a greater difference in ideas of the nature of kingship than between those Milton expresses in *Of the Tenure of Kings and Magistrates* and the ideal Dante offers in *De Monarchia*. In the one, kingship is provisional, deriving its authority ultimately from the consent of the governed;[15] in the other, the prince is uniquely responsible to God for the safe-keeping and just rule of his people and their development into citizens of the City of God. Yet both these writers appeal to ancient precedent, ancient events, ancient theorists, to support their arguments. And in Machiavelli's *Il Principe* (1513) – a book popularly supposed to have been inspired by the devil – the argument relies heavily on his reading and researches in Roman historians, especially Livy, coupled with his analysis of how people have behaved in actual recent practice. All therefore seek to prove their case from history.

We therefore need to look at the concepts of history our fathers held. Hegel cynically suggested that the only thing people learn from history is that people do not learn from history; Marx added the warning that

---

him; and he is the instrument of the punishment of those who are guilty. None of Richard's victims is guiltless of innocent blood; and when he has bustled about destroying them all, he is himself destroyed by Henry Tudor. See my *'Richard III': a Critical Study* (London, 1989).

15. Milton is no early theorist of constitutional monarchy in our sense, or of democracy. His outlook is far too – literally – aristocratic for that. He is developing the Elizabethan concept of the ultimate human authority in the state being not the prince, not Parliament, but 'the prince-in-Parliament'.

those who do not learn are doomed to repeat its mistakes. For us, history has become in the main the structural study of whole societies; the minutiae of parish records, cotton workers' diet sheets and one's grandmother's gossip are as important and relevant – to use a vogue word – as any number of political events. What seems to be the aim is the achievement of a feeling of 'what it was like', *how* things have got to the state they have – an understanding (doomed to be partial) of a vastly complex social machine without letting value judgements creep in. In the past, even the quite recent past, history was something else again. Dionysus of Halicarnassus first made the often quoted remark that 'History is philosophy teaching by examples', and we would do well to remember that for our ancestors philosophy – the pursuit of wisdom – was one of the highest of human endeavours. Wisdom is not just knowledge, but an understanding of the context and meaning of that knowledge; ultimately it aims at a moral, even a theological or devotional, end. There is good biblical authority for the importance of this quest in the Wisdom of Solomon, and good pagan authority, to mention only the works of Plato, or Aristotle,[16] or Epictetus. If history is, then, subservient to philosophy, as Dionysus's remark implies, it follows that the reading of history will ultimately be a moral activity, an attempt to understand the nature of the human predicament by the study of individual examples.

History is not only philosophical; it is a process with a shape to it. Whereas the Greeks (and the Romans) had seen history as merely cyclical, the Jews left to the West a vision of history as a process which had a definite beginning, showed the operation of God in human life and in the world, and would one day have an end when all should know as they were known. It was moreover purposive, full of meaning, and followed ultimately the will of God for his Creation. God Himself might intervene in it directly, as He had at the time of the Exodus, or, as Christians believe, supremely in the Incarnation of Our Lord. The consequence of this eschatological view, to use the exact term, was to see history as an as yet incomplete process: modern men continued a story their fathers had

16. Aristotle's remark in the *Poetics* that tragedy is more philosophical than history becomes rather important in the context of this book: both are concerned with the pursuit of wisdom, but because tragedy, which is only based on happenings (or what might believably happen), escapes the demands for factual accuracy that limit history, it is freer to search for significance and meaning and express those things through its form and shape. Aristotle is also suggesting that tragedy teaches wisdom in its own right, and is thus closely related to the highest discipline, philosophy.

begun.[17] English history too was therefore a continuum, where modern men were deeply affected by their forefathers and would equally deeply affect their sons. So even for people of slight education, English history – and the watching of plays about it – could not be other than relevant to their own concerns.[18]

Though these ideas are formulated and used by what today would be called academics, who are by definition more articulate than most people, we should not assume them to be untypical of what the man in the street thought. He might not have expressed his ideas so well or so fully, or had the range of reference to support him. But even today most people regard history at its lowest level as providing cautionary examples, and modern politicians often appeal to history – however bogus – to justify their particular stance to potential voters. 'Remember 1945' or 'Remember Munich' are simply updated versions of remembering Henry V or Richard II. The topical issues in Shakespeare's day could only be discussed by appeal to the evidence they had: that of history. A playwright who tackles these issues is going to find himself drawn inescapably to history. The history of England that is built into his plays is a history that allows author and audience to come to terms with themselves, to work out their values in a communal and serious activity, to formulate, express, evaluate their ideals. The playwright, then as now, both responds to and modifies preoccupations and issues in society and formulates them (it is arguable which comes first). A society much concerned about legitimacy of succession, succession itself, and the nature of the ruler's title – ultimately about man's position *vis-à-vis* God – must discuss these issues. In its understanding of the past – or at least in the isolation of its problems – it may well find the means to discuss those contemporary concerns which, because they were too intimate, too important to be easily handled openly, could not be approached by any other means.

17. This leaves fossils in our language: 'progress' suggests, implies, that history is moving towards some substantial improvement in the human lot; 'descent' preserves the medieval idea that modern men and their civilization are far inferior to Antiquity, and that the world is wearing out. It is a nice irony that the millenarianism of Marxism is a consequence of centuries of Jewish and Christian thought about history.

18. The force of a play like *King Lear* is quite different when you watch it not as fictional but a a dramatization of a real episode in English – that is, your own – history, where its plot is believed to be true. Despite the efforts of Polydore Vergil in the 1530s, many still believed the old account of Britain's history (as in Geoffrey of Monmouth), which starts with refugees from Troy founding Britain and goes on to figures like Cymbeline and Lear.

# Part II   The Ricardian History Plays

# 5. Mirrors of our Fickle State

Our first idea, fuelled by television serials and the comforting nonsense of popular novels, of the reign of Elizabeth and just after is of a brilliant brocaded world, where a brave little England trounced the monstrous power of Spain, where every other man was a poet and every other woman worth his poetry. Our ancestors would have been mystified by this picture. Their world, like ours, was a world of problems – not just metaphysical or academic, but real, pressing, political and economic issues that are entirely familiar to us. For example: in Shakespeare's own lifetime – a mere sixty years – the population of England rose by fifty per cent, with the attendant social problems and strains on the structure of society that entails; the value of money halved, and, as usual in times of high inflation, the gap between rich and poor widened dramatically and old wealth often became new penury. Jobs were scarce, and unemployment led to real and dangerous social unrest. There was a series of poor harvests, especially in the 1590s, and people really did die of hunger – which is not a nice death – in merrie England. The country lurched from one short-term crisis to another, and the fear of rebellion or subversion from outside was only too well founded. Religious dissent could easily flare into vicious civil war, as it had done in France, where a weak-headed king on one frightful occasion in 1572 repeatedly fired his arquebus into the terrified mob of his Protestant citizens driven past his palace by Catholic bravos. Elizabeth's brilliant balancing-act – and the skill of her great ministers, Burghley and Leicester – secured her own throne while she lived, and it won enough time for the immediate threats to change their nature; but it did not solve problems that were all too obvious and whose causes were not understood even as much (or as little) as we understand them today. Nevertheless the age was one of brilliant achievement as well as of crisis, of real hope as well as of fear and despair. It was then that the foundations of much that we value today were being laid.

## i *Topicality*

It is against the background of this paradoxical age that we must see Shakespeare's plays, and particularly the histories. The question of what a history play is – what it was intended to do – and how its first audience recognized it as such and responded to it is one to which I shall return, for the audience's capabilities deeply affect what an author can do and how he can do it. It is essential to grasp first the point that history plays were nothing if not topical. No artist who hoped to keep his audience and be treated seriously could fail to address himself to the important issues of his own day, however he framed them.

Before Shakespeare's time there were a good number of plays dealing with the events of English history. Where Shakespeare is remarkable is not only in the quality of his writing – and some others are pretty good – but in the way in which he avoids a saloon-bar, unthinkingly patriotic approach to, for example, the victories of Henry V; *The Famous Victories of Henry V*, which he certainly knew and competed with, is about as subtle as a meat cleaver and is jingoistic centuries before the idea was invented.[1] His histories may apparently close with a resolution of conflict, with a reassuring pat on the back of the audience who have the good sense to be English; but the impression is momentary, ambiguities come flooding into our memories, and the most apparently confident of them all, *Henry V*, the career of the Elizabethans' ideal king, closes not with triumph but with the Chorus's prediction of future strife and the loss of what has been so dearly won. Even the ending of *Richard III*, superficially a panegyric of the Tudor settlement after a century of civil war, underlines that that settlement by a marriage is organically connected to the kin-strife that preceded it. Shakespeare's deep ambiguity makes the play disturbing rather than reassuring, and the questions that are raised are also pressing contemporary ones.

The plays examine the way people behave politically, the way they are motivated, the way they justify their actions to themselves. Shakespeare deliberately jolts his audience into seeing the present in his recreated past[2] by putting in contemporary details they could themselves have experienced – for example, in *1* and *2 Henry IV* his audience would be more than familiar with the levying of troops, and with Falstaff's dodges, for this was a period when England was again under threat and the

1. It was nonetheless in tune with a major popular attitude. Since 1585 England had been drawn into the Dutch War of Independence against Catholic Spain, and disagreement about support for the rebels, *as Protestants against Catholics*, set the terms for the debate over foreign policy right down to 1640. An aggressive patriotism, fuelled by the Spanish war, easily saw England as an island of Protestant light menaced in a global struggle against Spanish Catholic darkness. James I was not popular when he made peace with Spain, despite the obvious economic good sense in so doing.

2. Which they were, in the reading of history, in any case accustomed to do: see pp. 70ff.

tramp of armies was heard in the land. The deep fear of civil strife is fully reflected in the plays. While nobody in the audience would mistake for historical fact the concern for ceremony in *Richard II*, or the clash between the man and the office he discharges (in *Henry V* movingly explored in Henry's speech before Agincourt), the issues do relate strikingly to Puritan controversies of the 1590s, and to the whole debate – indeed, the irreconcilable paradox that James I unwisely attempted to solve – about the prince's two bodies, the one political and eternal, the other human and mortal.[3]

In *Richard II* the very choice of subject is topical almost to indiscretion, for the parallel between the events of Richard's last years and those of the ageing queen was standard. When in 1601 the historian William Lambarde was showing Elizabeth the fruits of his researches in the royal archives and arrived at the time of Richard II, she broke in: 'I am Richard II. Know ye not that? . . .' In the rebellion of Essex she saw echoes of Bolingbroke, and Essex himself arranged with Shakespeare's company for the play to be produced on the eve of his London rising.[4] Yet Essex never intended the deposition of Elizabeth, any more – we may be sure – than Bolingbroke (either fictional or historical) did that of Richard. Bolingbroke and Essex both sent messages of submission to their monarch. What here was at issue was something that keeps cropping up in all the major history plays of the time, and is indeed crucial in *1* and *2 Henry IV*: the nature of political power and the influence of counsellors. It is a matter of fact that the personal authority of the monarch, especially in the Privy Chamber, now developing as the centre of executive government, was the cardinal political reality; those who enjoyed the Prince's favour were powerful, those who lacked it were not. The political world was thus divided into factions – the word had not yet acquired any pejorative sense – and clients of those factions who sought

3. See above, pp. 59ff. It is worth reminding ourselves that, despite the real personal power of the monarch through the royal prerogative, the ultimate legal authority in Tudor thought was the hybrid concept, the 'queen-in-Parliament'.

4. Though with hindsight we can see its immediate unlikelihood, to the Elizabethans the renewal of a civil war like the Wars of the Roses looked very possible indeed. Hence the dying Edward's stress on reconciliation in *Richard III* (II.i) is ironic in its dramatic context, but a topical injunction to the audience. Robert Parsons (probably – see pp. 68ff.) in *A Copie of a Leter, wryten by a Master of Arte of Cambridge* (1584) speaks of 'the olde contention, betweene the families of York and Lancaster, wherein so much English blood was spilt in tymes past, and much more like to be poured out now, if the same contention should be set on foote againe. Seeing that to the controversie of titles, would be added also the controversie of religion, which of all other differences is the most dangerous.'

power and influence.[5] Those out of favour inevitably felt that they could do a better job than those in; and so *Richard II* was peculiarly relevant in 1601, not because Elizabeth was senile – she was far from it – or mismanaging things as Richard had done, nor even because of Richard's deposition and Elizabeth's vulnerability; the main thrust was against the dominance of a corrupt faction at Court, what Essex and his faction saw as the malign influence of the Cecil–Ralegh interest. When Bolingbroke sentences the caterpillars of the commonwealth, the Essex followers saw their leader sentencing the hated Cecil and Ralegh. Power grew out of personal access to the monarch, which Essex had been denied and which Aumerle, in *Richard II*, insists on. It is on just such assumed access that Falstaff builds his false hopes, and his two plays show, among other things, the prince learning to choose the right group of counsellors – the Lord Chief Justice rather than the denizens of Eastcheap. One consequence of this political reality is that many of the evils of the time are blamed not on what we would now see as the true causes but on bad counsellors (as happened particularly in the next two reigns), on a sort of political immorality, on (to use the old word from the complaint and satire writing of the later Middle Ages) 'wasters' of the common weal. It follows that the road to a good commonwealth is similarly dependent on the character and qualities of the ruler and his counsellors. Thus in drama set in a historical period, Shakespeare – whatever else he is doing at the same time – is describing, evaluating, and exploring the political realities and controversies[6] of his own day; and we may be sure his audience was aware of the fact.

## ii *The handling of the past*

But history plays (plays in general, for that matter), despite their relevance and topicality, are not merely dramatized leader columns. They may relate to contemporary concerns, as for example *The Tempest* and *The Winter's Tale* seem to bear on the important political issue of

5. This keeps on appearing in the plays: Rosencrantz and Guildenstern in *Hamlet* are in a dilemma far more real and vital than we usually perceive, and thus we underrate the way Shakespeare has handled them. They were 'clients' of the heir to the throne in old Hamlet's reign, which was a promising position; but now all is changed. What should they do? To survive politically and to rise at all, they must follow Claudius. To maintain their integrity, they must stay with Hamlet. (Which is a comment on Courts and the demands they impose, and not unlike the points moralists like Skelton had been making earlier in the century.)

6. See, for a particularly striking example, the discussion of Oldcastle/Falstaff below, pp. 137ff.

England's support for the Elector Palatine.[7] They may deal with general theoretical and conceptual issues like the nature of rule, the subject's obedience, and the way politics fits in with a given view of the universe; But they are also interpretative fiction built on the facts of the real history of the ancestors of their audience, which attempts to help them to come to terms with what they themselves are. No one in Shakespeare's audience would have mistaken what he saw on stage for real history; he knew that those actors at the end of the performance would cast off their robes and return from the illusion of the play. He knew he was watching not the past described, but the act of describing and interpreting it, and his own expectations and knowledge would necessarily be called into play. So part of the material that Shakespeare worked with in his histories was his audience's attitude to their own past.[8]

The views of modern historians on the fifteenth century are, of course, self-evidently irrelevant to our present discussion; what is material is the view Shakespeare found in the majority of his sources – the received view, so to speak. Henry VII had commissioned the Italian scholar Polydore Vergil to write a history of England. There is no reason to doubt that Polydore was an honest man, but the fact is that his interpretation of the necessarily incomplete material he used was coloured by his own predilections and methodology, and by the fact that his patron was the centre of a Court that felt his accession had been, in the words of *1066 and All That*, a Good Thing. (After all, in common experience what one sees is modified by what one expects to see and one's angle of vision.) Polydore's account is the foundation of the main Tudor tradition of historiography,[9] and his angle is largely that taken by Hall in 1548

7. See Frances A. Yates, *Shakespeare's Last Plays: A New Approach* (London, 1975).

8. In view of my discussion below in Chapter 11, it is apposite to recall Sidney's emphasis on the poet's power and duty to create things not as they are or have been, but as they might or could be – a moral rather than a literal truth. And Francis Bacon, in discussing what he calls 'Idols of the Theatre' (that is, hindrances to clear knowledge imposed on the mind by the neatly satisfying complexity of systems of thought which may bear little relation to what actually *is*), uses a similar idea about the theatre: '. . . stories invented for the stage are neater, more elegant, and more agreeable to the taste than the true stories out of history' (*Novum Organum* (1620), Aphorism 62).

9. We must be careful not to oversimplify; there was a variety of opinions in Shakespeare's day about both Richard II and Henry V – the view of history was not uniform and monolithic. We need briefly to mention here what has been called the 'Tudor myth' of English history. Put at its simplest, it was argued until a few years ago that the Tudors encouraged their historians to take the view that the sacrilegious deposition of Richard II led inevitably to a period of civil strife in the reigns of Henry IV and VI, which was only resolved by the cataclysmic reign of Richard III, when all the guilty perished, and the divinely ordered

and by Rafael Holinshed in both his edition of 1578 and of 1587 (the one Shakespeare used). Henry VII is seen as the saviour of a broken England, worn out by the civil war and the suffering that followed inevitably on the original sin, the literal sacrilege, of the deposition of Richard II; for, as the Bible points out, shall not the sins of the fathers be visited unto the third and fourth generation, yet in the end the Lord will have mercy and hearken unto the prayer of the afflicted? Now Shakespeare does not – could not – deny this overall view, but he can and does make it considerably more complex. For example, his Richmond (Henry Tudor) in *Richard III* may be a Mr Clean, but (like Octavius at the end of *Antony and Cleopatra*) he does look pretty dull and a lot less interesting than the bottled spider he has just killed. The resolution does not settle the problem of the meaning of the real suffering that preceded it. Shakespeare's perspective on the fifteenth century, then, may well be largely Tudor, but he deviates because he is translating relatively formless chronicles into drama, taking major historical liberties out of the artistic necessity of dealing with time on the stage and of presenting the names in a chronicle as credible and memorable people who will walk and talk their brief hour. There are limits on his liberties, of course – Richard III can't win at Bosworth – yet he constantly changes the personalities of historical figures, conflates and alters times, and, particularly, personalizes. Whether or not history really is governed by the characters and choices of individual men and women as they respond to their roles – as was the classical view – the dramatist can only write as if it were. Shakespeare's people have an acute self-consciousness of themselves in their particular roles, a self-consciousness entirely consistent with the Renaissance understanding of how the role a man found himself in defined the values and nature demanded of him. He also shows extraordinary interest in the words by which his characters perceive and communicate what is happening to them. The mythic nature of contemporary life found an echo in a view of history that saw it too as not only containing literal but also mythic truth.

---

accession of Henry Tudor. Robert Ornstein's book, *A Kingdom for a Stage*, however, demonstrated that this is a serious oversimplification. Few chroniclers actually took this line, which, in some of its major elements, shows considerable Yorkist partisanship. The chronicler Hall glorifies the Tudor accession, indeed, but does it by denigrating (unjustly, as it seems) the Yorkist Richard III; he does not subscribe to the idea of a curse brought about by Lancastrian sin against the Lord's anointed. Alone of the major historians, Holinshed offers this view, and it is true that Holinshed was one of Shakespeare's chief sources for the Ricardian plays.

And, of course, Shakespeare was man enough to think for himself.

His eight histories have a real mythic coherence as a history of fifteenth-century England from the fall of Richard II to the accession of Henry Tudor. To pull Shakespeare up for his historical mistakes is merely tedious. Yet it must be remembered that for his audience, and for him, knowledge of the historical background was inevitably an important part of the theatrical experience – at the very simplest level it throws an ironic light, for example, over the whole of the career of Falstaff. There is every sign that Shakespeare put in this background with care, and used it entirely seriously: for example, Canterbury's tedious (to us) speech in *Henry V* (I.ii.33ff.) on the king's claim to France is too important to be left to a mere allusion or footnote. Inheritance, extending right up to the legitimate inheritance of the throne, was the basis of medieval and Elizabethan society; such details, essential parameters of the issues raised in the plays, matter to an audience who would expect to find them.

The history plays, then, depend a good deal on the audience's expectations, worries and prior knowledge. Shakespeare orchestrates these carefully. He is aware of what his audience can take: the complexity characteristic of Elizabethan plays suggests that audiences were fully accustomed to comprehending a large cast and an intricate plot. So his canvas is large, though – as the Chorus makes clear in *Henry V* – still far short of the reality. He can use cross-references between plays knowing that the material is already familiar in outline; and he can use for all he is worth the great bonus that the audience shares with the characters a knowledge of their past, but knows, as they do not, what is still to befall them. For central to the idea of the history play – of history itself – is time. History is about time, and the plays are significantly keyed to detailed space and time; we know where things happened, we know when they happened. The whirligig of time, in history as in plays, brings in his revenges, and playing over the whole fabric of the history plays is not only a sense of the irony of time provided by our knowledge of the outcome, but also an awareness that the historical time of the plays continues to our own, and that we are victims of a similar irony. One day our story too will be history. The Renaissance had no doubt that one day time would have an end, an *eschaton*, when all would be made plain and all judged. Paradoxically, both the permanent relevance of human life and its inherent precariousness is thus emphasized. Shakespeare underlines in Richard II, in Henry IV, in Falstaff, the inescapable march of the players towards their latter end; the shortness of the time left to his people and the coming of the night when no man may work is never far from his thoughts.

# 6. Hawks and Handsaws: Modes and Genres of the Plays

Lumping the plays together, as we tend to do, as 'histories' may be convenient, but it skates over some real difficulties. They are self-evidently not all the same in style or treatment of their historical material. Shakespeare seems deliberately to choose different modes in these four plays, and to signal different expectations, to focus his audience on specific issues. Moreover, we do well to bear in mind the idea in Elizabethan theories of art that outward form ought to show the inner nature of things. The structure of the plays, therefore, is likely to be intimately connected with what they are setting out to do and what category or genre they belong to.[1] *Richard II*, for example, would clearly come within Polonius's category 'tragical-historical'; equally clearly, none of the others would; in terms of imagery, as we shall see, all four are linked to – to use the comic term again – 'historical-pastoral' (see Chapter 7); but what do we do with the Falstaff elements in *1* and *2 Henry IV*?

## i *Richard II*

*Richard II* is clearly some sort of tragedy, and to see how it might be received we have to look at what values the term carried for its first audience. As Chaucer makes his Monk put it, in late medieval tradition

> *Tragedie is to seyn a certeyn storie,*
> *As old bokes maken us memorie,*
> *Of him that stood in greet prosperitee*
> *And is yfallen out of heigh degree*
> *Into miserie, and endeth wrecchedly.*
> (*The Canterbury Tales*, VII, 1973–7; B, 3163–7)

Note that there is no question here of any particular moral type of person – in fact the Monk's tales include people whom we would not

---

1. Polonius in *Hamlet* (II.ii) is comically made to have aspirations to literary theory, and he recognizes not only 'history', but also 'historical-pastoral, tragical-historical, tragical-comical-historical-pastoral'; the joke would lose its ludicrousness if Shakespeare could not count on his audience recognizing that plays could be written in different modes and that those modes would carry certain expectations with them.

call, even in a loose sense, tragic; it is the fall that matters, and the fall of the great exemplifies the great power of fortune in human affairs (see above, p. 11). Tragedy, as a genre, is thus both historical and cautionary; the chief lesson to be learnt is the instability of the world. It is important to realize that even when Shakespeare develops the idea of tragedy further than it had ever been taken before, in *King Lear*, he does not entirely abandon this link with Fortune; his insight is to connect the operation of Fortune with the moral activity of men. We can perhaps see him beginning to make this connection in *Richard II*.

'Tragedy' still carried a good deal of this old sense in this period. But other ideas were of course being introduced and explored. In one of the favourite reference books of the Renaissance, *Mythologiae siue Explicationum Fabularum Libri Decem* (Venice, 1568), Natalis Comes defines tragedy in Chapter III as a political fable – that is, a story whose secondary, concealed, meaning is not only more important than its surface narrative but which also has a direct relevance to the way men run their states. And the renewed interest in Aristotle's analysis of Greek tragedy in the *Poetics* had given rise to a good deal of serious consideration of the term – and indeed of the theory of drama as a whole, as I outlined above (pp. 50f.). We may be certain Shakespeare knew of this discussion, and of the concept of the three unities that was extrapolated from Aristotle, for he makes Polonius refer to it (*Hamlet*, II.ii). (Which also implies he expected some of his audience to be familiar with it, at least in outline.[2]) Aristotle emphasized that if tragedy were to achieve in the audience what he saw as the desirable effect of the purifying of the emotions of pity and fear (i.e. their redirection from trivialities to the serious issues of the human condition, and a sense of the dignity of man), certain things were necessary: the hero must be important, but he must also be recognizably a man like ourselves, who is neither impossibly good nor impossibly bad; his fall must spring from some flaw in his character, and must be the result of a chain of events that do not merely follow each other but are causally linked. His fall must also be just, however terrible it may be. Here there is a clear emphasis on the moral nature of tragedy. It is moral in the motivation of the plot, moral in the examination of the problem of the justice of events, and moral in the effects on the audience. The form becomes a means of interpreting our

2. *The Tempest* is a *tour de force*, which might have been deliberately written to show that he could, if he wanted, confound those critics, like Ben Jonson, who disapproved of plays not keeping to the unities; the represented time is the exact time of performance, the action is single, the place a small island.

human predicament, not merely of contemplating the instability of fortune.

In Marlowe's *Edward II* (1592), a play which has a good deal in common with *Richard II*, there are three 'tragedies'. There is the obvious and simple fall of Gaveston, who falls from great prosperity and ends wretchedly. One applauds, indeed. There is the more complex fall of Edward himself, who is certainly seriously flawed in character, and led astray as a ruler by flatterers and evil counsellors (see above, p. 78), but who is by no means wholly bad. (His end, however, is revoltingly painful and demeaning, and lacks any hint of the great dignity and power of the death of the imprisoned Richard.) There is the rise and fall of the ambitious Mortimer, who begins as a young noble with a good deal of right on his side, rises to the position where he controls the kingdom, and then misuses that power appallingly. At the very point where he is at the summit of his power and seemingly most secure, Marlowe gives him the line, in Latin to emphasize its importance and irony: [3] '*Maior sum quam cui possit nocere Fortuna*' ('I am a greater man than Fortune can harm') (v.iv.67).

At that point things start to go wrong for him, largely through a series of accidents, and he is soon totally destroyed. Edward's son wreaks a terrible vengeance. And we feel Mortimer deserved it, that his challenge to Fortune showed an overweening pride and self-confidence. Like Marlowe's own Tamburlaine the Great, he overreaches himself – though he lacks the extraordinary consciousness of himself as an instrument of a higher purpose which Tamburlaine shows in his line: 'And Tamburlaine, the scourge of God, must die' (*Tamburlaine*, Part 2, V.iii.248). The irony is that we do see Mortimer as an instrument of punishment called forth by the excesses of Edward and Gaveston. This play, therefore, in its triple 'tragedy', shows us something of the actual transition between the medieval idea of the nature of tragedy and more sophisticated ones.

*Richard II* marks an important step in the development of Shakespeare's thought about tragedy – and, perhaps, in his understanding of the appropriate dramatic form for it. The four natural 'movements' (see p. 113, below) of the play correspond remarkably closely to the four-part structure used in classical tragedy and regarded as peculiarly satisfying and shapely: *protasis*, where the characters and issues are introduced; *epitasis*, where the plot thickens; and *catastasis*, where the action is

3. He obviously expected at least some of his audience to be able to speak Latin. Those who did not could nod their heads sagely; they would at least know something important had been said.

heightened before the *catastrophe* or final dénouement. Shakespeare had used this structure before – for example in *Richard III* – but conceptually *Richard II* is much more adventurous. Earlier plays of Shakespeare that were called tragedies in early editions do not have that sense of the dignity of humankind and of waste we experience in watching Lear, Macbeth, Hamlet and Othello as, partly through their own fatal error, the machinery of the universe grinds them exceeding small. In Richard III's case the laugh is on him from the very beginning; the audience may enjoy his amoral energy, but knows that he will get his deserved and expected come-uppance at Bosworth. *Romeo and Juliet*, also called a tragedy, is quite explicitly about lovers who are 'star-crossed', whose love brings them on to a collision course with their situation. Their loss is terrible, pathetic, a dreadful waste of youth and promise, but it is not motivated by their own moral choice or mistake; the final catastrophe, indeed, is purely the result of accident. Where *Richard II* breaks new ground is in the way Shakespeare perceived, in the historical narrative he found in his sources, an ambiguity about the person and actions of Richard which allowed his fall both to be deserved and at the same time terrible and wasteful, an ambiguity which permitted him to develop the person of Richard so that he *grows* to be 'every inch a king' (like Lear) when he is one no longer. He is able to give him a self-consciousness that recognizes what is happening to him, sees itself against the great exemplars of betrayal, and challenges (not without irony) the idea that the universe really is just and ordered. Like the heroes of Shakespeare's great tragedies, Richard undergoes a process of progressive isolation – from his Court, his followers, his queen, even from his idea of himself as king – and his end, after reduction to the primal human being fighting for mere life, is an anonymous groan.

But the constraint of history that he should devote almost equal attention to Bolingbroke's rise to power allows Shakespeare a further advantage; in the career of Bolingbroke in this and the next two plays, Shakespeare was able to explore, in a remarkably delicate way, the tragic potential of a man who rises quite credibly to the summit of worldly power and comes precious close to losing everything that makes the holding of that power worth having. (This is a theme that he will later handle in the person of Macbeth, and perhaps glance at in Claudius in *Hamlet*.) Comparison of Bolingbroke with Marlowe's Mortimer shows just how much more profound is Shakespeare's understanding of the way in which a man can be forced, by a sequence of events he has himself set in motion, into positions that initially he would abhor. (He also gives Bolingbroke when he is king a self-consciousness that allows him to see the very vulnerability in his own situation that he exploited in Richard's.) The reciprocal movement of Richard and Bolingbroke – the one falling and growing by his fall, the other rising and losing something of his humanity by that rise – greatly deepens our perception of the problems involved not just in being a ruler but in being human at all; for with both of them we sympathize, both of them we censure, and both of them have made the real, touchable world that not only Shakespeare's first audience but we ourselves inhabit. For by signalling to the audience that the play is a tragedy, at the very least Shakespeare is telling them to contemplate the vicissitudes of human life; by taking his material from well-known and topical English history, he is removing the subtle barrier between what can be conveniently categorized as 'story' and what is painful in the here and now – exactly as today a play like Hochhuth's *Soldiers*, or television programmes about the recent past, or about heroic figures like Winston Churchill who are only recently dead, make the shoe pinch. This exploitation of historical event represents a challenge to thought and involvement, and rules out the indifferent response. Richard II really mattered in English history, and no Elizabethan could fail to have a view about him. Just as Greek tragedians took their plots from mythical history known to everyone, and accepted as in some way paradigmatic of the puzzle of existence, so Shakespeare takes his from the history he could count on his audience knowing, and turns their attention to the examination of the very nature of the world – political, ethical, moral, cosmic – they take so readily for granted.[4]

## ii *Henry IV, Parts 1 and 2*

Looking at *Richard II* in this way raises a larger issue relating to the next two plays as well. Richard's tragedy is serious and moving, but to all intents and purposes it is over by Act V, Scene v; all that is left for Richard is to die. Whereas in the later tragedies there is indeed 'nothing left remarkable beneath the visiting moon', this play ends in scenes which, far from tying up the issues raised, deliberately extend them forward in

4. It is, indeed, noticeable that with the exception of *Othello* all the plots of the tragedies are taken from what was believed to be real history. *King Lear* is no exception; though Polydore Vergil had disproved the account of English history that had been traditional since Geoffrey of Monmouth in the twelfth century, few listened. The story of Lear and his daughters is still part of the furniture of popular history, and appears not only as plays but in compendious poems like Drayton's *Polyolbion* (1622).

time beyond the play's end. Richard had to pay for the time he wasted as 'gardener' of his realm (see below, Chapter 7), and while divine ordination justly shortened his tenure of the kingly office, human action unjustly shortened his days as a man. This must be paid for too, because however complicated the motives of the men behind it, the moral universe cannot allow the wicked act to prosper. So in the last scenes of *Richard II*, which gather the four major figures and mention some chief concerns of the next play, Shakespeare is clearly planning the two plays that followed about two years later. He pushes us forward into a continuing saga of misrule, insurrection and response. There are close parallels between the two reigns. There are banishments and confiscations in each; the new king, Henry IV, has at least the potential for tragedy, and finds that his most admirable quality – the ability to motivate men – lays him open to the tragic mistake of motivating Exton. Hotspur, whose real age Shakespeare quite deliberately and unhistorically altered so that he could parallel both Henry IV and Prince Hal, is led by his sense of personal injustice to a crime that in motivation and action is very like Bolingbroke's. But it is unsuccessful, whereas Bolingbroke's, temporarily, was not. The constant references to the deposition of Richard in the Henry IV plays overshadow the entire action; such guilt must be paid for.

It seems that Shakespeare was building into *1* and *2 Henry IV* something that might well be called a tragic substructure, whatever other modes the play may use. That substructure centres round Hotspur in Part 1, and (it has been argued [5]) Falstaff in Parts 1 and 2. Both of them (particularly Falstaff) have clear symbolic importance (see pp. 133f., 140f.), but as persons their careers have at least the potential for tragedy. Both rise to positions of apparent security and power, and both gamble on their luck; but both are ruined by the logical extension of characteristics in themselves. It is worth briefly looking at each in turn.

Hotspur had admirable qualities and great gifts. His energy is attractive, his concern for honour (however qualified later – see below, pp. 133f., 185ff.), expressed in magnificent if hyperbolical language (Part 1, I.iii.199ff.) and his impulsive generosity (III.i.131–2) give him at least some of the magnanimity of the potential hero. He is a born leader of men, capable of inspiring affection and admiration. In his play he is very

5. Catherine M. Shaw, 'The Tragic Substructure of the *Henry IV* Plays'; *Shakespeare Survey* 38 (1985), pp. 61–8.

like the young Bolingbroke. Henry IV himself compares him favourably
with his own son even at the end of *Richard II*, wishes that he were his
father, and sees the parallel with himself. But he has bad qualities too;
just as Richard said of Bolingbroke and Mowbray,

> High-stomach'd are they both and full of ire;
> In rage, deaf as the sea, hasty as fire,
>
> (*Richard II*, I.i.18–19)

Hotspur is heir to that 'harsh rage' and 'want of governance' in Bolingbroke's character which led him ultimately to usurpation. Worcester
and Northumberland underline his similar failings: his impetuousness,
impatience, anger, sense of injury and lack of self-control (*1 Henry IV*,
1.iii.207–8, 233–5). Worcester spells his weaknesses out in no uncertain
terms:

> In faith, my lord, you are too wilful-blame,
> And since your coming hither have done enough
> To put him quite besides his patience.
> You must needs learn, lord, to amend this fault.
> Though sometimes it show greatness, courage, blood –
> And that's the dearest grace it renders you –
> Yet oftentimes it doth present harsh rage,
> Defect of manners, want of government,
> Pride, haughtiness, opinion, and disdain,
> The least of which haunting a nobleman,
> Loseth men's hearts and leaves behind a stain
> Upon the beauty of all parts besides,
> Beguiling them of commendation.
>
> (*1 Henry IV*, III.i.171–83)

Lord Bardolph later reminds us of where these weaknesses led him – to
rebellion and defeat and death:

> [He] with great imagination
> Proper to madmen, led his powers to death,
> And winking leaped into destruction.
>
> (*2 Henry IV*, I.iii.31–3)

The very qualities that make him attractive are political liabilities and
destroy him; it does not seem mere coincidence that Lord Bardolph is
given the energetic and impetuous verb 'leaped', for it reminds us of
Hotspur's memorable lines, said when at his most admirable and attractive:

> *By heaven, methinks it were an easy leap*
> *To pluck bright honour from the pale-faced moon,*
> *Or dive into the bottom of the deep,*
> *Where fathom-line could never touch the ground,*
> *And pluck up drownèd honour by the locks ...*
>
> (*1 Henry IV*, I.iii.199–203)[6]

However ambiguous a figure he may be, we care about the attractive, almost heroic, Hotspur, who risks and dares; his fall and death are emotionally very powerful. It is significant that Prince Hal, the adversary he holds in contempt but whom we know him to have seriously misjudged (as Richard misjudged the seriousness of Bolingbroke), feels real compassion for the man he has just defeated, and speaks over him an elegy that, while it in no way glosses over the grievous sin of 'ill-weaved ambition', underlines the serious loss of such a man:

> *This earth that bears thee dead*
> *Bears not alive so stout a gentleman ...*
> *... take thy praise with thee to heaven!*
> *Thy ignominy sleep with thee in the grave,*
> *Be not remembered in thy epitaph.*
>
> (*1 Henry IV*, V.iv.91ff.)

So powerful is this moment that it subsumes emotionally the fall of all the other rebels; and we see symbolized in Hotspur the payment for the crimes of 'gross rebellion and detested treason'. His fall is not only personal but paradigmatic; it underlines within the framework of historical event what *ought*, in a simple world, to have happened to Bolingbroke. Hotspur's fall, too, is a direct result of the chain of circumstance initiated by Richard's misrule, the shadow of which lies as long as the shadow of his murder.

Falstaff operates as a character in a number of extremely complex ways, and later it will be necessary to turn to him again. Here I want to draw attention to certain traits in his character which point to him being used to throw light on the nature of misrule, usurpation, and its ultimate Nemesis. He has reference to the persons of both Richard and Henry IV. We must, for the time being, take for granted, without the further examination that will be necessary, his enormous attractiveness and energy on stage.

6. Shakespeare underlines the irony of Hotspur's career here by making him connect personified honour with the instability of the moon, the image of fortune, and the changeable sea, governed by the changing moon.

The interesting parallel between Henry IV and Falstaff has first to be considered. Falstaff, in his disordered and riotous life, his contempt for all authority except that of his own desires, is of course a symptom, or consequence, of a national breaking of order. He has won to his company the heir to the throne, away from his father and explicitly away from his duties. Just as Henry IV is thus led to see Hotspur as a preferable, even ideal, heir, Falstaff sees *what he thinks* Hal to be as an ideal king – one who will subvert the settled rule of law, hang no rogues in England, and overturn the authority and hierarchy of government. Eastcheap, Falstaff's milieu and almost creation, thus comes to symbolize Falstaff's kingdom – a kingdom he explicitly and parodically plays king to in Part 1, II.iv. With breathtaking *lèse-majesté* he guys the actual figure of Henry, and Shakespeare gives him speech which, though prose, is not dissimilar to the sententious public utterance of Henry IV in Act I, Scene i. He acts out in visible form the moral reality of a kingship like Henry's, without the sanction of divine grace or due succession. In him we see the extension to a horrific conclusion of the misrule we saw in Richard and the usurpation it called forth. For him, rule is rapine, the magnifying of the self and its appetites at the expense of the commonweal; not the husbandry of a garden but its looting. He is, in fact, a King of Misrule, and Eastcheap is a glimpse of his kingdom.

For a time he has the illusion that power will soon be realized. Hal seems *to him* to treat him as a father, seems to promise – though he never does – what Falstaff wants. He trades on these expectations appallingly. He misuses the king's press cynically and cruelly, mutilates the body of the fallen Hotspur, lies about his own prowess, claiming – quite seriously, I think – an advancement in the hierarchy of rank that is different only in degree from that achieved by Henry IV and attempted by Glendower, Hotspur and Mortimer. Yet Hal in Part 2 chooses a new father in the Lord Chief Justice, who embodies loyalty, justice and order, the antithesis to both his real father and to Falstaff; and all that is left to Falstaff is the memory of the illusion of glory and power. His fall, externally (and dramatically) necessary as it is, is internally motivated, the fruition of his own ironic insight about the impermanence of the world in the very first moments of his first appearance in Part 1, I.ii. He is indeed a 'minion of the moon', and his fortune has ebbed and flowed like the sea, 'being governed, as the sea is, by the moon'. Prince Hal replies to him with an irony that cuts deep through Falstaff's own. Just so has the winning of the throne turned to dust and ashes in Henry's mouth.

But his reference in his fall extends beyond Henry to Richard. His weakness mirrors Richard's, as Hotspur's does Henry's. He and Richard both live off their realms, in actuality or intent. Both are egocentric, both charm others and deceive themselves with words, each constructing and believing in a world that is quite other than the one that is actually around them (see Chapter 11). God's angels do not descend to fight for Richard, despite his confidence; Falstaff's own image of his England is a lie and a cheat that he falls for. Both are blind to the signs of real danger; Falstaff ignores the explicit warning and detailed prediction given by Prince Hal in Part 1, II.iv.466, as Richard ignores – even fuels, by his smiling remark – Bolingbroke's 'high pitch' that is to destroy him (*Richard II*, I.i.109).[7]

He comes to a public humiliation, as Richard does, and also to an internal recognition of what his real state is. Richard comes publicly to the one, and alone in prison to the other; with Falstaff it is simultaneous, his public fall coinciding with his private realization of his aloneness, his only companions Shallow and Silence. His erstwhile companions Pistol and Bardolph become followers of the new king, just as Aumerle left Richard. He utterly deserves this fall, as Richard did his, as Macbeth does; yet he is pitiable and pathetic. Though he is not tragic, the outline of his career has the shape of tragedy and clearly echoes in a comic grotesque mode some major elements in the natures and careers of the main political figures.

Why this substructure is there at all in two plays that emphatically are not tragedies needs some attention. After all, Shakespeare seems to have thought it important; he altered the historical record he worked from pretty severely to allow the parallel between Hotspur, Hal and Bolingbroke to be developed, and virtually invented the Falstaff plot (see below, pp. 142ff.). The problem returns us once more to the idea of the history play. Given titles that suggest single heroes, nevertheless the real subject of these plays is not Richard or Henry or Hotspur or Hal, but England. They are about a real people caught in a trap of real history, a trap that actually happened. That people – England itself – suffer from generation to generation, expiating the original guilt of revolt, and acting out and suffering the inevitable consequences, until somehow the blood sacrifice is paid. Hotspur is one such sacrifice. But just as, as a result of original sin at the Fall, humankind is unable to regain that state of

7. Richard is given a striking image, whose irony only we, with our historical knowledge, can perceive: Bolingbroke, subliminally, is a falcon, flying at game – Richard.

innocence, so the deposition of Richard, specifically linked to the Fall, casts its shadow over all succeeding human life. Carlisle's prophecy is fulfilled to the absolute letter; Richard's own, in *Richard II*, V.i.55ff., is quoted by Henry IV in Part 2, III.i.71ff., to underline the entail of guilt into which they are all locked. He takes that guilt on his own head – and has to carry, alone, the guilt of murder (Part 2, IV.v.183ff.); he clears Hal, but the fall is not undone, the soiling remains. Hotspur and Falstaff are the symptoms of the disorder he caused, and agents of new trouble in their own right. The consequences of this primal act may remit for an interim, as in the reign of Henry V, but Henry remembers the blood of Richard in the moment before his greatest triumph; his son Henry VI loses the throne Henry IV had usurped. The fallenness of man's nature makes his finest qualities the seeds of his downfall. That hint of tragedy thus underlines for us the profundity of Shakespeare's understanding of the human condition and of the political life in which we are all inescapably involved.

But the Henry IV plays have other, more obvious, structural elements signalling the genre to which they belong and thus warning the audience about the type of response that may be demanded. An obvious feature they have in common is the consistent alternation of scenes between the political milieu and the world centring round or dominated by Falstaff. The political dimension is pretty straightforward; even we moderns readily recognize that we are watching and are being asked to judge political behaviour in a historical context – a chronicle play, in fact. (The simplicity of the idea should not suggest that the response need be simple.) What is more problematical is the relationship of the Falstaff scenes to these; clearly it matters a lot, or Shakespeare would not have so carefully intertwined them over a huge structure covering ten acts.

That ten-act structure is itself a problem. Here is probably not the place to attempt to settle the question of whether the Henry IV plays are to be seen as two independent works or as a single huge one, so long that it had to be split in order to be played on consecutive afternoons. There seems to be a thematic structure that does in fact run right through both, and this I shall discuss later. These points are clear, however:

1. Each part has a virtually self-contained rebellion within it (though they are far from unconnected); in each a different sort of challenge by a different set of rebels is dealt with.

2. They have in common the development of the career of Falstaff, with his apparent high point occurring after Shrewsbury, and each requires the other to present a complete picture of him.

3. They have in common the theme 'uneasy lies the head that wears a crown' – especially if that crown was won unjustly.

4. In both the relationship between Prince Hal and the crown is a developing and central concern, to the point where, at the end, he is seen outdoors in a grand public triumphal procession as king (a neat balance to the first time he appears, alone, indoors, accompanied only by Falstaff, making funny but rather unkingly wisecracks).

This might well suggest that, whatever the stage practice of the time, there are sufficient links between the plays to make it sensible to take them together.

The Falstaff scenes, particularly in Part 1, contain some of the funniest writing that has ever graced an English stage. They are therefore extremely memorable, and there is evidence that, like Charles I re-naming *Much Ado About Nothing* 'Beatrice and Benedick' in his copy of the First Folio, the plays were remembered and referred to by the names of *Falstaff* or *Oldcastle* (see p. 140). But such comedy can easily blind us, as moderns, to the realization of what sort of comedy it would have been recognized as by its first audience; and that recognition intimately affects the relationship with the political scenes.

It has long been acknowledged that Falstaff's dramatic ancestors inhabit the Morality tradition (see above, p. 53). We easily assume that phrases applied to Falstaff, like 'that old white-bearded Satan', 'Vice with his dagger of lath', and so on, are mere hangovers from this. But, as we shall see, there are very good grounds indeed for thinking that Shakespeare was deliberately writing something very close to a Morality himself in these scenes, or, at the very least, giving his audience a nudge to suggest they should consider them in a similar way. If we take a central issue of Parts 1 and 2 to be a discussion of the education of a prince – a Morality theme if ever there was one – we can easily see how the Falstaff scenes represent the temptation of the prince to misuse of power and self-indulgence: using the old word, to 'riot'.[8]

Now no temptation has much chance of succeeding if it is not believable and attractive, and Falstaff has to be felt to be damnably so. The writers of medieval allegories, sermons and Moralities knew this well, and there is no greater vividness to be found anywhere than in some of the detailed portrayals, as if they were real people, of abstract

---

8. Using this word reminds us of the splendidly Falstaffian allegorical portrayal of this quality in the person of Ryotte in Skelton's *Bowge of Court* (*c.* 1498). Skelton also wrote a rather good Morality drama about the nature, duties and vulnerabilities of a king, *Magnyfycence.*

93

qualities like Lust or Pride or Sloth. Moreover, Shakespeare gives us clues throughout, so that behind the illusion of the vast, pulsating, sweating bulk of Falstaff we are to see him being referred back to the allegorical character (see below, p. 144). We have already noted how he and his milieu symbolize the disorders in the realm of England itself. Behind the 'realistic' figure, then, lies something which in its symbolism and values relates closely to the Morality drama. This should not surprise us, for, as we mentioned above (p. 52), at this time people expected drama to discuss abstract moral issues through symbolic character and action. What is striking is how boldly Shakespeare uses the techniques and frameworks of the Morality.[9] But this is not significant simply in a discussion of Falstaff. As we saw, the alternation of scenes is consistent and noticeable. If one set of scenes is moralistic in the way I suggest, and if, as they do, the two sets eventually integrate at the crowning of Henry V, when all the characters in the play drop the masks they have consciously or unconsciously been wearing and take on their true roles, it is very good sense indeed to regard the Falstaff scenes as making manifest the issues underlying the apparent rationality of the political scenes; indeed, to see the interweaving as a means of maintaining a choric commentary on the political action. And, of course, the point works the other way too: the political scenes comment on the Falstaff scenes.

In watching the Henry IV plays, then, I think the audience is being given a number of overlapping categories into which to fit them. The first (in point of response as well of importance) will be the recognition that, whatever else it is, this play is chronicle drama relating to real events in real time. Almost immediately will follow the recognition – probably expected, in view of the legends about Prince Hal – of the Morality elements in the temptation and education of a prince (plus the irony that the audience will know about, expect and indeed desire Falstaff's eventual fall). Later the alternation of scenes will make them view the chronicle elements in a Morality light too – almost as if those elements were acting as exemplars for the generalized moral reflection prompted by recognition of Falstaff's ancestry. Finally will come the recognition of the tragic substructure that thematically links these plays to their predecessor and brings into our minds Richard's murdered body,

9. Exactly as he uses them in the Porter scene in *Macbeth*, II.i. The scene has direct verbal allusions to the comic scene in the Harrowing of Hell plays, where the Castle of Hell is guarded by a drunken porter who responds with comic chitchat to the knocking at the gate. He opens it to let in Christ. Not an insignificant clue to what has happened to Macbeth and Scotland, and to the significance of Macduff.

gored by many wounds like the body of England itself, a strikingly recurrent image (notice how many images relate to the idea of England as a gored body). To treat these plays chiefly as jolly comedies, therefore, with an irritating intrusion of politics, is to get them about as wrong as it is possible to do. It is remarkable how often people who should know better have done just that, for in them we hear far more than the chimes at midnight.

iii *Henry V*

The use of Rumour, painted full of tongues – an allegorical/Morality-type figure if ever there was one – to bridge the two parts of *Henry IV* and to introduce the important idea of public opinion (see below, pp. 132, 183ff.) may have given Shakespeare the idea for the extensive use of the Chorus in *Henry V*. A Chorus opening (or closing) a play is not that unusual in the drama of the 1590s, and indeed in the old Interludes writers often structured their material as a sequence of thematically organized, parallel, narratively distinct episodes, unified and framed by an explanatory Chorus. *Henry V* could thus be seen on a cursory analysis as a rather (deliberately?) old-fashioned play, but Shakespeare is in fact doing something highly innovative, quite unlike what initially we might expect. In no other play does he structure the entire narrative by a Chorus intervening at important points with significant information. Looking for a moment at this figure and what he says will help us to recognize the signals Shakespeare is giving his audience, and thus the parameters of the construction of the play.

The opening Chorus sounds a note that recurs in all subsequent ones: the impossibility of the playwright and actors conveying with any real verisimilitude the magnitude and importance of the action. Running through all these links is the insistence on the need for the audience's consenting imagination to fill out the inadequacies of the representation, a sense of the weakness of words and vision. This might well look like bravado, or indeed folly, for what if the audience did take these remarks at face value and agree about the inadequacy? Sales of oranges might well shoot up. But we can be sure that Shakespeare is underlining this point for a very good reason and that he is quite certain his audience will respond in the desired way.

The Prologue (who announces in line 32 that he is also to be Chorus) is instantly recognizable as not being part of the play proper, for it was standard stage practice for a Prologue to signal his nature by wearing a long black cloak. The job of a Prologue is to introduce the matter of a play and to suggest what sort of thing we are to see; the job of a Chorus is to comment and supply information. Now this immediately distances the represented action in a way that does not happen in the preceding three plays; and this distancing is immediately confirmed by the insistence through the subjunctive mood on the impossibility of the *present* actor really being like Harry the Fifth:

> *Then should the warlike Harry,* like himself,
> *Assume the port of Mars . . .*

The Prologue begins, then, with a statement of an impossibility in what is grammatically an impossible condition. He calls for a Muse of fire, knowing full well the scarcity of the species. Yet in that statement lies an important clue to what is happening. His opening lines in their grandiloquence focus round the idea of inspiration by the Muse; and this is like nothing so much as the conventional opening of an epic poem. The bold personification in the next lines of famine, war and destruction (like the dogs of war unleashed on France), emblematically pictured waiting for their master Harry's command, reinforce this hint, and the emphasis on the size and importance of the conflict that dominates the rest of the speech is exactly like the grand, serious, high-style openings of classical epic. It is clear, I think, that Shakespeare in making this allusion is asking his audience to get ready a certain set of expectations and responses, and we need to look at what those are.

There would be no one in the audience, not even the legendary groundlings, who would not have at least some idea of what an epic was. Anyone with any education at all could hardly avoid knowing at least parts of Virgil's *Aeneid*, either in the original Latin or in one of the several sixteenth-century translations. They might also be familiar with Homer, just possibly in the first part of Chapman's English version, published in 1598. They would first of all know that an epic was a very long and highly serious poem dealing with huge issues like the founding of a people, or a great and titanic conflict in which a whole civilization – even the gods themselves – were involved. They would know that the conflicts of epic centred round great, admirable, awesome but human figures with human feelings, like Achilles or Hector, Aeneas or Turnus. They would expect that the epic, traditionally the highest of all poetic forms, should be deeply concerned with the values and ideals of a whole nation. They would, finally, expect it to be relevant to their own thinking about the human condition, even to their own political framework. (This is true of Virgil, and exactly how Milton, writing some fifty years later, indicates he expects *Paradise Lost* to be read.) Sir Philip Sidney wrote:

As the image of each action styrreth and instructeth the mind, so the loftie image of such Worthies most inflameth the mind with desire to be worthy, and informes with counsel how to be worthy.

*(Defence of Poesie* (1595), ed.
Feuillerat, Cambridge, 1962, p. 33)

The purpose of epic poetry is to arouse moral admiration and encourage imitation of great deeds.

Henry V was by general agreement a fit subject for epic treatment. Aristotle's view, beginning to be widely known (see above, p. 50), that the material of epic fable should be historical and that the epic should have magnitude, would clearly admit his reign. Samuel Daniel in his verse epic *Civil Wars* (1595) does not deal with Henry's reign, but comments that 'new immortal *Iliads* might proceed' from such 'eternal matter'. His campaigns had already been rather clumsily handled in an attempt at epic majesty in the anonymous *Famous Victories of King Henry V* (1594?), which covers a longer period than Shakespeare's play. Of the appropriateness of the subject to the epic mode, or vice versa, there is no doubt. But the informed members of the audience must have sat up and taken startled notice when they began to receive Prologue's signals; for writing an epic poem and writing a play are, on sixteenth-century and classical critical terms, very different artistic activities. Shakespeare is doing something not just daring but revolutionary, and nothing had been seen like it on stage before. The urgently apologetic tone of the Prologue after the splendid opening is quite deliberate; Shakespeare knew he was risking the scorn of the learned and the judicious spectator.

Critical theory, either in Aristotle or in Shakespeare's friend and rival Ben Jonson, insisted that the magnitude of the epic was not something that could be compassed by a stage play. It also insisted that the action should be single (unity of action) and of a satisfying wholeness, and Shakespeare takes liberties with unity of action in nearly all his plays, including this one. The solution Shakespeare adopted was to write a series of historical tableaux, often alternating between contrary sets of values (the low-life scenes contrasting with the high politics), and pull them together by the device of the Chorus, all of whose speeches sound the epic note. The Chorus is thus being used like the messenger in classical tragedy, to 'recount thinges done in former time or other place' (Sidney, *Defence of Poesie,* ed. Feuillerat, p. 39), and would be recognized as so doing by the more learned members of the audience. His important structural and narrative function frames the tableaux and secures something like a unity of action and (another of the three unities derived from Aristotle by the Italian critics) unity of place, for, as his words make constantly clear, the action is taking place as much in our minds as anywhere else.

The appropriateness of Henry as epic hero need not be doubted. *Henry V* is moral in the epic way – a 'loftie image' stirring us to virtuous emulation – because of Shakespeare's portrayal of his hero. This we shall of course have to discuss more fully later; but for the moment it is enough to say that as near as makes no matter he is made to embody the classical and Renaissance conceptions of the ideal king, ideals which coincide with the uncommon nobility yet the essential humanity of the epic hero.

The mode that is being signalled to us as we begin *Henry V* is radically important to how we take the play. To see a deep irony on Shakespeare's part, a deep ambiguity about the figure of Henry, is fatally to misread what its first audience could have seen. There is ambiguity; but it is not the ambiguity a late twentieth-century Western liberal would like to see. Shakespeare's Henry V is, above all, admirable; his career, exemplary.[10]

## iv *The plays as a sequence*

Tragedy, chronicle hybridized with Morality, epic – the plays are clearly so different in conception, genre and expectation that we have to recognize that looking at them as a tetralogy can obscure issues of real importance, and, particularly, may lead us to see them reductively as merely 'history plays', as we commonly and loosely use the term.

Nevertheless, Shakespeare does seem to have envisaged them as a

10. Henry V was seen by the vast majority of people in Shakespeare's day as an entirely admirable king. For example, when the son of James I, Henry Prince of Wales, died in 1612, the profusion of elegies on the loss of that young man (of whom far more was hoped than he could ever have lived to deliver) constantly compare him with the admired heroes of the past, like King Arthur, Achilles, Mars, Alexander, the Black Prince – and Henry V. Our perfectly proper horror of war was not always shared by our fathers, who could see it as something glorious and noble; and though there is much that is complex in Shakespeare's treatment of Henry V and his campaign, it is simplistic to see him as subverting the values many attached to it. Moreover, even if he had been doing so, it is hard to see how an audience could have so received it. But see the discussion below.

sequence of some sort. *Richard II* seems deliberately to leave loose ends and point forward to a play as yet unwritten where the fulfilment of Richard's and Carlisle's prophecies will form a major part of the action. A lot of its ideas are simply not fully worked out. Moreover, it is from Hotspur (v.iii.16) that we first hear of the dissolute behaviour of Prince Hal that will occupy so much of the next two plays, and from II.iii we know Shakespeare to have already made in his mind the crucial alteration to Hotspur's age to allow him to be so strongly contrasted with Hal. But that the succeeding plays were not yet in any detailed form in Shakespeare's mind is suggested by the fact that the central figure of Falstaff is not mentioned in V.iii, whereas the other Eastcheap features of robbery, taverns, loose companions and debauchery are. The Oldcastle legend (see below, pp. 137ff.) which developed into Shakespeare's Falstaff was so well attached to the prince that had Shakespeare thought of using it seriously he could hardly have left out the name of the misleader of youth.

And so four plays intervened between 1595 and Shakespeare's return to this period of English history in (probably) late 1597. Both Parts of *Henry IV* (1597–8), however, clearly look back to the previous play, not only in mechanical connection to it but in thematic relationships and verbal echoes. Both look forward in no merely general way to *Henry V*. The two parts are clearly interdependent: each has a complementary rebellion, each rebellion a dénouement which complements the other by, among other things, highlighting the nature and behaviour of Hal (Prince John and Hotspur throw a lot of light on him). Over all ten acts our attention is focused on the gradual establishment of the value and worth of the prince's character. Part 1 opens with him (apparently) at a nadir – a wastrel prince, unfit to rule; Part 2 closes with a justly applauded coronation, picking up the very themes of legality, authority and justice Falstaff quite seriously mentioned in Part 1, I.ii.56ff. Similarly, at the end of Part 2 Falstaff has finished his gradual but (to him) unperceived fall from the highest point of the 'security' he thought he had reached at the beginning of Part 1. One of the central concerns in Parts 1 and 2 is, after all, the education of a prince; the goods are hardly delivered until Henry V's campaigns in France demonstrate true royalty in action – an event openly expected by Prince John in *2 Henry IV*, V.v.108–10. Further, the Epilogue's promise at the end of that play, to

continue the story, with Sir John in it, and make you merry with fair Katherine of France; where, for anything I know, Falstaff shall die of a sweat, unless already 'a be killed with your hard opinions, seems to be a serious declaration of a part-planned play. There is excellent evidence, too, that it was fulfilled, and that the first performed version of *Henry V* had indeed a substantial part for Falstaff.[11] As it stands, the references back to the audience's memory of the two parts of *Henry IV* are obvious; at a crucial moment before Agincourt, Henry remembers Bolingbroke's crime in *Richard II*. We can therefore be pretty certain that in these three plays (*Henry V* dates from 1599) Shakespeare was thinking of sequels and expects us to do so as well.

It is of course of the very nature of history for sequels not just to matter but to be of the essence. It therefore makes sense for us now to look briefly at those issues that, it can be argued, are common to more than two plays in the group, and often to all four. The changes of genre do not rule out the notion of thematic concerns than run right through them.

11. See pp. 169ff. *The Merry Wives of Windsor* was probably written between *2 Henry IV* and *Henry V*. Queen Elizabeth is supposed to have been so taken with the figure of Falstaff that she asked for a play about him in love. It forms no part of the sequence; its comic thrust is an extension of the Gloucestershire scenes and the *senex amans* comedy of Falstaff and Doll in *2 Henry IV*.

# 7. This Blessed Plot: Husbandry and the Garden

The very fact that these are history plays which deal with the detailed consequences of a single historical event, the deposition of Richard, presupposes that a central interest is what is meant by the concept of England. That the audience is interested in history at all suggests not a mere curiosity about the happenings of the past, which could be much more easily and simply satisfied than by a play, but rather an attempt to understand the nature of the political and moral issues that beset them in their own time by, as it were, isolating them in the test-tube of history. This was an age, after all, when the relationship between the ruled and the ruler was of passionate and overwhelming interest – to the point where death itself was not too high a stake; when the obligations of the one to the many (and vice versa) were problems not merely of morality but also of politics; when a sense of distinctive nationhood was fostered by insecurity at home and trouble abroad; when, finally, men and women were hesitantly, but to at least some extent, consciously, mapping out the sort of society they felt to be just and to strike the right balance between the things that are of Caesar and those that are God's. The old image of the body politic acquires a new force; it is made up of its many members, but how are those members to agree together in a common purpose?

As I made clear above, Shakespeare's vision of English history is by no means an unthinking acceptance of any Panglossian myth that all is for the best in the best of all possible worlds as long as a Tudor gets the throne in the end. He is aware that Tudors too are fallen beings who judge wrongly and destroy things of value: the dignity he gives Wolsey in his fall, and the heroic patience and pathos he gives Queen Catherine in *Henry VIII*, make that abundantly clear. Even the political victors and the heroes are flawed; Bolingbroke never knows peace, mental or political, after Richard's death – the opposition to him would literally dismember the body of England to satisfy their own desire for power; and his son is aware, almost to despair, of the huge moral burden the king must bear as a ruler, as well as of the inherited burden of guilt and injustice. Shakespeare is exploring, it seems, the very nature of rule and of political relationships in the body politic. One of the most interesting aspects of the plays dealing with historical material lies in the way that material opens up the issues of order and harmony in a state, which are all very well when outlined theoretically – as they are by Ulysses; but, alas, the theory so rarely accords with the observed practices of men and nations. The body politic's distempers in the past may suggest a better understanding – even, perhaps, a way of coping – for those in the present.

A striking image right at the beginning of *1 Henry IV* looks back to the strife of *Richard II* and ironically forward to what is to come:

> *No more the thirsty entrance of this soil*
> *Shall daub her lips with her own children's blood . . .*

A mother greedily eating her own children is a fit dominating image for a play following on from the casual carnage of the best blood in England that marked Henry's accession (*Richard II*, V.vi),[1] and including within itself the death or execution of so many nobles and commons. Yet the image is more than grotesque; it is pointedly unnatural, is meant to be so by Henry, and derives its unnaturalness not just from the idea of a motherland but from the idea of the body politic. This image of the state as body[2] remains with us throughout the next three plays. It is perhaps glanced at in the bloated form of Falstaff, creation of these distempers and distempered himself; it is hinted at again in Canterbury's beautiful speech in *Henry V* about the harmonious kingdom of the bees (I.ii). But Henry continues,

> *No more shall trenching war channel her fields,*
> *Nor bruise her flowerets with the armèd hoofs*
> *Of hostile paces.*

(*1 Henry IV*, I.i.7–9)

Here our point of reference has been shifted; we are now talking about gardens, husbandry and agriculture. Shakespeare has linked up the basic idea of the motherland/body politic with the central theme that runs through all four plays: the garden and how it must be cultivated.

## The garden symbol

We moderns have virtually forgotten the extraordinary symbolic power of gardens, and before we can get anywhere at all with Shakespeare's

1. The image echoes, surely, *Richard II*, III.iii.95–100.

2. *King John*, probably written in the early part of the same year, exploits to a remarkable degree imagery of the state and polity as a suffering body.

images and symbols of them we have to do something to recover the original force of the idea. It is of central importance in our four plays.

An age better versed in its Bible[3] than our own would recollect that, as Francis Bacon said, 'God Almighty first planted a garden', and gave it to man to look after. That 'happy garden state' where man 'knew not the doctrine of ill-doing' remained a potent image of perfection for literally thousands of years. It was, naturally, elaborated; the changes in the seasons and their accompanying discomforts were unknown, the plants gave their fruits in due time, and the lion lay down with the lamb. But man's desire (or, to use the old and more correct term, his *cupiditas*),[4] led him to seek a role and powers that God had not given him, and so he fell. With his Fall the whole of Creation was affected (see above, pp. 15ff.), and nothing could ever again be innocent and perfect.[5] He was cast out of the Garden, and condemned to eat his bread in the sweat of his brow (Genesis iii) – in other words, work became the norm of his existence, and the failed gardener became a farmer. (This notion of farming as the *best* fallen man can do is important, as we shall see.)

The biblical idea of an unfallen state of perfection received support from classical sources too. Ovid, for example, in the first book of his widely read *Metamorphoses* suggests the pristine state of the world, when evil was unknown. He also suggests what happened when man transgressed. These two strands (which are clearly, in some unimaginably distant past, related to one another) converge on the medieval and Renaissance idea of the garden-*topos*[6] and contribute to its usual characteristics of singing birds, a pleasant season, harmonious

3. It is a matter of historical fact that the Bible, with the classics, has had a huge and continuing influence on Western culture right down to the present; it was constantly read and studied until a generation ago, and men and women used it (among other things) as a means of understanding their own situation and the moral imperatives surrounding their personal and political action. *It cannot be stressed too strongly that students of our culture and literature will get virtually nowhere in understanding them unless they get themselves a Bible – and read it.*

4. That is, selfish desire as opposed to real love, self-giving and self-forgetting *caritas* – St Paul's 'charity' of I Corinthians xiii.

5. For English readers, the finest statement of both the intuition of what the unfallen Garden was like and the consequences of the Fall is to be found in Milton, *Paradise Lost*, IX and X.

6. The word *topos* introduces a very useful concept. The Greek means 'commonplace'; and as we saw in our discussion of convention above (p. 37), the commonplace both constitutes a norm and sets out the area of agreement between author and audience. An author is thus free to evoke a set of responses very economically and to use them to fit his current purpose. Pastoral uses many conventions and *topoi*.

human relationships and all other possible delights. Real gardens, of course, are in a fallen world, and thus can only glance obliquely, as it were, at the real thing to which they refer; but even there the symbolism operates, and in the formal Renaissance garden with its complex mathematics and patterns there is an attempt to evoke something of the perfection of Eden.[7]

We need to be very much on our guard, therefore, as soon as we stray near an Elizabethan flower-bed; reconstructing the signals contained in the idea of 'the garden' can lead us to some illuminating readings of poems, plays and pictures we thought we knew well. Thomas Campion's 'There is a Garden in her face', for example, takes on a wholly new force and set of references when we recognize that its subtextual discourse is built round Eden, the Fall of man and the angel with the flaming sword (Genesis iii).

But it was while in the Garden that man fell. And that primal sin has changed the world for ever and a day; there is no undoing what once has been done. But the mercy of God gave man work to do, so that from the ruins of his original destiny he could painstakingly build something of real value. Law and hierarchy were, according to the theologians, instituted by the mercy of God to temper the effects of the Fall – as Augustine put it, *in remedium peccatorum*. This has quite unmistakable general reference to the theories of kingship we discussed in Chapter 4, which operate in these history plays; but it also has specific application to *Richard II*, III.iv, the garden scene. This opens with the Queen asking two of her ladies how she shall 'drive away the heavy thought of care' in this garden – a remark that reminds us, if we need such a reminder, that this likeness of Eden is only a distant echo. She rejects all four suggestions that are made, and at that point draws aside with her ladies to observe the conversation of the Gardener and two servants. The Gardener, as a good gardener should, is making proper use of his subordinate to look

7. See, for example, the discussion of planting in Sir Thomas Browne's *Garden of Cyrus* (1658).

There is no room here, alas, to go into the fascinating history of landscape gardening over the seventeenth and eighteenth centuries in England. What happens is more than a mere change in fashion; it is a serious debate about the role of fallen man in fallen nature, and there is a central moral and philosophical interest in the planting of knot-gardens or of apparently 'natural' clumps of trees. Lord Chesterfield, indeed, in the eighteenth century, ironically referred to the amount of writing this controversy generated as being inspired not by the 'poetic madness' (*furor poeticus*) of Horace but by 'garden madness' (*furor hortensis*). Intelligent and curious wandering round a couple of representative gardens or parks can be more instructive about a temper of mind than a lot of critical books.

after his charge: to support the plants that need supporting, to prune the rank growth and uproot the weeds that harm the good plants. His imagery underlines the parallel between his role and that of a ruler. His man makes the parallel come very near home; England is the 'sea-wallèd garden' of line 43, but her gardener has neglected his duty sadly, and she is in a mess, running to waste.[8]

England's gardener has got his just deserts. The Gardener pushes the image a step further – Richard is more than just a gardener, he is a mighty plant, a tree (oak? – see p. 14) that sheltered less worthy men, and is now uprooted. (Surely there is an echo here of Our Lord's warning that 'every tree which bringeth not forth good fruit is hewn down and cast into the fire'? – Matthew iii.10.) The imagery of bad husbandry is sustained to line 66 in a remarkable *tour de force*, which explores in considerable *and memorable* detail the duties of a king. The conceit hammers itself into our consciousness as a potent way of valuing and understanding the fall of Richard and *why* it has inevitably happened; the management of realms and gardens are related arts. The Gardener's lines, too, are not only an admonition in a play, not only of general relevance; they shoot straight out of the play and challenge the mighty of Shakespeare's own day to defend their stewardship. The ideas of kingship so memorably stated here clearly have to be borne in mind when we look at the reigns of Henry IV and Henry V, and this discussion connects up with the ideas of the duty and person of the prince both as a mortal man and as the immortal symbol of the identity of the nation (see pp. 59ff., 77, 112).[9]

At this point the Queen steps forward. Shakespeare has her make quite explicit the point that has lain dormant since the Gardener entered: he is 'old Adam's likeness' in a garden that has been entrusted to him, but is now speculating on things above his station. She in her passion sees this as a parallel to Adam's primal Fall, and links this naturally with ideas of his betrayal by the one he most trusted – Eve – who has been betrayed in turn by the devil in the guise of a serpent. The imaginative force of this is profound. It links to Richard a new idea that we shall see

8. 'Waste' is more than just what we mean by the word; it is the evil misuse or misdirection of the goods of a State. Much medieval satire is directed against 'wasters', and Bushy, Green and Bagot are, in Shakespeare's and his forefathers' terms, 'wasters'.

9. Shakespeare returns to the idea-complex 'gardening/true breeding/royalty' several times – not least in *The Winter's Tale* when Perdita, in a sort of primitive Gardeners' Question Time, advises Polixenes on the relationship between art and nature, and, implicitly, on the duties of a king. (She thus shows her own as yet undiscovered royalty.)

develop in the rest of the play – an idea of innocence betrayed, that he is a man more sinned against than sinning; it supports the bold subliminal linking between the (supposed) betrayal of Richard with Judas's betrayal of Christ (III.ii.132–4), and pushes our idea of Richard along the road to true tragic sympathy. But the crucial thing is that the Queen sets up in our minds the fall of Richard as the primal, original, sin of the Henry plays – nothing can ever be the same again.[10] The world is different from this point on, and only with incessant care will a shaken and wan Bolingbroke keep his hollow crown.

The idea of England as a garden that through sin – Richard's bad gardening, the Fall of Richard – turns into a farm, requiring hard work, takes us into a discussion of farming imagery in these plays.[11] There is a vast amount of it from the beginning of *Richard II* to the end of *Henry V*, and it links these plays together in a way quite unique in the canon. To look at this imagery and its importance in the light of its probable source, the agricultural poems of Virgil, is useful as there seems indeed to be a detailed correspondence between Virgil's four *Georgics* and Shakespeare's four plays.

There can be little doubt that Shakespeare's 'small Latin' – which by our standards probably means quite a lot – had enabled him to cope with Virgil's *Georgics*. This book was, after all, on every schoolboy's reading programme, and even the Latinless could hardly avoid acquaintance with the poems since they were borrowed from extensively, and translated: Ben Jonson – a fine classical scholar – owned a copy of A. Fleming's version of 1589. Virgil wrote these poems, apparently of country life and good husbandry,[12] after the end of the terrible civil war that began with the conflict of Marius and Sulla, and continued with

10. The recurrent images of betrayal, particularly in *Richard II*, often allude to the serpent's betrayal in Eden; they strikingly recur in exactly the same terms, even to the inclusion of Judas, in Henry V's impassioned speech in response to the intended treason of Scroop, Grey and Cambridge (II.ii.79ff.). We notice, too, that Falstaff, a corrupter of youth, is also fleetingly seen as a devilish tempter – a 'white-bearded Satan'.

11. In a fallen world – be it an Ovidian or Christian Fall – 'country' poems, whether pastoral or on good husbandry, can powerfully suggest, and keep alive, the possibility of a great Universal Garden tended and brought to fruiting by a supreme and loving Gardener – an ordered and harmonious cosmos, in the terms so movingly explored by the Elizabethan philosopher Richard Hooker in his *Laws of Ecclesiastical Polity* (Books I–IV, 1593; Book V, 1597).

12. Virgil, following Lucretius, was working within the convention of didactic poetry; originally such verse manuals had been designed as easily remembered manuals of instruction. (There are sixteenth-century examples, like Thomas Tusser's *Five Hundred Points of Good*

that of Pompey and Caesar; extended by the murder of Caesar and
the vengeance exacted by the uneasy alliance of Octavian – the future
Augustus – and Mark Antony on his murderers, Brutus and Cassius,
it only ended when Octavian defeated Mark Antony at Actium in 31
B.C. Augustus's task was somehow to bind up the wounds of a world
torn by three generations of vicious internecine strife, to bring peace
to a ravaged Italy, to turn men trained to a life of fighting their
countrymen back into peaceful farmers and citizens. Virgil was fully
aware of the magnitude of Augustus's achievement in pacifying the
world, yet was also keenly conscious of the fact that not only had he
done it at huge cost, even to the dispossession of farmers from their
fields to enable Augustus to pay his soldiers, but also that the bloodshed could not simply be forgotten: the farmer's plough turned up the
bones of those who died at Philippi, and the shed blood was recalled
in the redness of the new wine. His discussion of country life is therefore unavoidably political.

Shakespeare cannot have known the *Georgics* without noticing that
Virgil sees history itself as a sort of agricultural process. The *Georgics*
celebrate peace, but the memory of devastation lies behind every promise of fruitfulness and seems almost to be one of the conditions for
it. The ruler may, by wise rule, achieve a fruitful peace, but the Golden
Age could never be restored and the settlement was always precarious.
In the middle of Book I, for example (I.316ff.), a terrible storm
suddenly breaks just as the harvest begins; it is, significantly, seen in
military terms, and its effects are described (ll.322–34) in terms of epic
combat:

> *Saepe ego, cum flavis messorem induceret arvis*
> *Agricola, et fragili iam stringeret hordea culmo,*
> *Omnia ventorum concurrere proelia vidi,*
> *Quae gravidam late segetem ab radicibus imis*
> *Sublime expulsam eruerent; ita turbine nigro*
> *Ferret hiems culmumque levem stipulas volantes.*
> *Saepe etiam immensum coelo venit agmen aquarum . . .*

(Often, just when the farmer was setting the reaper to work in his golden fields,
just as he touched the brittle-stalked barley, I have seen all the squadrons of

*Husbandry*, London, 1557, a guide to matters agricultural in clay-footed verse.) But this
practical purpose is no longer central to Virgil, and he is discussing other more pressing and
moral issues behind the details of hoeing, vine-trimming and beekeeping.

the winds rush together, far and wide tearing the heavy crop from its very roots and tossing it up; in its dark whirlwind the storm carried away the light stalks and the straws. Often too a great battle-line of the waters gathers in the sky . . .)

The third book, on the management of animals, closes with a long section (ll.440ff.) on their diseases; and the fourth ends, surely symbolically, with the magnificent and haunting story of the failed attempt of Orpheus the poet to win back, by his love and music, his wife Euridice from Hades to the light and colour of the upper world, to restore that perfection and unity which had been lost.[13] Virgil sees the farmer's, and, by implication, the ruler's life as a constant struggle against the forces of disorder and darkness: they are only just under the surface:

> *Scilicet et tempus veniet, cum finibus illis*
> *Agricola, incurvo terram molitus aratro,*
> *Exesa inveniet scabra robigine pila,*
> *Aut gravibus rastris galeas pulsabit inanes,*
> *Grandiaque effossis mirabitur ossa sepulchris*

(I.493ff.)

(Indeed, the time shall come when in those very fields the farmer, after working the land with his curved plough, shall find pikes turned up eaten with rust, or with his heavy mattock shall hit upon empty helmets, and will marvel at the great bones from the graves that have been broken open.)

It is easy to argue a general debt to the *Georgics* in the four plays on the level of images of agriculture. In *Richard II*, I.iii.127–8, we are reminded of Virgil's image, quoted above, of the plough turning up the reminders of civil war; in IV.i.137 Carlisle's warning to Bolingbroke recalls strongly Virgil's plains of Haemus twice manured with Roman blood. The Gardener overheard by Isabel talks about the pruning of trees exactly in Virgil's tones (III.iv.29ff.) In *2 Henry IV* Shakespeare makes Henry use both gardening imagery (which reminds us strongly of Richard) and then bee imagery to express his disappointment in Hal (IV.iv.54ff., 79–80), even picking up Virgil's image of the bees' nest in rotten carrion (*Georgics*, IV.281ff.). Later he sees himself in terms of the industrious bee, who, ironically, in the end loses all it has won. In *Henry V* these bee references culminate in the description the Archbishop gives of the ordered commonwealth of the bees (I.ii.184ff.), which is taken

---

13. L.P. Wilkinson, *The Georgics of Vergil* (Cambridge, 1969), pp. 108ff., reminds us of the commentator Servius's assertion that Virgil used the Orpheus section to replace a politically delicate passage.

from Virgil's discussion of the bees (with some dependence on Wil-lichius's commentary, which first appeared in the Venice edition of 1544). In II.iv.39–40 the good gardening of Virgil's husbandman[14] is used to warn the French of what Hal's harvest is likely to be. But the connection seems to be more interesting than merely this borrowing of details; there are structural parallels of some consequence. Virgil's Book I is devoted to the tilling of the land, the second to planting, the third to the manage-ment of animals, and the fourth to beekeeping. The four plays, which as a whole explore the moral sickness and the sterility of civil strife, seem to mirror Virgil's fourfold structure. *Richard II* uses extensively images of tilling the land or garden; Gaunt sees England both as a garden and, later, as a mismanaged farm; Richard in his prophetic lament (III.iii.161ff.) sees his tears, the result of his fall, as a storm that will 'lodge the Summer corn/And make a dearth in this revolting land'; the two Henry plays are full of images of England's earth gaping to receive the blood of her sons, and of animal passions. Canterbury's model of an ordered commonwealth is a Virgilian beehive,[15] and the bees, as Henry IV knows, lose their honey each autumn. This parallel is interesting enough, but it doesn't in itself settle anything. It does, however, suggest we should look more deeply.

Virgil's perception of the tension in human life and politics between order and disorder[16] seems to have helped Shakespeare to articulate his own political and moral vision, his own perception of the unresolved tension in English politics and history between 'winning' and 'wasting',

14. The fullest description is in Virgil's picture of the good husbandman, who labours against his difficulties and is happy *as a king* with the beauty and goodness he has wrested from the hard earth. See *Georgics*, IV.125ff.

15. Note the irony, however; Canterbury uses it to encourage Henry not to peace, but to war: as if the hard-won instant of peace in England can only be preserved by aggression against France.

16. He sees the very conditions of existence as full of struggle:

> ... *sic omnia fatis*
> *in peius ruere ac retro sublapsa referri,*
> *non aliter quam qui adverso vix flumine lembum*
> *remigiis subigit, si bracchia forte remisit,*
> *atque illum praeceps prono rapit alveus amni.* (I.199ff.)
> ... *labor omnia vicit*
> *improbus, et duris urgens in rebus egestas.* (I.145ff.)

(So everything is fated to rush to the worse, to slip back, just like a man who, just managing to row his boat against the stream, if he should rest his arms for an instant, the boat carries him the way the stream is running.

Relentless labour overcame everything, and in hard circumstances need is pressing.)

natural and unnatural behaviour, progress and relapse. It is as if he sees human society as subject to brief intervals of fragile order which grow out of the previous suffering and themselves contain the seeds of future strife. The history he handles seems to be conceived of as a precarious agricultural process. For example, Hal is specifically made to be a Good Gardener – an Augustus, indeed[17] – in contradistinction to Richard, who was not. At the very moment when he is victorious and England knows a unity and peace and justice she has not experienced for a generation, Burgundy's speech (*Henry V*, V.ii.23ff.) pulls together all the images of agriculture in the four plays in one huge and elegiac image of neglect and devastation. The neglect and devastation in *both* realms can only be repaired by the marriage of the rightful king, who has proved his right to rule and his ability to do so, with the princess whose delightful, innocent and vulnerable femininity in this most masculine of plays reminds us of the vulnerable femininity of another princess of France, Isabel. Between the two women lies the image of the bleeding mother that is tormented England. And the irony is huge; for in the reign of their son, legitimate heir to both crowns, so 'many had the managing' of his state that all was again lost in a welter of kin-strife.[18]

The central metaphor for these plays, then, draws on biblical and Virgilian insights into the human condition. England is an estate to be managed, all too often woefully misused, fearfully dependent on her gardener. Gaunt's speech is a complaint against the husbandman who has neglected his patrimony and rented it out for private satisfaction; Henry IV's bee-like diligence has taken place against the background of an England whose furrows run with blood; the rebels' war aim in *1 Henry IV* (III.i), made dramatically memorable by the prop of the map, is the literal dismemberment of Mother England. Two scenes in the four plays, moreover, are set in actual gardens, and discuss the management of them quite openly and symbolically; it is tempting to see them as deliberately contrasting. The garden scene in *Richard II* underlines what a king should do to tend his realm, and what Richard has not done, and connects both ideas with the irrevocable and – in itself – hopeless fallenness

17. Virgil never actually equates Augustus with the Good Farmer – the *Georgics* and *Aeneid* are models of what *should* be, and warnings against certain traits in Augustus's character. But, with hindsight, Elizabethans could look back at the reign of Augustus as golden, and at him as a ruler to be emulated.

18. It is interesting to compare the predictions of Elizabeth's future greatness at the end of *Henry VIII*: the promise is genuine, but the experience of the audience must make it seem less than the whole truth. These plays deal, after all, not only with models of what might or should be, but also with models of what problematically and untidily *was*.

of human nature. In *2 Henry IV*, we glimpse in Shallow's orchard the ordered life of the Gloucestershire countryside, a world where real work is going on: Shallow grafts his own trees, while Davy interrupts, seeking advice on the management of the farm and on whether to plant the headland with red wheat. But its stewards are foolish and unjust: Davy seeks favour, not justice, from the Justice, and Falstaff, gross image of that disordered growth the bad tending of the realm has allowed, irrupts into this world bringing disorder with him, and the memory of misspent youth – a time of wasting that foolish age longs to regain. The person of the gardener, then, is of central significance, for though the king be but a man, he must bear all. O hard condition!

# 8. Passing Brave to be a King: Richard II

The description in Chapter 4 of the attitudes to the person of the prince and to his role outlines the parameters of Shakespeare's discussion. A most important element in that discussion is the concept of the king's two bodies, the one public and immortal when acting in *proper* concert with his realm, the other fallible, mortal, the private human being called to move in a great sphere. The tension between the man and his office is central to these four plays, and it is probably most convenient if we look at the discussion of the gardener's role in the order Shakespeare gave it, by taking each play in turn.

The garden scene (*Richard II*, III.iv) is, strictly, unnecessary to the development of the narrative, but its appearance within the central block of the play is clearly meant to concentrate our minds powerfully. Its symbolism we need not look at further; but in relation to the rest of the play it pulls together and makes visibly explicit, in the metaphor of the proper role of the monarch in the management of his realm, the gardening/farming images elsewhere in the language of the play. Richard has failed in this job; he has allowed the caterpillars to eat the growing shoots, and has not trimmed the weeds that in the previous scene have just choked him. But the scene also introduces a multiple ambiguity, for it has a reference beyond this play into the subsequent ones and so provides a standard of evaluation against Richard for Bolingbroke. Bolingbroke is a potential gardener. He sees himself in *Richard II* as engaged in a tidying-up and cleansing of the estate (II.iii.165–6). York echoes this in his warning to Aumerle (V.ii.50–51); Henry actually is a gardener, in effect, in the Henry IV plays. It turns out that his garden too is full of weeds. And, finally, we see that he himself is one of the weeds Richard's bad husbandry has allowed to grow.

The play cannot therefore be seen as a straightforward contrasting of the figures and behaviour of Bolingbroke and Richard – though indeed they are contrasted to a minutely balanced and visually exact degree in scenes that comment on each other like two sides of a diptych. Each figure displays a tension between the person and the role the circumstances of history force him to play, and neither resolves it satisfactorily. The failure to resolve it leads to waste, kin-strife, war and the ultimate breaking of the most basic of human communities, the family: the

112

upheaval of Bolingbroke's rebellion leads York, whose *every* choice must be a failure to keep faith, to cry for his son's condemnation; and (apparently) the well-meaning and troubled Henry IV can no more rule his own son than can the devious and unreliable Northumberland rule his.

I have already discussed (pp. 82ff.) the theoretical basis of the play as tragedy. It divides naturally into four movements. The first extends from the beginning to II.i.223 (effectively the end of a 'scene'[1], where we see the crises (some of them deriving from his actions previous to the play) that Richard as king faces with unwisdom and worse. The second movement, down to the end of III.i, deals with the shifting of the real power into Bolingbroke's hands. From III.ii to V.i we concentrate on the deposition of Richard, his humiliation – indeed, what has been called his 'Passion'; this is counterpointed by IV.i, a scene which deliberately echoes visually the trial scenes of Act 1. Here Bolingbroke is using the power Richard has lost. Finally, from V.ii to the end Bolingbroke is king and is capable of mastering a political crisis; but the storm clouds are gathering. This movement is counterpointed by the magnificent last moments of the deposed but now truly kingly Richard.

The opening scene is visually splendid: a king in all the panoply of rule, under the picture of the ordered heavens and among his ordered Court, God's vice-gerent about to give judgement as is his proper function. (Our memory of this state opening is visually cued by IV.i, a clear parallel to it, and the last scene of the play, V.vi; this makes us reflect on what Bolingbroke is and what he has done.) But the matter under judgement is effectively the involvement of Richard in political assassination – murder. As I.ii makes clear, even those who want to support him have a duty of blood-vengeance against him, yet to take up that duty involves the sacrilege of fighting against 'God's substitute'. When the king himself is guilty, what can the subject do? Richard recognizes the explosiveness of the issue, and tries to evade it by refusing judgement. But to do so impugns the honour of the opponents, and the combined insistence by Richard and Gaunt on reconciliation between them is unsuccessful.

1. See above, p. 36. Act divisions are of course quite imperceptible, and it makes a lot of sense to look at Elizabethan plays as a sequence of scenes (as indeed some texts are printed) in a significant order. Where one scene ends and another begins is difficult to perceive except by entrances and exits (which is, in fact, the conventional division in classical French drama). As Mark Rose (*Shakespearean Design*, Cambridge, Mass., 1972) and others have shown, Shakespeare and other dramatists deliberately balanced scenes against each other, often using visual memory of a pattern made by actors on stage across the whole stretch of the play to highlight a later scene – as happens in this play, of course.

Richard has lost some control already. He then takes the only way out open to him; to order trial by combat. When in I.iii the trial is about to take place, Richard again impugns the honour of the combatants by refusing to allow them to fight; and then banishes them with clear injustice and inequity. However we may see Richard's difficulty – that to allow the issue to come to a fight necessarily involves himself and his guilt – this is no kingly behaviour; in ignoring the claims of the combatants' honour it strikes at the very roots of feudal loyalty. His weakness of command in Scene i and his partiality – born of fear[2] – in Scene iii show him in a very bad light indeed.

The murder of Gloucester was evil in itself. Richard's handling of its sequel challenges the established rights of justice and chivalry on which his own royal power depends. He now goes on to break the laws of inheritance by which he himself holds the throne when, to cope with his financial difficulties (a perennial problem of governments, including Elizabethan ones), he confiscates without a shred of legality the estate of Gaunt. Not only is this wrong; it is folly, for it makes Bolingbroke irrevocably and justly his enemy, and breaks the chain of law, obligation and justice that binds king and realm together. Shakespeare prepares for this moment very carefully. First, in I.iv, he shows the king most unattractively joking with his flattering counsellors about really serious matters, and at the end wishing for the death of Gaunt, who has been loyal to him even against the interests of his own son, brother and sister-in-law. Then he immediately juxtaposes with this the fine scene of the two old dukes, pessimistic York warning the dying Gaunt of the emptiness of his hopes that good counsel may turn the youthful Richard from his 'rash fierce blaze of riot' to sober rule. Gaunt is provoked into his great complaint, whose justice we have already seen, about the wasteful misuse of Richard's great office. The complaint presents both an ideal of England to which the audience cannot but subscribe and a prophecy of what the audience know to have actually happened. It underlines the fact that Richard deserved his fall and was personally responsible for it. The attack on Richard in person reinforces this, and Richard is forced back on petulant abuse of this great man. We should note here the ironic parallel between this moment and that between another old man and a young one – King Henry's recalling of Richard's misrule in his own chastisement of an apparently wastrel prince in *1 Henry IV* (III.ii); the

2. In I.iv, lines 20ff. show clearly that Richard has, with real disquiet, noticed Bolingbroke's cultivation of his popularity.

great difference is that Gaunt appeals to an ideal of England, Henry to political practicality. But this prince will not learn. His immediate seizure of Gaunt's property on the news of the latter's death strains the loyalty even of old York[3] – Richard himself notices his disturbance (II.i.186) – who is moved to spell out that Richard's action strikes at the very root of Richard's own claim to the throne (ll. 195ff.). The Richard we have seen so far may be a legitimate monarch, but he is a tyrant, ruling without mercy or law and perfectly conscious that he is doing so. This man, dominated by fear and self-will, is inadequate to the office he holds, and is, indeed, fundamentally unattractive.

Immediately after Richard's exit at II.i.223, Shakespeare shows us the consequences of his actions. His vassals recite a catalogue of his tyrannical misdeeds; and canny Northumberland, after seeming to blame the king's flattering counsellors rather than Richard himself, begins to sound out Willoughby and Ross on the possibility of actual rebellion. It is quite clear that this is not a new idea for Northumberland, or for Bolingbroke; the news of the heavily armed expedition to (as Northumberland euphemistically puts it) 'make high majesty look like itself' has been known to him for some time. Now the blame is quite clearly Richard's – this is one of the weeds of his realm, too; but equally, the perplexity of York (II.ii.109ff.) underlines that the *choice* to rebel or not is the fearful moral responsibility of the rebel *even if the king is tyrannical*. Northumberland's lack of qualms, a neat foil to York's own attitude, shows how right York was in saying that Richard had destroyed the very basis of the commonwealth. The news of the actual landing follows fast – ironically in a scene where the attractive speciousness of the counsel given by Bushy has been neatly exemplified – and the movement of power to Bolingbroke gathers momentum. Everyone, from Bolingbroke downwards, is presented with an insoluble moral conundrum and no one comes out of it with entire credit.

This detailed picture of misrule and what it causes haunts Henry IV as he looks at the behaviour of his unthrifty son; and indeed, did we not know better, we could see him as 'ambling up and down,/With foolish jesters and rash bavin wits' like Richard. It is constantly referred to throughout the remainder of the tetralogy. There is in it a strong

3. The movement of first Gaunt and then York against Richard is significant. These old men embody a sense of history, the 'customary rights' of time; for them to consider breaking, and then actually to break, their oath of fealty to Richard is the severest possible moral condemnation of what he is and has done. Even Richard recognizes that York is 'just, and always loved us well' (II.i.221) – said, ironically, after he has gone right against his advice.

emphasis on the personal responsibility of the king not only to himself as monarch but also as guardian of the fabric of the realm. Richard failed, as we have seen. But the play does not end there. What Shakespeare now proceeds to do by exploring the contrast between Richard and Bolingbroke, is to examine what can happen to the man who *does* rule successfully and efficiently. The 'king-becoming graces' listed in *Macbeth*, IV.iii ('justice, verity, temperance, stableness,/Bounty, perseverance, mercy, lowliness,/Devotion, patience, courage, fortitude' – cf. above, p. 61) are entirely absent from the early picture of Richard, but they are in large measure present in Bolingbroke. Richard is grasping, discourteous and unmerciful; Bolingbroke is courteous, comes (apparently sincerely, at least at first) 'but for his own' (II.iii.147–8), is merciful to the potential assassin Aumerle even against his father York's anguished advice, and intends generosity and mercy to his enemy Norfolk (IV.i.86ff.). Bolingbroke is placed in scenes of judgement that deliberately echo the judgement scenes of Richard, shows decisiveness where Richard was arbitrary and feeble (I.i. and I.iii), and has a consonance with public opinion that Richard ignored. Yet, full of golden opinions as he is, something strange begins to happen to him. His actions begin to have an air of calculation, to be not quite what they seem; the man who comes 'but for his own' very soon acts like a monarch in condemning Bushy, Green and Bagot to death – which he certainly has no obvious right to do. It even begins to look like private vengeance (III.i.16ff.). Yet it was politically necessary – and, after Act I had shown their effects, desirable – that they should be removed. It is at this very point, when he has the effective power but not the name of king, that he is tempted to assume the throne itself (IV.i.113). It is a temptation that he could have refused: Carlisle is horrified, and sees absolutely no justification for this step. Shakespeare gives Carlisle a most powerful speech, full of images of the horrible manuring of the ground of England that will follow such an act, predicting the strife that the audience knows will come. But Bolingbroke, silently, ascends the throne; he does not answer Carlisle, and Shakespeare deflects our outright condemnation from him by making the odious Northumberland, without a shred of justice or legality, arrest Carlisle on capital treason. From this point on, Bolingbroke is drawn into act after act of political expediency. Late in the play he is quite ready to applaud the liquidation of those who rose in support of Richard (V.vi); again, he had to – once they opposed him they had to go. But where is the attractive, popular and dashing Harry Hereford now? By the end of the play we are looking at a worried, guilty man, for whom things are already going wrong. Shakespeare gives him the last image of the play, an agricultural one: a plant growing, fertilized by the blood of Richard; and the final note is guilt.

But the rise of Bolingbroke, interesting and compelling as it is as a study of political consequences, moves reciprocally with the absorbing development of the person of Richard in his fall. While Bolingbroke has all the political initiative, and is an interesting character, Richard is the referent of all his – and everyone else's – actions. His very existence forces the other characters to a definition of their moral selves and an understanding of their roles. The emotional centre of the play still lies with him. His fall is deeply interesting because it is not just fortune that casts him down;[4] it is a self-inflicted downfall (see above, pp. 82ff.), and yet we cannot but see it as terrible and cataclysmic. The cosmic images Richard uses of himself, which Salisbury and the Captain are made to echo in the complex images of dearth, sunset, the end of the world (II.iv.7ff.), have real validity, for Richard is an anointed king, he is God's vice-gerent. But, like Lear, he hath ever but slenderly known himself; he would accept no good counsel, as Gaunt and York realize, and like a king in a Morality, gave himself up to 'riot'. His inevitable fall forces him to know himself, and his fall is a fall upward to self-knowledge and an understanding of what being a king means.

A great deal seems to happen in a very short time after II.i.223 before we next see Richard. Shakespeare has deliberately telescoped historical time to give us the impression of events moving very fast against Richard, beyond his control. He goes out of the play on the Irish expedition, a perfectly proper enterprise in the national interest, but financed quite illegally by Bolingbroke's inheritance. Bolingbroke returns, and Richard's nobles hasten to offer their service to him – a movement epitomized in Harry Percy's tendering him his service. (The irony of this act, in view of subsequent events, cannot be lost on the audience.) Bolingbroke replies to York's challenging the legality of the whole affair

---

4. The contrary wind (II.ii.122–3) which fatally delays him in Ireland (II.iv) may seem mere accident; but Salisbury's image in II.iv.18ff. suggests that even the heavens have ranged themselves against Richard's misrule. Gaunt's lines,

> *God's is the quarrel – for God's substitute,*
> *His deputy anointed in His sight,*
> *Hath caus'd his death; the which if wrongfully,*
> *Let heaven revenge . . .*
>
> (*I.ii.37–40*)

suggest the ambiguity both of Richard's position and our response to his fall.

(II.iii.86ff.) – a challenge which also underlines the potential horror of civil war – by citing the illegality of Richard's action. He points out that Richard has offended not only against natural justice but the very fabric of feudal law, an act which affects all his nobles – as Northumberland (who may well not be saying here all he thinks) clearly sees (ll. 147ff.). Yet York recognizes that while Richard is wrong, and has alienated his whole peerage, to 'find out right with wrong' (l. 144) is equally illegal.[5] Richard's greatest supporter now makes clear not only his moral anguish, but his tacit support for Bolingbroke's case. The fairest thing he can do is to remain neutral. The scene has shown Bolingbroke's support and forces growing from moment to moment, while immediately afterwards the Welsh troops desert Richard, and Salisbury understands that this is the beginning of the end for Richard.

Act III, Scene i, like IV.i (see below, p. 123), visually echoes I.i and I.iii – a 'trial' scene. The sense of events moving against Richard intensifies: here Richard loses Bushy and Green, his closest counsellors. Bolingbroke's action in this scene demands our close attention. So far he has had a good deal of everyone's sympathy, but even he is clearly uneasy about what he is doing, and seeks to wash their blood from his hands by citing their public 'crimes' (ll. 5–6). But the catalogue of what could be classed as the wrongs caused by evil counsel soon turns into a catalogue of wrongs suffered by Bolingbroke himself. Like bad farmers, they have 'fed upon my signories,/Disparked my parks, and felled my forest woods' (ll. 22–3), and there can be no doubt in our minds that private vengeance on them is one of his major motives. In condemning them to death (the ever-ready Northumberland sees to it), he is certainly acting beyond what is his legal right. Bushy and Green go to their deaths with dignity, and their last lines, however *parti pris* they must be, make us question both Bolingbroke's justice and what he will do to England. Indeed, the last lines of the scene, containing the only mention of Glendower in this play, look forward to the civil wars of his reign; but Bolingbroke is not yet king, though he is talking and acting as if he were.

Act III, Scene ii, the middle scene of the play, makes a strong contrast. Visually it seems to emphasize kingly power: there are a good number of people on stage, and it opens, according to the Folio text of 1623 which in all probability preserves the stage practice of Shakespeare's company, with all the signals of an important military scene. But in it Richard

5. Once again, the play presents us with men caught in a trap where no course of action is right and just at the same time.

hears news of disaster after disaster. Richard already knows of Bolingbroke's coup, but the news successively of the desertion of the Welsh, the loss of Bushy, Green and Bagot, and York's support of Bolingbroke show him his increasing isolation. At the very least, we might find pity for him in this; but the scene so re-establishes him as a character that we feel something far more complex.

So far he has seemed almost totally unattractive – the only hint of anything different has been in the affection the queen, Aumerle and the favourites have for him. Here for the first time we see a Richard who, however histrionically, loves his country, and sees it as related to him in an organic way (ll. 4ff.). He is self-conscious enough of his overstatement of the bond between king and land to turn to his (smiling?) companions (l. 23) and repeat in all seriousness his intuition that England will tolerate none but her true master.[6] The extraordinary range of reference and extreme vividness of his speech sound a note of passionate concern for England we have not heard in the play since Gaunt's death, and Richard is suddenly no longer to be dismissed as simply a bad, weak king. He has become extremely interesting. His next speech (ll. 36ff.), with its bold and detailed application to his present predicament of the standard conceit of the sun's likeness to the king, may show what we know to be a false, impracticable confidence in the short term – Aumerle (ll. 33–5) recognized that images do not win battles; but it is a powerful statement of his divinely sanctioned role, in utterly memorable terms, which has more truth in it than is immediately apparent. Richard may not have practical wisdom, but he has an understanding, an insight, that goes a good deal deeper. For the comparison of himself with the sun, returning at daybreak and revealing deeds of darkness for what they are, contains much moral truth. His very presence is a challenge to those who have deserted him, whose breaking of order is more terrible than his own, and even after his death, in the Henry plays, each political character defines himself by his attitude to Richard and his fate. Richard also recognizes that the man and his role are inseparable – that unkinging a king is something which is literally impossible.[7] Yet these intuitions, which Richard sees as being of *immediate* comfort, are promptly put in an

6. The irony is seen to be double-edged as soon as we project our minds forward to the Henry plays.

7. Lear, seeking to lay down the burden of rule, does not see this; the course of his tragedy forces him to recognize that his kingliness is integral to himself, that he *cannot* deny his nature and role. He is never more king than when he is crowned by Nature with a crown of wild flowers.

ironic light by the succession of bad news. Richard's reaction to the loss of the Welsh is consternation, almost immediately replaced by an access of courage, and reliance on York. But hard on the heels of his mention of York comes Scroop's description of the whole country arming itself against the king, and of the loss of Bushy, Green and Bagot. When he knows the truth of their loss, Richard is forced to concentrate on the contemplation of what he has just said was impossible: the loss of his crown. In the course of a remarkable speech (ll. 144ff.) he gains enormously in moral stature. He is being forced to a wisdom that power and prosperity could not teach him – the vulnerability of kings, the fact that the world does not always run according to theories of how it should, the emptiness of the power he once enjoyed. Like Lear, he is obliged to recognize – and willingly accepts – his common humanity with his subjects (ll. 172ff.), the temporariness of power, the fact that the king's lot is one of sorrow. The scene ends with an entirely new note: a sense of responsibility for his followers. In its last lines and in a return to the earlier sun images, he discharges them to make their peace with Bolingbroke. He cannot take them to their ruin.

This scene has shown Richard moving rapidly from hyperbolic overconfidence, a passionate love for the idea of the bond between a king and his country, to a new wisdom and understanding of the much more complex relationship between them and of the humanity shared by king and subjects. There is a lot more to him than the weak and capricious tyrant of the first act. Shakespeare has given him a level of utterance that compels our attention and interest, full of precise visual conceits that stick in our minds and shoot out of their context into our experience of the whole play. Who can look at Bolingbroke as king and not remember the antic Death within the hollow crown? Richard has at last recognized that all men are under judgement, kings included, and from that new humility his true royalty grows.

The next scene (III.iii) opens with an obvious parallel to what we have just seen. The openings visually comment on one another: here is another military expedition, but, unlike Richard's, this is succeeding. The parallels are explicit and powerful. Just as Richard emphasizes that the title to the throne was derived from Heaven, so too York reminds Bolingbroke that 'the heavens are over our heads'; and just as when Carlisle reminded Richard that 'The means that heaven yields must be embraced' (III.ii.29), Bolingbroke replies: 'I know it, uncle, and oppose not myself/ Against their will' (ll. 18–19). These reflecting exchanges keep in the front of our minds the whole issue of the power of Providence in human affairs. Again, Richard's wishful hope that his mere return will chasten Bolingbroke and reduce him to obedience is balanced by Bolingbroke's open threat, significantly couched in images of storms and tempests of blood, to use his power unless Richard redresses the injustice he has done him. Both of them personify England as a mother (III.ii.8ff.; III.iii.47). When Richard and his entourage appear above (i.e. on the upper level of the stage), Bolingbroke applies to Richard the image used by Richard himself of the rising sun dispelling the clouds (II.iii.62ff.; cf. III.ii.36ff.) This imagery, reiterated by his opponent, 'places' Bolingbroke's own action, and reinforces the idea of Richard's organic royalty as a fact that neither can deny. The parallel between the two scenes so far not only emphasizes the irony of the complementary situation but also underlines the moral parameters within which both Richard and his opponent are working. Richard's first speech after his appearance is a challenge to his enemies. In the course of it (ll. 72ff.) he shows that he is fully aware – perhaps more aware than Bolingbroke will admit to himself – of Bolingbroke's aims – or, at least, of where the logic of his moves will drive him. His use of the royal plural underlines that community of king and realm threatened by Bolingbroke's action. In another of those grandiloquent conceits he shows too that he has virtually accepted the fact of his own eventual deposition, and foresees the terrible consequences Shakespeare's audience already knows will follow from it. All this while Bolingbroke is silent. Shakespeare makes Northumberland not only take the first assault of Richard's attack, but also act as Bolingbroke's spokesman, thus once again distancing Bolingbroke from the immediate odium.[8]

Richard's reply to Northumberland is conciliatory to the point of weakness, and the audience might easily take it as merely spineless. Shakespeare gives him the brief aside to Aumerle (ll. 127–30 and 133ff.) to indicate that Richard is, rather against his natural courage, playing for time; it is not easy. He is fully aware of the weakness of his position, and is moving deeper and deeper into an introspection that leads him almost to a willing, if agonized, acceptance of the inevitable. The balanced lines of 144ff. image the reversal of fortune: the king and his accoutrements occupy the first halves of lines 146–54, while the second

8. This is quite important: Shakespeare cannot allow Bolingbroke to be a mere villain in this play as he is actually very interested in his moral dilemma, and in the Henry plays (if at this point he was planning them) needs him as a sub-tragic hero. Northumberland – Bolingbroke's lightning-conductor throughout – has no moral qualms and an enormous sense of his own advantage.

halves explore the ideas of retirement, solitary life, prayer – and solitary death. He almost seems to long for the life of a hermit, a beadsman, or a palmer, praying for the sins of the world and expiating his own before being consigned to the only land a man can ever call his own, the grave. Seeing Aumerle weep in pity (a cue for the audience, surely) Richard has compassion on his sorrow and delicately explores the whimsical conceit of them digging their graves by the erosion of their tears. Such sensitive sympathy would have been beyond the Richard of I.i. or I.iii. Shakespeare is not only making Richard much more interesting than he was earlier, but also much more attractive. The fall of the powerful is always chastening to observe. When they are dignified and noble, as Richard is beginning to be, it can be painful; when we watch that fall involve the victim in a total reconsideration of what and who he is, it can be harrowing; and when, as we are beginning to realize and from now on are not allowed to forget, the fall throws a whole kingdom into chaos and calls in question the very parameters of the universe we take for granted, it can be terrible.

Richard is summoned to the lower court. The symbolism of his move from the upper stage to the same level as Bolingbroke is too obvious to need stating. He is effectively now unkinged, and both he and Bolingbroke know it. Bolingbroke uses the power he has won, but faced with the presence of Richard he is clearly uneasy and embarrassed – as he was not in III.i. The person of Richard, like his memory later, is, as Richard himself ironically guessed, a moral challenge to everyone else in the play. He prepares for his descent by yet another sun image, but this time one that severely modifies his idea of himself;

> *Down, down I come like glistering Phaethon,*
> *Wanting the manage of unruly jades.*

(III.iii.178–9)

Those who knew their Ovid would remember that Phaethon drove the chariot of his father the Sun against all advice, following his own self-will. He was unable to control the horses of the sun, and drove so close to earth that a huge tract of it was scorched and laid waste. Out of pity for the dwellers on earth, Jupiter struck him dead with a thunderbolt before he could do more damage. The parallel, conscious or not on Richard's part, is exact – the self-will, the refusal of advice, the mad career out of control in a rash, fierce blaze of 'riot', the rebelliousness of the horses, the eventual intervention of Heaven – and the terrible damage.

Act IV, Scene i continues and strengthens this radical re-polarization of our understanding of the two principals. Like I.i., it is a major Court assembly, of visual splendour, a splendour that signals the importance of what is to be represented. In the first movement a decisive Bolingbroke reopens the issue of Gloucester's death; murder (the sin of Cain) cannot simply be forgotten. (The irony is that Bolingbroke as Justice is, by the end of the play, guilty of exactly the same sin as Richard, and subject to exactly the same condemnation – as he well sees in V.vi.43.) As in I.i., the issue results in a challenge to trial by combat, that legal form where God himself takes a hand. Here, however, the challenges are multiple, and a whole peerage seems to be uniting against Richard's lieutenant Aumerle and thus against Richard himself. At this point of crisis, Bolingbroke, like Richard, postpones the decision. But while Richard postponed it out of fear, Bolingbroke postpones it out of magnanimity. The difference between the two men could hardly be more strikingly underlined. The second division of the scene we have already glanced at: the report of Richard's willingness to abdicate, Bolingbroke's readiness to accept the dubious legal fiction offered by York (ll. 107ff.) and ascend the throne (almost certainly present on stage, an important symbol, so far empty), and his silent rejection of Carlisle's impassioned warning of the crime and its consequences. The third section of the scene starts with a great visual irony: Bolingbroke is seated on the throne *like* a king in judgement, summoning Richard who arrives *like* a subject. Richard is accompanied by officers carrying the crown, visible sign of royalty and power, and from then on he completely dominates the scene and takes the initiative quite away from Bolingbroke.

Richard is at bay. His very presence, let alone his words, challenges the disloyalty of the whole assembly, and he sees his betrayal as a parallel to the betrayal of Christ whose vice-gerent he feels himself to be. While he seems impelled subconsciously to abdicate – as York suggests (l. 179) – because he is temperamentally unsuited to his role, he finds the process not just painful but almost inconceivable: he resists the idea while he accepts the fact of it. Shakespeare underlines this paradox and illuminates what is happening to both the principals by making Richard force Bolingbroke to reach out and take hold [9] of the crown he has not yet

9. 'Seize' is a better word. It has the sense in which we usually understand it; it also has the legal sense of 'take seisin', when a fief was given to a vassal, or when a piece of land changed hands. Richard is ironically treating Bolingbroke as his vassal, yet the word also reminds us of Gaunt's charge against Richard that he treated his land as mere 'tenement or pelting farm' that could be bought and sold.

relinquished. The two hands on either side of the golden circle are a potent visual symbol, emblematic in nature, of the central conflict of the play, and an image of the moment of fine balance when Fortune has not yet passed the crown from one to the other. (Like an emblem, too, the image has a deeper suggestion: the crown *defines* each man, is more than a possession.) As if it were a ritual – which, in fact, it is – Richard now develops a simile from this position; he employs the conventional image of Fortune's buckets rising and falling in a well to underline (like the verses of an emblem picture might) what is happening to Bolingbroke and to Richard himself. The irony is that the image emphasizes not only his own but Bolingbroke's vulnerability. This idea of reciprocity is exploited in the following lines (194ff.), where the extreme artificiality of the rhetorical patterns of *contentio, chiasmus, anaphora* and *parison* convey the transference not only of power but care between the two men. This sequence moves to a climax in Richard's punning reply to Bolingbroke's 'Are you contented to resign the crown?': he is, and he is not, for his identity goes with it and he ceases to be himself when his role is gone; he is reduced to a nothing, a zero. This is a moment of self-realization for Richard, when the full consequence of what has happened is suddenly clear. He proceeds, again in highly patterned, formal verse, ritually to divest himself of the accoutrements of kingship. The stage directions implied in these lines clearly indicate ritualistic action as well, but the real focus is on the reversal, undoing, of the ceremony of coronation, the unkinging of Richard's nature.[10] Yet in divesting himself of the trappings of rule he grows enormously. Northumberland's attempt to get him to read over a list of his misdeeds draws a rebuke that is kingly as no previous rebukes have been; he stands before them as a physical reminder of their own most heinous sin, a man more sinned against than sinning now. The 'trial' is linked to the tribunal of Pilate (ll. 239ff.), he himself to Christ delivered to the torment of the sour cross, a king suffering for the sins of his people.[11] He has become a conscious

10. Even here, Richard's awareness of language and symbol allows him an irony whose bitterness we can easily miss: 'send him many years of sunshine days' (l. 220) looks at first like mere (ironic?) good wishes, but when we think of how closely he has previously linked the notion of kingliness to the sun (see above, p. 119), and III.ii.50, III.iii,178; cf. II.iv.21, III.iii.63ff.), we see he is mocking Bolingbroke, whose days the audience would know were anything but sunshiny. The idea is repeated in l. 261, where Bolingbroke's sun melts Richard's appearance of kingship into tears.

11. I do not think it has been remarked before that Richard's resonances extend beyond mere comparison almost to blasphemy. 'All of you that stand and look upon me' (l. 236) reminds us forcibly of 'all ye that pass by, look on me' – part of the *Improperia* or Reproaches

sacrifice, whose self-perception dominates and values the entire assembly.

Richard unkinged is Nobody – no name, no title (ll. 254–6). He has to face this new self, to see it. The mirror that is brought to him works on many levels. Richard holding it is the visible symbol of that self-love which led him to ruin, but in common iconography the virtue of Prudence – a composite of memory, understanding and foresight – is often depicted as a queen (a royal personage) holding a mirror. Richard, I think, is here being made to embody the memory of his own power, failure and folly, his understanding of what is at present happening, and his foresight of the terrible harvest in England (cf. III.iii.72–100) that will be reaped after this act has come to fruition. He knows himself for the first time. But in the startling device of the shattering of the glass Shakespeare makes him destroy not only his own reflection. It is a comment on the brittleness of the glory Bolingbroke has won, and Bolingbroke's resulting quibble pushes Richard to a recognition of where the real tragedy in himself lies: not in the externals of kingship, but in an integral kingliness that cannot be divorced from his self.

Bolingbroke, so apparently successful and powerful, is completely upstaged by all this. We cannot even loathe him, for Shakespeare once more has Northumberland draw the odium on himself and away from Bolingbroke in the matter of the articles of abdication. The most curious thing of all is that we experience almost a sense of pity for Bolingbroke who has taken on what Richard has relinquished, and a sense of release for Richard, as if he has moved beyond the cares of state. The 'brittle crazie glasse', which is man, has to be shattered to be made again in a new likeness, as Richard is being. Our pity for Bolingbroke is justified, for by the end of the scene opposition to him is growing, and the first of those plots is being hatched that will dominate his reign and exact punishment for the deposition of Richard. Bolingbroke never knows another quiet moment.

The last words of Richard in this scene act as a choric comment on what we have witnessed: we have seen him grow to be a 'true king' and his subjects defined as 'conveyors' (thieves). Almost immediately, in V.i, the words 'true king' recur, in Isabel's bitter lines (ll. 5–6). The scene is moving in the extreme; we are brought to realize that Richard was loved,

of the Good Friday liturgy, when Christ is imagined speaking from his Cross to his faithless people. The 'water [that] cannot wash away your sin' is both an allusion to Pilate's washing of his hands, the tears of the onlookers (a cue for the actors), and the water that did wash away sin, which flowed from Christ's pierced side.

and the pathos of the parting with Isabel underlines the disjunction of Richard with his country as well as with his loving wife. Isabel voices, as it were, what England herself might feel at the loss of her king. The delicate effect of lines 80ff., almost musical in their patterned reiteration of ideas of parting, loss and contradiction, reminds us perhaps of Richard's own patterned verse when he uncrowned himself; here is another divorce, and here again, in this discord of concord, Northumberland takes a part.

The pattern of the verse is not merely pretty, and the passage conveys more than might appear at first sight. Several pairs of characters in plays of the early 1590s divide couplets or quatrains between them in lines of parallel rhetorical structure (for example, David and Bethsabe in Peele's play of that name, or Thomas Kyd's Soliman and Perseda). Shakespeare's Romeo and Juliet speak a sonnet between them at their first meeting. What all these have in common is that their loves are linked in a shared suffering, a shared destiny, and they are forced to highlight this through the exigencies of shared rhyme, rhetoric and form. Romeo and Juliet's sonnet, for instance, coming after the Prologue's revelation of the doomed nature of their love, bitterly reminds us of the two becoming one in the love to which the sonnet form can be so appropriate, yet of that unity being forced apart by the stars. Richard and Isabel are in parallel case; and the participation of Northumberland in their rhyme, a ground bass intruding on their elegiac duet, underlines that he too is caught up in a process of division that will eventually claim him also.

The division of the primal human bond, that between man and wife, is not only a symbol of the division between Richard and his land; it is symptomatic of the breaking of all human bonds on which civilization depends. It intensifies, brings to fruition, the division Richard himself had made in the family by the separation of son from father in banishing Bolingbroke; the crisis of Richard's reign is symmetrically bracketed by these two actions. The next two plays encompass a world where nobody keeps faith with anyone else, and the first stirrings of this are immediately noticed in the next scene, where father is set against son and is quite prepared – however agonizedly – to call for his execution. York has reluctantly broken faith with a king he could no longer support, and with the passion born of guilt he is determined to be true to the new king even if it means sacrificing the son who tried to keep faith with the old. But before we reach this point the deeply affected York describes the entry of Bolingbroke and Richard into London. The two descriptions are of more or less equal length – two pictures, vividly composed, bringing more powerfully to our minds than could any attempt to stage it the contrast between Bolingbroke at the height of Fortune's wheel and Richard at the nadir. Bolingbroke is mounted, as we later realize (V.v.78ff.), on Richard's own horse, which carrying him went 'So proudly as if he disdained the ground' – the horse is a symbol of the kingdom and the voice of popular favour Richard has lost.[12]

There is surely an ironic echo of Christ's entry into Jerusalem in the popular acclaim York describes, for the description of Richard as a man sacred yet insulted, accepting with 'grief and patience' his passing and the hardening of men's hearts against him, shows him suffering as the suffering Servant suffered. A mere thirty lines illuminate the contrast between the political reality of Bolingbroke's temporary power and the moral strength of the deposed Richard. York clearly sees the figure of Richard, now fallen, as a reproach to all those who pass by. Yet he accepts, as men do – and, Shakespeare hints, perhaps must do – the reality; and, in an echo of Gaunt's 'God's is the quarrel . . . Let Heaven revenge' (I.ii.37–40), declares a faith that even in these events Providence is active.

Shakespeare in these scenes is opening up a major distinction between the reality of power, the actual possession of it, and true royalty: an idea much handled in the next two plays. His final analysis of the royalty that is in Richard is to be found in the scene of his death. Scene v opens with Richard's soliloquy, his only one, in which he explores his own fall. In prison he can see (as Lear does) the folly of great ones, who ebb and flow by the moon, but it is a more profound analysis than that. He sees in himself as in his captors the central problem in human nature, that it will never be content, and that mental response and attitude alter the meaning of external circumstance. He knows himself not as a fallen king now, but as something deeper still, a fallen man. The playing of the music draws a further response of rare complexity, for the music (as so often in Elizabethan art) is a symbol of the harmony of the ordered universe, in which man should take a part.[13] It is a challenge to Richard to know himself as he is known, and also a vindication of the order he has broken as a bad gardener. The momentary faltering in the

12. That the horse is called Barbary may be significant too; cf. York's use of 'barbarism' in V.ii.36. Richard's loss of his loved horse may well recall, too, his own image of himself as Phaeton, unable to control the horses of his realm.

13. Cf. *The Merchant of Venice*, V.i.1ff. It heals Lear's madness (cf. the irony here of line 61), and Pericles hears the music of the spheres in the moment of his restoration.

rhythm (l. 42) echoes his own disorder, when he did not keep the 'concord [harmony] of [his] state and time' as God's vice-gerent should. The image shifts now from musical time to time itself, which Richard wasted – significant word! – with the inevitable result of his own 'wasting'. The extraordinary conceit that follows, where Richard sees himself as a weeping dial marking out the hours for Bolingbroke, is not merely pathetic, though it is certainly that. It underlines the vulnerability of Bolingbroke to time and the same condemnation that Richard now accepts.

The music also shows, as Richard realizes, that even in his fall there are those who love him. The Groom who enters is a symbol of those who still do, for no advantage; and such loyalty is costly. But ironically the Groom brings news that cuts Richard to the quick: his loved horse has readily transferred his affections to Bolingbroke. Richard can lose no more.

Except his life. It all happens very quickly, without the gratuitous cruelty Marlowe put into *Edward II*. But here at last is the man of action Richard should have been. All his life he has been incapable of acting decisively, yet now he seizes a weapon and dispatches with vigour two (at least) of his assailants. He responds heroically – and if Shakespeare followed Holinshed and in his stage practice gave Richard eight mur-derers, he is even more heroic. Exton's blow looks positively cowardly; and we are quite ready to believe, now, that it is sacrilegious.

Not infrequently Elizabethan dramatists gave the onlookers or their dying heroes 'last words' which either openly or by implication suggested the right response the audience should make. Shakespeare does both here. Richard sees himself as assured of heavenly bliss: he has expiated his faults. But he also sees his land as stained, polluted by the crime we have just seen. Exton agrees; Richard was indeed valorous, and the blood liberally spilt – as it probably was on stage – makes him realize the devilish nature of his crime. He is from now on an outcast, the sin of Cain, and worse, on his head. Kings are dangerous in their deaths, as in their lives.

# 9. This Royal Throne of Kings: Henry IV, Parts 1 and 2

The tragedy of Richard, his divorce from his England, has arisen out of his own nature, but the initiatives that led to that fall lie with Bolingbroke. In *Richard II* Shakespeare presents him not only as a mere foil to Richard, but as a man whose own actions and nature are problematical and who is feeling his way step by step in a political maze. He is drawn on by the logic of his actions to the point where he has to assume the name of king, as he has assumed the power of monarch. I do not think we should see him as a machiavellian plotter who was aiming at the crown all the time; that he is forced to assume it by the logic of his own actions is borne out by *2 Henry IV*, III.i.70ff. (Northumberland, by contrast, clearly does contemplate and accept the possibility of Richard's deposition from the very beginning, and sees potential profit for himself in it – a neat foil to Bolingbroke.[1]) At the end of the play most – but not all – of our sympathies lie with Richard, valorous and full of royal blood, yet the last notes of it are given to a sad and chastened Bolingbroke, aware of his own guilt. This is the man who now has to take on the 'manage of unruly jades', and already we have some sympathy for him.

Shakespeare is clearly interested in a problem the analysis of which continues in the Henry plays. He seems to be asking whether it is possible for the kingly office to be exercised properly without severe damage to the man exercising it. Henry is shown to us as a conscientious ruler who clearly cares deeply about his land, works extremely hard, and genuinely seeks peace with as much justice as is politically possible. But his early attractiveness (in *Richard II*) is gone; even the acts for which he deserves praise come to seem the result of 'policy' rather than inner virtue,[2] and he is an old, cold figure, full of reproof and punishment. But he is more interesting than this summary might suggest. Shakespeare has hinted, in

1. Richard recognizes clearly Northumberland's nature and motives; he sees that without him Bolingbroke would have been powerless, and that once Northumberland has broken faith with the anointed king, Bolingbroke will never be able to trust his loyalty, nor will Northumberland's greed allow him to be loyal (*Richard II*, V.i.55ff.). The image of disease in the body politic is apposite (ll. 58–9).

2. His attractiveness and popularity in *Richard II* are, in *1 Henry IV*, III.ii.39ff., made to seem – with hindsight – politically calculated.

Henry's talks with his household and in his soliloquies, that behind the public figure there is a man and a father who thinks and feels. He sees the crown as a killing duty – as Richard never did – and can even envy his poorest subjects; he is in some sense poorer than they. He is aware that his path to the crown has left him morally tainted, his head lies uneasy, and he seeks a peace of mind he glimpses only in death. Yet he is a fundamentally decent man, betrayed by those whose hearts he won as young Harry Hereford. He is paid in his own coin, and carries to his death the guilt of what he did to Richard.

We have already looked at Henry IV as potentially a tragic hero (Chapter 6.ii). He presides over a realm torn by revolt, and his life is a constant battle against disorder. His opponents in Part 1 are hardly attractive; Worcester and Northumberland – despite the plausibility of their case – are clearly just out for what they can get, although they claim to be avenging Richard, and they are using the military clout of Hotspur for their own advantage. Northumberland, indeed, is calculating enough to wait and see the outcome of the Hotspur–Glendower campaign before he commits himself, and is prepared to see his own son go to his death. Hotspur is a political innocent, and despite his rashness he is easily manipulated by these two terrible old men. The war aims outlined in Part 1 (III.i) are nothing less than the dismemberment of England, the parties cannot even meet without acrimony and selfish pride causing quarrels, and we are given a vision of a future – should they win – which is chaos. What sort of country will it be where the course of rivers is taken as a personal affront, 'robbing' one of the rulers of what he wants; where husband does not trust wife (Hotspur and Lady Percy); and, further intensifying the hint of chaos, wife and husband cannot even understand each other's language? (See below, Chapter 11.) Hotspur is deaf to all harmony, be it the music of the world or the music of a Welsh harp. The rebels are right, both in Part 1 and Part 2: Henry is a guilty man, whose claim to their allegiance, once advantage is removed, is weak. Yet *even so* he is the crowned king, and their rebellion against him is as heinous as Henry's was against Richard. He does defeat them and hold the realm together. Thus the final paradox is that his troubled reign sees a successful mopping-up of the internal dissension, so that his son inherits a secure throne.

But the memory of Richard – as reproach, as warning – will not go away. Henry is haunted by Richard's folly and unwisdom and waste, and sees his own son apparently repeating Richard's mistakes. The political wisdom, the shrewdness of man-management, that he possesses his son does not seem to want to learn – and the ironic parallel with Richard's disregard of York's and Gaunt's counsel is complete. We should accept as quite genuine the grief and fear that Shakespeare gives him on this account. All he has worked for, all his hopes, seem to founder on Hal's dissoluteness. In the first scene of Part 1 he sees the sharp contrast between the energetic Hotspur and his own Harry, and the thought is too painful to dwell on (I.i.91). But it is here, in Hal, that the major interest of the play lies, and it is in and through his career that Shakespeare continues his analysis of the 'king-becoming graces'.

The importance of the structure of alternating political and comic scenes in the Henry plays has already been discussed (p. 94), as has the connection with the Morality, that mode of drama peculiarly suited to the discussion of an abstract idea. Just such an idea must now concern us: the education of the prince for rule. In these two plays Shakespeare is exploring the maturing of a prince to the point where he takes the lineally descended crown with sadness and circumspection, with a willing embrace of justice and good counsel and a concern for the wise government and welfare of his realm. He acts with mercy and justice in dismissing Falstaff and his companions. In *Henry V* we see a study of that good prince in action.

Each Part of *Henry IV* looks at a different aspect of the education of the ideal prince. In each part he is played against the figure of another young man – Hotspur and Prince John respectively – and over each Part plays the opposition of the Lord Chief Justice and Falstaff as the counsellor he will choose. Over the whole ten acts there operates, too, an irony only the audience sees: it is historical fact that Henry V was a pious and successful king, that he rejected his bad companions and defeated a (much older) Hotspur at Shrewsbury. Furthermore, Shakespeare gives Hal at the end of his first scene a soliloquy (I.ii.193ff.) which explains to the audience with absolute clarity the complex game he is playing.[3] We tend to see this as pretty mean, but Shakespeare's audience

3. An important point needs to be made here, the first occasion on which it has been relevant (since *Richard II* has only the one soliloquy). We take soliloquies for granted because of our experience of Elizabethan drama, and easily forget that they do a quite specific conventional job. As in the Interludes, or the Moralities, soliloquy can act like a chorus – as the confessions and self-descriptions of Moralities do – to make sure the audience follow the *implications* of the represented action. Their use is a function of the idea of character in drama we have glanced at above (Chapter 3.ix); characters can not only be symbolic objectively, but point their own moral in a suspension of the time–space of the play. Even in plays like *Hamlet* where soliloquies are very important, these points stand; and it should finally be pointed out that Shakespeare makes *far less* use of the soliloquy or aside than do his contemporaries.

would see it as desirable political wisdom, remarkable and praiseworthy in one so young. Hal shows himself to be every bit as aware of public opinion and its relationship to power as is his father (cf. III.ii.39ff.) – and, indeed, a better psychologist. His imagery is of contrasting metals, of foils, of the regal sun breaking through clouds:[4] images that alert us to the structure of his career as Shakespeare has composed it. It affects our reception not only of the Boar's Head scenes but also the contrasts that his father had just made between Hal and Hotspur and will make between Hal and John. For what we see as Henry IV's misjudgement (cf. *Richard II*, V.ii.4ff.) cannot but be seen as an example of that public opinion which is so easily misled but which is one of the roots of real political power – a theme Shakespeare touches on several times in these four plays[5] and which he also explores in *Coriolanus* and *Julius Caesar*.

The first reference to Hal in Part 1 (I.i.77ff.) picks up where Bolingbroke left off in *Richard II* (V.iii.1ff.). But now Hal is specifically compared with Hotspur, a comparison that dominates Part 1. The theme of Part 1 is the revelation in the prince of an honour and chivalry that is not only as great as Hotspur's, but also of a distinctly higher order. There is never any doubt in our minds that it is there – after all, we know the story; what the play does explore, through the contrast, is the *nature* of kingly honour and chivalry in action. Hotspur is in a real sense Hal's 'factor' – an agent gathering material for the use of the owner. Thus this part of the play is strictly less about the education of the prince – his reclaim from dissoluteness to stability, as the incautious reader (though not auditor) might guess – than the qualities that education should develop. (Other areas, indeed, *are* about the need for the prince to know, recognize and reject vice and welcome virtue – though the issue is never in doubt.)

Hotspur is without cavil a splendid soldier and a very brave man. He is attractive in his energy, and in his playfulness with his wife – though that should not blind us to the fact that he is treating her pretty shabbily. But his concept of honour, however glamorous, is sterile. Notice how in I.ii.158ff. his discussion of it grows out of anger, of hurt pride; for his hearers to 'redeem/Your banished honours' (ll. 178–9) entails either the king's abject surrender to his disgruntled nobles, or his deposition, or

---

4. The reminiscence of Richard's imagery is clearly deliberate.

5. It is unfavourably illustrated, for example, in York's description of the entry of Bolingbroke into London. See my discussion in Chapter 11.iv.

both. Worcester tries to use Hotspur's energy to discuss a properly political course of action; but, as we have seen above (pp. 87ff.), Hotspur's hot-headedness again takes over, this time with the extraordinary idea that danger is worth having for its own sake. The soaring images of his next speech (ll. 199ff.) – which ironically link honour with the instability of fortune – rest finally on the idea of selfish pride:

> *So he that does redeem her thence might wear*
> *Without corrival all her dignities.*

Much spirit and little sense; and not much that is admirable. It is this sort of silly honour, the murmur of men's admiring tongues, that is so firmly undercut by Falstaff's reduction of the concept to empty 'air', that is useless even to the dead possessor, in the battle at Shrewsbury. Moreover, notice how Hotspur's honour is of very loose morals. He can without a qualm make alliance with his former opponent Douglas, his country's enemy, but out of pride and pique he can't easily remain on good terms with his friends. His rudeness to Glendower and Mortimer in III.i is not only inexcusably discourteous but politically silly. This man loves a quarrel for its own sake, and sees no more morality in honour than in a game of conkers. He is completely unsuitable as a potential monarch.

Furthermore, his attitude to Hal gives us another line on what honour means to him. He is mean and ungenerous in the way he talks about him. In *Richard II*, he had without sensitivity or consideration gleefully told the king the worst about his son (V.iii.16–19), and delightedly perpetrates the pun 'unhorse/un-whores'. In this play his first reference to him is contemptuous – he accepts unthinkingly the common view of Hal, this 'sword-and-buckler Prince of Wales' (I.iii.237), and his lack of nobility is shown by his even entertaining the thought that he would 'have him poisoned with a pot of ale'. Before Shrewsbury (IV.i) comes another contemptuous reference: 'Where is his son,/The nimble-footed madcap Prince of Wales' (ll. 94–5), and Vernon's reply, describing a new Hal, suddenly revealed as a person to be reckoned with, gets no warm welcome:

> *No more, no more! Worse than the sun in March,*
> *This praise doth nourish agues.*          (ll. 110–11)

He almost seems to grudge Hal any praise that could be directed at himself; he wants praise 'without corrival'. And immediately afterwards he takes off into exalted bombast about 'sacrifices' and 'the fire-eyed maid of smoky war'. Hotspur's language betrays the unsubtlety of his mind – raw, oversimplified, violent, thinking in rhetorical clichés and ignoring the need for considered thought (see Chapter 11).

His uncle and Vernon dare not relay to him, until it is too late to be accepted, Hal's offer to settle the issue of the battle by single combat; they know he would jump at this chance of glory without (as usual) a single thought about its political or military advisability. When he is told, and in his turn wishes there could be single combat (V.ii.47–50), it is for motives quite different from Hal's. Hal sought to save innocent bloodshed (V.i.99)[6] and urged it courteously, with generous and sincere compliments to Hotspur (V.i.85ff.), but Hotspur seems to want to fight out of hatred, and Vernon's praise of Hal's courtesy (V.ii.51ff.) calls forth once again contempt and scorn, and mean puns alluding to Hal's supposed sexual dissoluteness. Nor can he even, ironically, consider the possibility of his own defeat.

When the two rivals clash (V.iv.60ff.), Hal's key idea is that they are *both* stars, and that England is a sphere not large enough for the two – a generous and honest estimate of his enemy. Hotspur merely wishes, in effect, that Hal were worth fighting (ll. 68–9). Yet Hotspur's honour is 'cropped', as Hal promised his father it would be: defeating such an enemy makes Hal subsume the reputation of Hotspur. And Hal's valediction is dignified, generous, even loving. There was something in Hotspur that was valuable, but Hotspur could never have glimpsed the generosity of mind that could comprehend an enemy and treat him as a person.

The repulsive behaviour of Falstaff and the appalling treatment of Hotspur's body that immediately follow are more than mere comic relief after a tense moment. Falstaff hopes to profit by it; and hopes to con people into believing the unbelievable. Shakespeare is surely underlining that honour that is *mere* reputation ('air'), as Hotspur's was, can easily degenerate into Falstaff's amorality, where what matters is the front put up to the world. By contrast, what we have seen revealed in Hal is an honour that is moral and internal, that is not dependent on public repute – Hal is generously prepared to let Falstaff take his chance with his lie – but is part of a man's sense of his own integrity and his own selfhood. It is precisely this honour that Shakespeare has shown us in Hal, carefully distinguishing it from the jingoistic military glory Henry V could easily seem to represent. For the world admired Hotspur for sufficient reasons:

6. And the king agreed, knowing it was politically dangerous – a contrast to Worcester.

he was a good soldier and a good leader, a man of enormous courage and skill. It is in exactly these qualities that he is compared with Henry V, and Hal has shown he possesses them – and more. Shakespeare is putting down a marker for the French campaigns.

Prince John has a far smaller role in Part 2 than Hotspur has in Part 1, but his presence is important. Like Hotspur, he is used to point up the royal qualities of Hal, but is also set up as a contrast to Hotspur. A good and dutiful son, already a man skilled in war and peace, he is fully worthy of trust. In Part 1, III.ii.32–3, the king chides Hal that John has taken his place in the Council (another example, like his longing for a son such as Hotspur, of Henry's misjudgement), and in Part 2, IV.i, he is Henry's general, with 'a full commission,/In very ample virtue of his father,/To hear and absolutely to determine' the settlement of the rebellion. The cool intelligence and calmness that Hotspur lacked is his main trait, and he is circumspect and calculating to a fault. He is given a powerful speech reproaching the Archbishop in Part 2, IV.ii, in which the very tones and cadences of his father may be heard. Whereas in this situation a Hotspur would have rushed without thought to the arbitrament of arms, this prince calmly accepts those parts of his enemies' case that seem just, promises redress of grievances – and then, by a deliberate disingenuousness in exploiting their over-confidence, traps them. This is not exactly glamorous conduct, and he is reproached for it by the rebels; but the fact of the matter is that he has saved many English lives and put down the rebellion efficiently and finally. His conduct here, in fact, anticipates that of Henry V before his French expedition, when he traps Cambridge, Scroop and Grey in an exactly similar way. Neither breaks word or promise or honour. Both princes are being made to show the 'policy' Elizabethans thought necessary in a true prince, which both Richard and Hotspur so signally lacked.

There is little dash or verve in Prince John, and one cannot imagine him leading men into the storming of Harfleur or the desperate action of Agincourt. But he is not unattractive: he has more than adequate courage, as we see in Part 1, V.iv.16ff. and 128–9, when, having not only fought well but actually taken on Hotspur himself, he wins his father's and Hal's sincere praise. He is very pleased to be sent by Hal to relay to Douglas Hal's generous freeing of him without ransom.[7] Indeed, he shares more than a few of his brother's qualities, and it is interesting to note how each reacts to Falstaff's conduct in battle. In Part 1, V.iii,

7. Note that Douglas, as a Scot, is not a rebel. Nevertheless, his magnanimity – a mark of true kingliness – reveals quite a lot about Hal.

Falstaff's idleness and fooling irritate Hal in the extreme; similarly, in Part 2, IV.iii, John chides Falstaff for his late arrival on the field. After Hal has killed Hotspur, he allows Falstaff to perpetrate his lie, and even generously promises to 'gild it with the happiest terms I have' (Part 1, V.iv.157). In Part 2, IV.iii, John shows a comparable indulgence; Falstaff's ludicrous self-advertisement for having 'captured' Sir John Colevile does not take John in – 'it was more of his courtesy than your deserving' – but he promises he will 'better speak of you than you deserve'.

We are not at any point allowed to forget the parallel between the two brothers, and the course of the plays shows a gradual convergence between the public estimate of Hal – we as audience see him differently, of course – and the reputation his brother already enjoys. Their linking is emphasized by, of all people, Falstaff. His speech in praise of sack (Part 2, IV.iii.85ff.) opens with a sneer at the 'young sober-blooded boy' who has just been signally kind to him, whom he clearly does not like – and whom he completely underestimates, for John is anything but a fool and a coward. At the end of the speech he ludicrously attributes Hal's valour to sack. That it is Falstaff who, in such a context, sees such a contrast between them makes us notice, in fact, the similarity; and see, moreover, that Falstaff is quite upstaged by an irony that began with Hal's 'I know you all' speech (Part 1, I.ii.193ff.). He is confident he knows where he stands with Hal, but Hal is actually playing just the sort of circumspect, deadly serious game with Falstaff and with public opinion that John played with the rebels. At the end of the speech, Falstaff also contrasts Hal with Henry IV, and again the effect is to make us see the common ground. Hal has all of Henry's political qualities, and what seems like praise of his wild youth turns into a reminder of his soberness of judgement. Falstaff uses, in this speech, the agricultural images I discussed above, and is thus, without realizing it, confirming (while apparently rejecting) the values and symbols of real kingship the plays have set up:

*Hereof comes it that Prince Harry is valiant; for the cold blood he did naturally inherit from his father he hath like lean, sterile, and bare land manured, husbanded, and tilled, with excellent endeavour of drinking good and good store of fertile sherris, that he is become very hot and valiant.*

John is always a good son to his father, a figure of order and settled life. On his father's death it is he who sympathizes with the apparently dreadful prospect before the Lord Chief Justice, and 'would 'twere otherwise' (Part 2, V.ii.32). Hal is still a mystery to John. He has not understood his nature or his tactics any more than Hotspur did, and both underestimate him. Just as Hotspur's good qualities were 'cropped' and taken over by Hal, so too are John's. He trumps his courage and his policy, and at the end of Part 2 he embraces the Lord Chief Justice – the justice itself John thought Hal would reject. John and Hotspur show Hal to be a bigger and more august figure than either of them, who possesses in fuller measure and completeness the 'king-becoming graces' that each of them glimpse. Hotspur puts down one marker for the victor of Agincourt; John puts down another for the just king and the architect of the peace. And both point to that magnanimity and strength that is fully developed only in *Henry V*.

The heart of Shakespeare's discussion of the education of the prince and of true kingliness in Parts 1 and 2 must ultimately centre on Falstaff. His presence in both parts, often in deliberately parallel situations – the two battles, for example – constantly keep these issues alive, for he is a 'corrupter of youth', a 'white-bearded Satan' at loose in the world of the play. Falstaff's physical grossness is a visible image of that distemper in the realm only true kingship can cure. But before we can look at him properly, his curious history must be outlined.

### Falstaff/Oldcastle

It has long been known that behind Falstaff's name itself lay a problem. Shakespeare's sources for these plays were not only the Chronicles, but also earlier plays on these events and on popular tradition concerning them. In that popular tradition the legend of the wastrel prince who is suddenly reformed and becomes a model ruler had remarkable tenacity – perhaps because it had a considerable similarity to a motif in folk-tale and romance. The real Prince Henry had been an associate of the Lollard knight Sir John Oldcastle, who was actually burnt for heresy in the reign of his prince. Oldcastle in the popular tradition becomes a rogue, and appears as such in the *Famous Victories* which Shakespeare certainly drew on. (It also gave him, probably, suggestions for the treatment of the incident of the Dauphin's tennis balls in *Henry V*.) One or two references still remaining indicate that when Shakespeare wrote *1 Henry IV* he called his rogue Oldcastle.[8] It is now clear that those references hide an earlier, performed, version of the play in which Falstaff was

8. For example, 'My old lad of the castle' (Part 1, I.ii.41); 'Oldcastle died a martyr, and this is not the man' (Part 2, Epilogue).

called Oldcastle throughout, and we need to examine the implications of this.

Oldcastle was a major historical figure and a focus for sixteenth-century discussion of contemporary concerns in religion and politics. A play making him a central character could not avoid sharing the explosive topicality of many Elizabethan plays that we noticed above. The first version of the play may well have been a *succès de scandale*, and the publication of the first Quarto in 1598 may have been hurried through to publicize a change of names demanded by the censor.[9]

The original Sir John Oldcastle (*c.* 1378–1417) was High Sheriff of Herefordshire and became Lord Cobham, in right of his wife, in 1409 (he was thus connected with the Lord Cobham of Shakespeare's day, a man of considerable influence). He was a valiant captain and a 'hardie gentleman' in the French wars,[10] so Holinshed tells us, high in Henry V's favour, but he became a supporter of the Wycliffite or Lollard heresy. Henry V personally tried, but in vain, to win him back to the orthodox faith; he was hanged and burnt.

Controversy over this figure continued for some two centuries. Was he to be seen as a martyr to a sort of proto-Protestantism, as a gallant man, or was he a traitor to the king who befriended him? In the mainstream historical tradition, represented by chroniclers like Fabian, Hall, Grafton and Stow, he is a robber, a traitor and a heretic. Worse, he was a hypocrite, hiding foul designs under a cloak of righteousness. His confession at his trial of his youthful misdeeds is quoted: 'In my frayle youthe I offended thee (Lorde) moste greeuously, in Pride, Wrathe, and Glottony, in Couetousness and in Lechery' – a good number of the Seven Deadly Sins. He intended to destroy his king, God's law, and 'all manner of policie, and finally the lawes of the land'. But this view was not accepted by the Puritan writers, who were always ready to look back

9. Censorship was usual. Before publication, a manuscript could be submitted for perusal and approval, but with a play where publication in book form was not intended initially (for sound commercial reasons), the censor could not operate until after seeing the first performance. If he objected, he might ban performances; or, if the matter was important enough, he might insist on immediate publication of a revised text.

Many modern critics would have us believe that Shakespeare was an out-and-out subversive of the values – political, social, religious – of his time. If he was so, it is very odd that the censors, who were far from stupid, didn't spot this rather important fact. Perhaps the critics are making him in their own image . . .

10. The original version of *Henry V* almost certainly fulfilled the promise of the Epilogue to *2 Henry IV* and had a part for Falstaff in France; some of Pistol's and the Boy's lines are best explained on this hypothesis. See pp. 169ff.

into the dark Romish past and see men who hinted at the glory of the clear wisdom and rightness that had been revealed in themselves. The fourteenth-century poet Langland, for example, is much praised for his 'satire' of the abuses of the Church – an important but far from central issue in his poem. Foxe, whose *Actes and Monuments* (commonly called the 'Booke of Martyrs') was in every parish church in the reign of Elizabeth, spends twenty pages defending Oldcastle and rebutting the case against him. It can be seen, therefore, that an attitude taken to Oldcastle was a pretty sure symptom of one's religious stance, and therefore of one's political views – even, given the international situation at the end of the century, of one's views on what England's foreign policy ought to be. We may begin to guess why the censor was worried.

Shakespeare's treatment of his character clearly shows few Puritan sympathics. In Falstaff it is only *Puritans* who are satirized. The religious allusions, of which there are many, are entirely appropriate to his original identity, and they are all hypocritical. Oldcastle's very presence emphasizes the plays' religious motifs, in particular Henry's constantly reiterated desire to go on pilgrimage to Jerusalem – an ironic metaphor for the life of man on earth, in which all the characters are tested. The victims of the robbery in Part 1, I.ii, are said to be 'pilgrims going to Canterbury' (ll. 124–5), to St Thomas's shrine – innocent travellers seeking their salvation through penance; yet the Puritans considered Oldcastle to be a man more saintly than St Thomas à Becket. A good number of references to the historical Oldcastle underline the impression that Shakespeare has taken an anti-Puritan line, and also that he was seeing in the historical figure an archetype of moral chaos who could fitly be associated with the popular tradition of the wild youth of Prince Henry. For example, in Part 1, I.ii.144–5, Falstaff's 'By the lord, I'll be a traitor then, when thou art King' surely alludes to the fact: Oldcastle did become a traitor when Henry V became king, and he did turn upon the 'true prince' of Part 1 (II.iv.263). Henry V did try to re-convert Oldcastle, and this seems to be the point of the allusion in Part 1, I.ii.96–7, 'I'll be damned for never a king's son in Christendom'; and in lines 119–20, 'Then art thou damned for keeping thy word with the devil.' The historical Oldcastle was burnt; Falstaff is compared at Part 1, II.iv.440, to a 'roasted Manningtree ox'. The historian John Stow records the story that Oldcastle at his execution said he would rise again in three days; Falstaff 'rises from the dead' at Shrewsbury. In the charade of Part 1, II.iv, two portraits of Falstaff are given, one as a virtuous man, the other as a corrupter of youth, a reverend Vice; this looks like a clear allusion to the opposing views of Oldcastle, and we are in no doubt which one we are to take. At V.iv.162–4, Falstaff promises – conditionally! – a conversion, a conversion the historical Oldcastle described in his trial. All these allusions make it clear that Shakespeare has not only portrayed a Protestant martyr as a hypocrite, but has entered the controversy with relish and a streak of cruelty.[11]

There are of course inconsistencies in the figure of Falstaff/Oldcastle between *1* and *2 Henry IV* and *Henry V*. The change of Oldcastle's name after Part 1 was produced may have affected the way Shakespeare could handle Hal and Falstaff in Part 2. The real Oldcastle betrayed the real Henry V, and Henry V attempted to save him; in Part 2 Falstaff does not betray, but is rejected – not without generosity – for political expediency. There is, moreover, a change in Falstaff's character between the two Parts, as we shall see.

Having established that Falstaff was originally the controversial Oldcastle, it follows that one implication of his association with Hal, particularly in Part 1, is that Shakespeare is suggesting the prince's preparation for rule should embrace true religion and reject false – and that the false religion to be rejected was that of the extreme Puritans. (There are numerous examples elsewhere in the Shakespeare canon that suggest, at the very least, Roman Catholic sympathies, and in 1611 John Speed seems to have thought Shakespeare actually was a Roman Catholic.) This is of some topical importance. We must now look at how Shakespeare used this issue in the discussion of kingly qualities and their development.

The alternation of scenes in these two plays reminds us that Hal, as no other character, straddles two worlds, that of the Court and its values and that of Eastcheap. The course of Parts 1 and 2 shows each world demonstrating its true nature and values, and Hal taking from each what is valuable and necessary to him as the hero king who unites England. Inevitably he must reject Eastcheap, but not before he has observed it fully and recognized that he is king *as well* (as John could

11. The topicality of all this is clear. Philip Henslowe, of the competing company (see above, Chapter 3.viii), in 1599 put on a cooperatively written potboiler called *The first part of the true and honourable historie, of the life of Sir* IOHN OLD-CASTLE, *the good Lord Cobham*, written specifically in reply to *1 Henry IV* to clear Oldcastle's Protestant good name. There are many similar references in the two plays. Later, in 1639, the first version of Part 1, called *Oldcastle*, was performed at Court, where the queen was a fervent Catholic, at the Cockpit theatre in Whitehall Palace on 29 May – the Prince of Wales's birthday. Appropriate!

never be) of the disordered and frivolous and corrupt, and must take responsibility for it. After all, at the end of Part 2 very generous and merciful provision is made for Falstaff; he is sent to honourable custody in the Fleet pending examination, and he and his companions will be 'very well provided for' (V.v.102), the only condition being that they must not come near the royal presence until they have reformed (see pp. 169ff.). We see in the structure of the Henry plays and in Hal's choice something very similar to the favourite Renaissance theme – in emblems, paintings, poems and plays – of the Choice of Hercules. In this old story, which originates in Xenophon's *Cyropaedia*, Hercules is confronted by two women, one of whom, Virtue, offers him wisdom and understanding, while the other, Vice, offers sensual pleasure. (In visual treatments, Vice often holds a beautiful mask before her hideous features.) Like Hercules, Hal *could* choose Vice – despite his soliloquy; that this is a real possibility *for those without the audience's hindsight* is indicated by the ease with which those of Eastcheap think he is already theirs and those of the Court are quite sure of it. In keeping with many treatments of the Hercules legend, Shakespeare is showing, in Hal, that a true hero is master of pleasure and a follower of Virtue. There is no doubt at all that Hal enjoys a lot of the fun in the Eastcheap group; but note that he never actually touches the pitch of the proverb that Shakespeare makes Falstaff quote euphuistically in Part 1, II.iv.405–6 (self-valuation indeed!), and much of Hal's humour in these scenes is directed against Falstaff's false values. His very first speech to him in Part 1, however it is spoken, is an attack on Falstaff's vices and sins.

The temptation, even if we know the outcome, is real enough, and it is often forgotten, even by readers of *Paradise Lost*, that tempters are not tempters if they are not deeply attractive. Falstaff is just such a 'tempter of youth', and I have already discussed his connection with and dependence on the Vice of the Morality plays, who solicits the allegiance of young men through his wit, humour and good company and his offers of food, drink and sex. But Vice is the devil in another guise; and Falstaff is, after all, called a 'white-bearded Satan, a corrupter of youth'. Where Shakespeare is extremely daring – and provocative – is in conflating this figure with Oldcastle. If the character of Falstaff, this aged whoremaster and drunkard, this gluttonous coward, thief, extortioner and murderer,[12] is aimed at the extreme Puritans, there is a good deal

---

12. What other word fits his treatment of his 'food for powder'? – Part 1, IV.ii.63ff.; V.iii.35ff.

more than humour involved: there is direct challenge to their notions of the state and of the little world of man – and to their good faith.

In popular opinion in the Henry plays, Hal has cut himself loose from his real father and what he represents, and we see him in the process of choosing a moral father. The relationship with Henry is coloured by misunderstanding, for Henry is all too ready to judge by appearances and report; his misunderstanding of Hal's taking of the crown is a case in point, for after Hal saved his life at Shrewsbury he ought to have judged his son better. On this head alone Hal is symbolically set apart from his father, for he is never taken in by mere appearance; that fault dogged Richard, and Henry Bolingbroke who trusted Northumberland. The important opposition, however, is between Falstaff, who treats Hal with the familiarity appropriate to a son, and the Lord Chief Justice, whom Falstaff insults and who fears Hal's accession – and to whom Hal says, 'You shall be as a father to my youth' (Part 2, V.ii.118).

The young are always attracted to riot and intemperance, and the Lord Chief Justices of this world – and others! – have the job of containing their excesses while they grow up. Hal was no different: in Part 2, V.ii.73ff., the Lord Chief Justice refers to the occasion (dear to the popular tradition of the wild prince, but which has no foundation in history) when Hal struck him 'in my very seat of judgement' and was, quite properly, imprisoned for it.[13] But in Part 2 Hal is away from Falstaff for most of the five acts, and his reconciliation with the Lord Chief Justice is public. Shakespeare is showing Hal beginning to take his part as a responsible and indispensable part of the machinery of state, whose place is on the field or in the palace. The confrontation is clearly between the attractions of the old Vice, Falstaff, and the sternness – but not inhumanity, for Shakespeare portrays him as a compassionate and feeling man – of the Lord Chief Justice. Falstaff and the Lord Chief Justice both have speeches that turn on their expectations of what will happen when Hal comes to the throne. Right at the beginning, Falstaff asks, '. . . shall there be gallows standing in England when thou art King? And resolution thus fubbed as it is with the rusty curb of old Father Antic the law? Do not thou when thou art King, hang a thief' (Part 1, I.ii.58–61). He does not take Hal's reply seriously. (When king, Hal does indeed hang thieves – Bardolph, for instance.) The Lord Chief Justice expects the worst, and so do those who support him (V.ii.26ff.). Part of the dramatic pleasure is that we know they are both wrong. The irony

13. Notice that Shakespeare makes Hal quote Henry IV's approval of this action (V.ii.108ff.) – a small but important indication of Henry's honesty and seriousness as a king.

allows Shakespeare to give the Lord Chief Justice a powerful apologia for the impartial justice and political stability that follow when the royal house itself is under the law. In Part 2, on hearing of Hal's accession Falstaff promises Shallow: '. . . choose what office thou wilt in the land, 'tis thine' (V.iii.122–3). The only 'justice' Falstaff can offer is typified by the ridiculous Justice Shallow: partial, bribable, self-seeking, an old man who wishes for the powers of youth – but only to commit more folly and lechery.[14] Falstaff and his world exist, and always will; but they should not come within ten miles of the royal presence.

Given the parameters of the discussion in the plays, then, in Falstaff we know what type of figure to expect. The details, however, are unusual. I have discussed above the paradoxical links he has with the notion of a tragic figure (pp. 90f.); there is a complexity in him that makes him dramatically interesting. His energy and wit engage both us and Hal by, as Dr Johnson said, the 'most pleasing of all qualities, perpetual gaiety, by an unfailing power of exciting laughter, which is the more freely indulged, as his wit is not of the splendid or ambitious kind, but consists in easy escapes and sallies of levity, which make sport but raise no envy'. There are hints of complexity: the jokes about his conscience, Oldcastle or no Oldcastle, round him out in the dramatic context; a coward and cynic, when he has to fight or be killed he fights – and then shams dead. But the main thing Shakespeare gives him is a capacity for development. In Part 1 we see a gradual revelation of a complex, but to all intents and purposes static, character. But after Shrewsbury a new and much less likeable Falstaff begins to appear as he thinks power is growing. Immediately after Falstaff's outrageous lie about Hotspur's death, a new pride (another deadly sin) and arrogance is seen in his dealings with both superiors and inferiors. He even assumes his interest with Hal will be of use to Prince John. He is impossibly rude to the Lord Chief Justice (Part 2, II.i.102ff.), and in the earlier confrontation (I.ii) between them – where he takes some very hard knocks – his humour seems for the first time to be merely silly (ll. 143ff.). He spends his time with the common whore, Doll, and treats her and Mistress Quickly with utter cynicism and cruelty. In Hal's absence, Falstaff now sees him without the apparent affection of Part 1, merely as a source of good fortune; and we actually watch him thinking how he can use Shallow not only for his own

14. In Shallow, but more obviously – crucially – in Falstaff, Shakespeare has used the idea, part of the comic stock throughout the Middle Ages and the Renaissance, of the *senex amans* – the old man in whom sexual desire has outlived performance. Seeing him with Doll on his knee reminds us forcefully of this; see below, p. 144.

advantage (Part 2, III.ii.316ff.; IV.iii.125ff.) but as 'copy' for jokes to amuse Hal (V.i.71ff.). His conception of honour, funny enough in Part 1, is seen in action in Part 2. He sends his men into the hottest part of the fight to their deaths so that he can claim the pay of those killed.

Finally, if this development were not enough to make even the stupidest audience see what was going on – and Shakespeare knew enough about audiences to make his plays dolt-proof – he is careful to point up what Falstaff is, what he embodies, by clear visual signals – just as he defines what is happening to Richard. Two examples will suffice. In Part 1, II.iv.371ff., in the charade at the Boar's Head, Falstaff acts the part of a king: 'This chair shall be my state, this dagger my sceptre, this cushion my crown'. There is a clear cue here for the visual staging, and once we formulate it properly against the emblems and symbols of the time, interesting things happen. The chair becomes a throne (one meaning of 'state'), yet it is a mere 'joint-stool' – a fake; the sceptre of justice becomes a dagger of violence and rapine; and the cushion on his head, his 'crown', is emblematic of sloth, one of the Seven Deadly Sins. That focuses it all, for Falstaff 'is' Sloth – the rejection of spiritual good and the ignoring of all higher calls than those of the body. This is Falstaff's real nature, and this is what a kingdom ruled by his values would be. Again, consider Part 2, II.iv.209ff.,[15] where Falstaff asks Doll to give him a kiss. The comments of Hal and Poins, observing, make us see this almost allegorically – 'Saturn and Venus this year in conjunction'; old age sits ill with lust. Falstaff and Doll's own words turn on the idea of the death they must both die – and there is no sexual pun here. What is visually communicated to us is Falstaff as lust, another deadly sin, reduced to the ludicrous ugliness of its real self in this presentation. Shakespeare is using here, almost unchanged, the allegorical tools of the Moralities; and not for the last time, as readers of *Macbeth* or *King Lear* will know.

It is his language – as Johnson saw – that gives Falstaff the illusion of life and the surface attractiveness that makes him compelling (see Chapter 11). But despite its brilliance, his language itself is a moral symptom. In his speech, words run mad into pun and clench and *double entendre*; his language inverts a perception of reality as his conduct wishes to invert the real thing. He is even, with the Lord Chief Justice, momentarily reduced to meaningless repetition – 'gravy, gravy, gravy'[16]

15. The parallel structure of Parts 1 and 2 is beautifully exemplified here. Both of these crucially defining Boar's Head scenes occur at the same point in their respective plays.

16. Gluttony, surely suggested here, and exemplifed visually in his sleep behind the arras in Part 1, II.iv.513ff., is another of the Seven Deadly Sins.

– but the torrent soon gathers fresh strength. Only at the end, rejected by Hal, does reality momentarily break in: 'Master Shallow, I owe you a thousand pound.' (He has other debts – he 'owes God a death'.) He tries to take off again into the illusion of language, but fools no one, for Shallow returns his own earlier pun: 'A colour that I fear you will die in, Sir John.' His last words are an appeal – which will be heard – to the Lord Chief Justice whose good sense he rejected. But even this point, concerning the distance between Falstaff's language and reality, is cued visually. He is set in contrast to the near silent Silence in Part 2, III.ii and V.iii, another old man whose remarks centre round death, a lost past, and, after dining liberally with Falstaff, drunken fragments of half-forgotten songs. This is the inner Falstaff, the withered applejohn.

The complexity of Falstaff, then, is central to our understanding of the progress of Hal to the realization of what true kingship entails. Before the play opened this prince was educated to distinguish vice from virtue, responsibility from irresponsibility, but his kingdom and the audience have to go through a process of thought and learning. The plays are generally relevant; they are also a signal warning, in what everybody knew to be Queen Elizabeth's declining years, to those jockeying for positions of advantage in the succession. Falstaff is both warning and challenge.

There is no sweet fruition in an earthly crown, as Marlowe's Tamburlaine the Great thought. In Part 2, IV.v, that 'golden rigol' which Richard had held out to Bolingbroke as a symbol of fortune and of care lies on Henry IV's pillow as Hal watches. Here is where Shakespeare leads the man who is to become the Henry of *Henry V* to explore the pain and responsibility of kingship; like his father, he envies his poorest subjects. But, seeing no sign of life in Henry, he takes it with dignity and sorrow – and a consecration of himself as ruler to God's protection.

But Henry is not dead. Hal's explanation of his act powerfully illuminates his action in taking the crown. He took it to 'try with it – as with an enemy/That had before my face murdered my father'. He sees what it has done to his father, what the crown had cost in terms of humanity and love; he upbraids it – 'thou . . . Hast eat thy bearer up'. Shakespeare, through him, points us to the theme we first looked at in our discussion of *Richard II*: the cost of kingship to the king. Our pity for Henry is increased by his confession to his son of the 'by-paths and indirect crooked ways' by which he came to his kingship. He cannot undo what his own action led him to do, he cannot undo the unhappiness of his whole reign, and must carry responsibility for it to his grave. Yet Hal may inherit it with 'true peace'. Neither Richard nor Henry knew that.

This scene, IV.v, is an important qualifier of our reaction to Hal when he appears after Henry has died. He has succeeded to the crown with pain and fear; we can accept his assurance that he sees it as a 'joint burden laid upon us all', that he will 'bear your cares' (V.ii.55ff.), as quite without hypocrisy; and his first act as king is to embrace Justice. With this, the body politic torn apart by Richard is restored, and 'limbs of noble counsel' (l. 135) chosen to ensure that, just as his own body is now properly governed (his 'affections', l. 124, having been buried with his father), England too will be 'in equal rank with the best-governed nation'. That hope is examined in *Henry V*, the final test of kingliness.

# 10. This Sceptred Isle: Henry V

In *Henry V* there are so many references back in time to the events dramatized in the previous plays that, while the play is, naturally, able to stand quite independently, it gains enormously from being seen against the well-known events of the reigns of Richard II and Henry IV. Even more does it gain when seen against the background of the discussion of rule and the ruler in Shakespeare's treatment of those historical events.

In watching the movement of Hal from Eastcheap towards the crown, a redefinition of his self, and an acceptance of the implications of his role, we have been constantly reminded (not least by Henry IV) of the movement of Richard away from the crown to his discovery of a new self in his new nonentity. The careers of both – and of Henry IV too – centre round their possession, or not, not only of legitimate title to the throne, but also of the Cardinal Virtues of Prudence, Justice, Temperance and Fortitude. In *Henry V* these virtues are seen for the first time united with legitimate possession of the throne; the earlier plays demonstrated how necessary they are to a ruler by showing men engaged in power struggles who possessed them only partially or not at all. Richard, for example, lacked both justice and temperance, and was imprudent to a degree; in his fall he learned fortitude and, when it was too late, the three divisions of prudence – *memory* of his own misdeeds, *understanding* of what was happening to him, and *foresight* of what would happen to his realm.[1]

Henry Bolingbroke's fortitude we can take for granted; he possessed a sense of justice and was temperate, but he was led into a course of events whose outcome he did not foresee and whose consequences dog his reign with unhappiness and rebellion. In the *Henry IV* plays, Henry tries hard to understand and foresee his problems, but ultimately is a responder to events rather than a controller of them; his sympathetic portrait is neatly set against that of the unlikeable political schemer Worcester, who possesses almost a parody of prudence. (Worcester is also contrasted with Northumberland – a vacillating man, given to misjudgement.) Hotspur has a complete lack of the virtue of prudence –

1. This threefold division is a medieval and Renaissance cliché. The interdependence of these qualities is well demonstrated in Titian's 'Allegory of Prudence'.

he has no policy or forethought, can control neither his tongue nor his actions, and lacks the broadness and generosity of mind that is essential to justice. Falstaff's cunning is shortsighted, working on assumptions we know to be false, and takes no thought for the time that will come when no man may work. He shies away from prudent consideration of the ultimate end of man when he tells Doll not to speak like a death's-head, a *memento mori*, to him (Part 2, II.iv.229–30ff.). In his lechery and gluttony he is a very figure of intemperance; he is mean and unjust in his treatment of the Hostess, his soldiers, and – had he been able – would have been so to Shallow and Silence. The idea of connecting fortitude with Falstaff is ludicrous, and the nearest the Eastcheap group come to a perception of fortitude is in the ridiculous posturing of Pistol – which hides a deep cowardice.[2]

Against all these is set Hal. He has prudence in full measure; his behaviour throughout Parts 1 and 2 indicate an awareness of his family history, an understanding of public opinion and people as well as political reality, and a foresight that allows him to turn his possession of the throne into a mark for later ages to aim at. This quality is also shown in his examination of the evidence in the council in Act 1 of *Henry V*, before committing himself to war. That council also shows his concern for a cause that is just; and his justice is shown not only in the treatment of Scroop and Cambridge but also of Bardolph, who is caught robbing a church. He is fair and just to both the Hostess and Hotspur.

The justice that Hal comes to exemplify is neatly underlined when he plays the part of his own father giving judgement in Part 1, II.iv (a picture deliberately set against the icon of misrule we have just seen in Falstaff), and in the confirmation in his speech to the Lord Chief Justice of the visible symbols of justice, the sword and the scales (which still surmount the Old Bailey). The mercy (of which more later) that goes with justice is shown in his treatment of Falstaff and his companions. His fortitude in battle and hardship is obvious, and we have seen how in the midst of intemperance in Part 1 he remained temperate. Henry in *Henry V* is thus not only a legitimate king, but also a good man.

He is also a Christian. The emphasis on this in *Henry V* is very noticeable, and the play examines, among other things, the implications

2. Pistol's dramatic ancestors include the *miles gloriosus* ('boastful soldier') of Roman comedy, a stock figure who appeared regularly on the Elizabethan stage. The number of quotations from Marlowe Shakespeare buries in his speech suggests he was less than impressed by the hyperbolic heroics Marlowe gives his royal figures, particularly Tamburlaine, to speak.

of a deeply held personal Christianity for the ruler. The Prayer for the Church in the First (1549) and Second (1552) Prayer Books is virtually identical to that in the 1662 Book of Common Prayer; it beseeches God to

defend all Christian Kings, Princes and Governors; and specially thy servant Elizabeth our queen; that under her we may be godly and quietly governed: And grant unto her whole Council, and to all that are put in authority under her, that they may truly and indifferently minister justice, to the punishment of wickedness and vice, and to the maintenance of thy true religion and virtue.

The prayer stresses the powerlessness of the ruler without God's help, his duty of good government, and of impartial justice. These are exactly the issues that the play deals with in the series of tableaux framed by the Choruses (see Chapter 6.iv), and furthermore it scrutinizes what is involved in being a Christian prince. Henry in this play has to blend his role as a conqueror and legitimate ruler with his inward, personal Christianity. The tension has the potential for tragedy, but through it Henry discovers his true identity and reaches a triumphant synthesis.

The first act of *Henry V* is so structured as to bring these issues into consideration. Shakespeare often uses in his political plays a big Court scene at or near the beginning to introduce us to the issues the play will raise, and to the persons involved. The staging of such a scene necessarily reminds us of the hierarchy in the state that mirrors the *ordo* (see Chapter 1.i) in the universe; we have seen this at the beginning of *Richard II* and *1 Henry IV*. Frequently too (but not invariably) he structures these scenes so that we have a short introduction by some minor characters who prepare us for what we are about to witness, then the big state entry, then a third division commenting on some of the implications of what has happened.[3]

Act 1 opens with Canterbury and Ely talking about the king. They both agree he is 'full of grace and fair regard' and 'a true lover of the holy Church' (I.i.22–3), and Canterbury goes on to enumerate his perfections. The inevitable reference to his reformation is couched in terms specifically religious, echoing the Baptism Service of the Prayer Book of 1560; the prince's 'consideration' (repentance) has, as it were, undone the Fall and left a perfect man, the proper abode for the Holy Spirit. (It is

3. For example, cf. *King Lear*. Sometimes, as in *Henry V*, Shakespeare uses what are marked in the text as separate scenes to build up this structure (cf. *Julius Caesar*, I.i, I.ii; and *Hamlet*, I.i, I.ii).

noteworthy that already we have, as we did in Gaunt's complaint about Richard's mistreatment of England, reference to the Garden of Eden and that other garden, the Paradise of the blessed.) His character is more than just reformed. He can understand the subtler points of theology (ll. 38–40); he is skilled in civil law (ll. 41–2); he can speak eloquently on the art of war (ll. 43–4);[4] he is an expert in statecraft or 'policy', and can by reason solve problems that would have driven even an Alexander to use his sword.[5] He speaks with all the admired arts of rhetoric, and has married the 'theoric' and 'practic' sides of life as a good Renaissance prince should. What is being described is nothing less than the Renaissance ideal of the *uomo universale* we see in Sidney or Castiglione, a man who is master of himself and master of the pleasure that would corrupt other men (l. 51; cf. above, p. 141). Ely – who holds a bishopric that, as we know from *Richard III*, has something of a reputation for strawberries – replies with garden/cultivation images (the strawberry thriving under the useless nettle, and so on) to suggest that there may have been an organic connection between the king's early wildness and his present excellence.

After this prologue comes the state entry. We should envisage a stage crammed with people – even if we only allow two attendants per noble (mean by Renaissance standards) there would be twenty-one people on stage before Canterbury and Ely enter. This company obviously must have been organized as nearly as possible in a pattern like that of the Elizabethan Parliament. Henry's opening of the matter of his claim to the French throne shows exactly those qualities Canterbury has enumerated: mastery of the legal issues, eloquence, a readiness to defend his right by battle, a recognition that the king bears a heavy responsibility under God for his actions. He is a king who is far from trigger-happy, but cares deeply about justice. He is aware that the rightness of his cause is not one he alone can decide (I.ii.10–12) and warns Canterbury not to

4. We ought not to let our perfectly proper horror of war blind us to the fact that our ancestors saw it as potentially glorious, an activity that called for nobility and self-sacrifice, and an art utterly desirable for the true ruler to possess.

5. This reference to Alexander's 'unloosing' the Gordian knot, of which it is prophesied that he who undid it would rule the world, is quite important, and anticipates Fluellen's linking – comic in expression, but to be taken quite seriously – of Henry to Alexander. The link cannot be openly made without overstatement, but it can be suggested with force; and Alexander was one of those Nine Worthies who set up a standard for all other military men. These were the three Jews (Joshua, Gideon and Judas Maccabaeus), three pagans (Hector, Alexander and Julius Caesar) and three Christians (Arthur, Charlemagne and Godfrey de Bouillon who captured Jerusalem from the Saracens in 1099).

'fashion, wrest, or bow [his] reading' to suit what he thinks Henry wants to hear. A far cry from the flattering counsellors of Richard! Canterbury's reply is to be taken seriously, however difficult we find it to do so; it emphasizes the justness of Henry's claim and the legitimacy of his decision to pursue it by war if negotiation fails.[6] Henry is adamant on this point: 'May I with *right and conscience* make this claim?' This careful weighing of the legal and moral rights shown by Henry is highlighted by the parallel with his father, for although Bolingbroke had right and law on his side, this careful consideration never crossed his mind. He was pulled by the logic of his own actions into rebellion and the deposition of an anointed king.

Ely supports Canterbury, and caps the latter's roll-call of English heroes and his reminiscence of the well-known story of the Black Prince at Crécy with a call to Henry to live up to their valiant example.[7] Prophetic; for Agincourt was, like Crécy, a desperate throw against huge odds, and Edward and Henry did, in 1356 and 1415, 'forage in blood of French nobility'. A lesser king would immediately be swayed by such a volume of ecclesiastical agreement; but Henry still holds back. The 'policy' Canterbury described is exemplified in his concern to protect his realm from the incursions of the Scots. But, as his counsellors agree, here is no Irish expedition of a King Richard; this realm is properly and harmoniously organized, and Canterbury's memorable speech about the mutual interdependence of the commonwealth of the bees finally convinces Henry of what he should do.

Yet this part of the scene is not quite so simple as this makes it sound. For a start, the support of two senior bishops is pretty powerful; and we ought to remember that Bolingbroke's actions to seek the throne were strongly opposed by Carlisle, and his continuance on it by the Archbishop of York. Both appealed to divine sanction for their opposition; but Canterbury and Ely represent such a sanction *supporting* Henry. The

6. Which raises the issue of the *Just War*. The theology of this idea ultimately derives from Augustine. In the thirteenth century St Thomas Aquinas laid down three conditions in which arms may be taken up: it must be on the authority of the sovereign, the cause must be just, the belligerents must have a rightful intention – for example, to prevent a greater evil. (Some thinkers also added that it was a good idea to make sure you had a good chance of winning.) Henry's war is made out to be just on these terms; and likewise the French, resisting their lawful sovereign, are fighting an unjust one. The issue is a topical one, in which the Elizabethans were much interested.

7. The imagery is of lions. We recall Henry's own call before Harfleur to 'imitate the action of the tiger' – a royal and noble beast, but violent and destructive. Note the imagery below – the Scots are doggy, wolfish, weasels, mice; the English eagles, lions, cats.

contrast with his predecessors could hardly be more powerful. Secondly, Canterbury's speech about the bees holds up an analogy to the well-ordered state, an ideal to be worked for, rather than offering a description of what actually *is*. There is an implied conditionality in his lines,

> *I this infer,*
> *That many things, having full reference*
> *To one consent, may work contrariously*

(ll. 204–6)

which reinforces his earlier suggestion that 'obedience' (i.e. this inter-dependence in the state) (l. 187) is 'an aim or butt' to be worked for. It may not yet have been achieved, and the achievement may be temporary. The confidence – and it is a real confidence – of this scene is set off by the recognition that the ideal is not automatically achieved; the details of the hive of England are, in fact, examined in subsequent scenes. Henry has to be the 'sad-eyed justice' delivering over to execution, at whatever personal cost, those who break his trust and their own faith.

But that painful act of self-control is still in the future. A more pressing one is immediate. To highlight Henry's nature, Shakespeare made a significant change to his sources at this point. In the sources the Dauphin's insult arrives *before* the decision is taken to press Henry's claim. Here it is clear that the decision has been reached in fair and open concert of the prince with his counsellors, working together like the commonwealth of the bees, and that the Dauphin's insult does not affect the issue one way or another. What it now serves to do is to underline that, as the ambassadors report (II.iv.29ff.), the rest of Europe must take note of the change in Henry as his own country has had to do in *2 Henry IV*.

The ambassadors enter with a good deal of trepidation. Henry re-assures them:

> *We are no tyrant but a Christian king,*
> *Unto whose grace our passion is as subject*
> *As in our wretches fettered in our prisons*

(I.ii.242–4)

– a reply which not only endorses the law of nations, but reminds us of the standards of kingship we are to apply to Henry and of the justice in him that controls both his subjects and his own passions. His own passions need that self-control, for he is clearly deeply offended and angry at the Dauphin's joke. He contains his anger, even turns it into a series of bitter puns and images, but it is clear that the irresponsibility of the Dauphin, a more foolish Hotspur, must bear a good deal of the blame for the decision to refuse Henry's demands, and thus for the war that will devastate France. Five times in the last twenty-five lines of the first act Henry emphasizes that he is acting in God's name and that his cause is just, and there is no reason to suspect any irony on his or Shakespeare's part. After all, the historical tradition attributed to Henry V a piety and seriousness about religious issues that there is no reason to doubt; he is known to have had long and earnest theological arguments with Oldcastle to win him back to the orthodox religion so that he could save him from execution. Shakespeare has already made Canterbury endorse this, and the whole of Act I has been focused on demonstrating what qualities make him a credible 'mirror of all Christian kings' (II,Chorus,6). Shakespeare could have left the matter there and merely taken Henry off to a gung-ho expedition to bash the French. But he does something much more interesting. He shows Henry developing those qualities in action that the mere statement by Canterbury might not be enough to convince us he possessed, and developing a piety and humility that reflect, perhaps, Richard's later consciousness of his place in God's sight. Henry grows and develops in this play not only as a ruler but as a man conscious of his huge moral responsibility, at the cost of his own personal feelings. The justice Canterbury speaks of is shown not only in the patient searching of his own title to the French throne, where he stands to gain a good deal, but also in the extremely painful and wounding confrontation with the conspirators in II.ii.

He clearly knows all about the treason of Scroop, Grey and Cambridge before he asks them their opinion about the treatment of the wretch who committed *lèse-majesté*. Those who themselves would have betrayed him advise severity – the advice of flatterers who say what they think he wants to hear. But he shows the wretch the royal prerogative of mercy; and their own mouths have denied the conspirators the chance of mercy for their more heinous crime. All their betrayals are bad enough; but the one that is particularly wounding is that of Scroop, for clearly Henry loved the man. He is given a long speech of reproach (II.ii.79–144) in which the tones of the public man give way to the broken cadences of a betrayed friend. The most common grammatical structure is a pained, reproachful question; the second person singular (signalling the intimacy of the reproach) dominates, and the imagery moves from money to extortion (l. 99), to devils tempting a man to fall, then to the devils' ability to deceive with fair-seeming, and finally to the open mention of what had been more and more insistent in the subtext: the Fall itself. Like Adam, Scroop has fallen from grace, and has committed the sin of Judas in betraying his master. The reminiscence of Richard is inescapable in this, the last betrayal, as that of Richard was the first. The speech is full of the tones, even the very rhetorical patterns (ll. 127ff.), of Richard; yet their positions are antithetical. Richard was powerless against his betrayers, and had to fall to learn what being a king meant; Henry knows what being a king entails, and has to use his power to punish, however unwillingly. Against the desires and pain of the private man they must be punished. Henry assumes again the royal plural in their sentence, for this is a necessary act of policy. His passions are indeed in prison. We may applaud so just a prince, but we are made aware of the cost to the man.

Memory of the other plays again highlights this moment. When Bolingbroke indicts and condemns Green and Bushy (*Richard II*, III.i), there is more than a hint of personal animus in what purports to be justice; and neither of them accepts either his authority or the justice of his condemnation. Worcester, when condemned by Henry IV (*1 Henry IV*, V.v), can merely 'embrace this fortune patiently', and does not accept Henry's right though he must accept his power. Mowbray and the Archbishop of York (*2 Henry IV*, IV.ii) are also indignant at Prince John's stratagem – which is not, incidentally, so unlike his brother's here. But these traitors not only accept Henry's justice and right, not only repent of their crimes and ask for God's pardon, but also applaud his action. There could be no stronger endorsement of Henry's kingship than this, from those who would have destroyed him.

Scene ii extends the private self-control of I.ii into public action. The world is having to notice this prince who indifferently ministers justice. The contrasting comic scenes, II.i and II.iii (of which more later) give some idea of the sort of people for whom Henry has responsibility; even there, as Falstaff lies dying, his heart 'fracted and corroborate' by the king's rejection, Nym accepts 'the King is a good king'. In II.iv the news of the formidable nature of this prince reaches France. Here is another of those visual parallels Shakespeare used so often; the court of England in I.ii, presided over in harmony by Henry, is contrasted with that of the France he claims. Here is no country acting in concert. In the face of external threat, the counsellors disagree. The Dauphin shows a foolish and imprudent disregard of Henry as a monarch, and speaks with the contemptuousness of a Hotspur, while the Constable urges that the ambassadors' report of his excellence must be taken seriously. King Charles wisely agrees, remembering Crécy and the tree of which this prince is a shoot. When Exeter and his train are announced, again the Dauphin foolishly butts in, implicitly comparing the English to a pack of dogs and the French to the noble deer; the irony of which he is unconscious is that the deer is hunted and pulled down by the dogs (II.iv.69–70). Exeter's message to the king reveals a good deal about Henry. He is not entering on this war lightly, and, like the French king himself just before, is terribly aware of the horror of war and its insatiable appetite (ll. 104–5;109). He beseeches Charles 'in the bowels of the Lord' whom they both acknowledge (l. 102) to deliver up the crown to save the suffering of the innocent. To the Dauphin he sends back insult in the same terms as he received it; and that foolish young man desires nothing more than the arbitrament of war without thought of the cost. His folly, over-confidence and silly pride masquerading as honour keep alive in this play, as a coarsened and distorted reflection, the memory of Hotspur whose character was strongly contrasted with the inner honour of Prince Hal.

In Act III, war has arrived. Henry's physical courage, fortitude and prowess does not need exploring in this play; had Shakespeare wished to do so, he could have dramatized the famous and historical combat with the Duc d'Alençon he found in his sources – he alludes to it in some detail at IV.vii.150ff. What is explored as the play goes on is his inheritance, and more, of his father's gift of inspiring and leading men. The speech before Harfleur (III.i), the favourite old warhorse of anthologists, would never have acquired that status had it not been indeed inspiring. It belongs to a recognized genre for which Shakespeare and his generation must have known a plethora of classical precedents – 'the general's address to his soldiers before the battle' – and a masterpiece of rhetoric was obligatory, particularly in an 'epic' play. Its first half centres round a striking image: a peaceful human face physically distorted by rage into the mask of 'grim-visaged war', nostrils flared, teeth set, eyes staring. The second half appeals to pride of family and of country, to a consciousness of national worth about to be tested, before Henry's own face distorts in the roar of the battle-cry. The material on which he must bring his inspiration to bear is immediately underlined by the next scene. Shakespeare obviously cannot – as he keeps reminding us through the Chorus – show the siege of Harfleur, but he can illustrate the responses of the combatants. Bardolph's first line is a broken, comic reminiscence of Henry's own – quite serious, though; but the old sweats and bravos of Eastcheap, Nym and Pistol, are finding things too hot for their liking, and the poor Boy would rather have a pot of ale than any amount of glory. (There is more than an echo of Falstaff here: see pp. 169f.) Fluellen enters in high rage and drives them on, leaving the Boy behind. Alone, he outlines his contempt for their cowardice and their thieving – and their silliness in both. It is such men that Henry has to turn into heroes.

But Fluellen, Captain Jamy and Captain Macmorris are another matter, comic as they are. (There were stage Welshmen, Irishmen and Scotsmen in Elizabethan theatre, as there are in our own.) Their disputes are comic and longwinded, but they are about the art of war and the serious matter in hand – unlike the ludicrous quarrel of Nym and Bardolph in II.i; here are representatives of the whole of Britain uniting in the king's service and sinking their pride and difference in a common purpose.

Shakespeare has not given Henry a simple attitude to war. Henry has been convinced his war is just, and we ought to accept that the audience would have agreed, whatever our own feelings. Shakespeare shows him proceeding on the course that he lays out for him very carefully and thoughtfully – even cautiously. If his claim to the throne of France is just, then the war the French engage in by rejecting his claim is a civil war – 'impious war', as he calls it at III.iii.15. He is therefore acting according to Elizabethan ideas with every bit as much – and more – justice and legitimacy as Henry IV did in putting down the rebellions of his reign. His ambassadors gave the French a chance to agree, and warned them of the consequences; by refusing, they accepted the graphically realized horrors of an invasion. So Henry proceeds to his first campaign at Harfleur. But before committing his troops to the sack of the town, he stops, and gives the Governor another chance to acknowledge his lordship. His speech at III.iii.1ff. is imperious, frightening; he spells out what happens when a city is sacked – something Elizabethans knew all about, from the upheavals in the Low Countries. It is not a nice picture. The images of violence, pain, fire, devils and monsters swirl in and out of the speech to make a picture that chills the blood. The soldier whose blood is up is like a hunting-dog, 'fleshed', mowing down without remorse children and young girls, deflowering[8] them even while they shriek and their old fathers have their brains knocked out against the walls. This hellish picture is further intensified by images that send us

8. The imagery is extremely complex in lines 13–14. We think of death as a reaper of all flesh, which, as the Bible says, is grass; but superimposed on this is a strange and grotesque mixture of sexuality (death was often at this time pictured as a grotesque lover) and spring-like growth unnaturally destroyed. Indeed, once again Virgilian agricultural images come into play, but Virgil never achieved this astonishing denseness of reference.

back to the Mystery play of the Massacre of the Holy Innocents – babies spitted and jerking on the swords and spears of Herod's men while their mothers look on.[9]

Henry does not want this to happen – he is himself horrified by the picture – but he has the wisdom to know the limits of command: no general, in wars from Troy to Vietnam, has ever been able to control his troops in victory. And he is trapped; he cannot raise the siege and end the war now, for what is done cannot be undone. He has to play the role of king through to the end. The only way out of this horrible fate is for the town to acknowledge his lordship. When it does, instead of the punishment it might deserve for resisting in the first place he commands Exeter to 'Use mercy to them all'. For mercy (see below, p. 168) becomes the throned monarch better than his crown.

The daring juxtaposition of this tense moment and the little scene with Katherine (III.iv) works interestingly. The scene is charming. After the noise and heat of battle that the language has conjured up, there follows this picture of peace and quiet and innocence, with a delicate play of cross-language bawdy (see Chapter 11, pp. 188f.). The violent rapes of Henry's imagination give way to hints of peaceful and willing dalliance. The scene serves a particular purpose: it shows us the future Queen of England, whose femininity will complement and complete the manhood of her king. But a darker side shows in this symbol of the innocence that war might have destroyed. The war, however just, is a terrible risk, and might destroy the very thing it sought to win.

However glorious and admirable as a war-leader Henry may be, therefore, Shakespeare has not presented us with a simplistic view either of human conflict or of the man himself. Throughout the four plays, from Richard's and Carlisle's prophecies onwards, the horror of war has constantly been realized. The little people do suffer in the conflicts of the mighty, and the vulnerable and guiltless new growth is uprooted by its terrible storm. The question must be asked: how can a war be just, fought (as Henry's is) in the name of a just and merciful God, and yet perpetrate such unjust cruelty? The answer, which the play faces squarely, lies in the very nature of man in his fallen state. As we have seen above (Chapter I.ii and vi), God gave man not only a nodal position in the chain of being, but free-will so that he could be a responsible moral person and not a mere automaton. That freedom necessarily

9. A stained glass in St Peter Mancroft, Norwich, shows this scene from the cycle of plays. Dolls would be used, of course, which could be made to jerk realistically by shaking the sword.

entails the possibility of refusing to do God's will, and this means that man's decisions will have effects far beyond himself. Man fell in Eden and the whole earth subject to him inevitably suffered, not for any sin of its own but because its governor had failed in his responsibility to it. In his mercy, as Augustine said, God instituted states and law to contain the effects of the Fall (see above, p. 104), but the Fall could not be undone, nor could the intimate connection between man's actions and the world he lived in be severed. Strife became a condition of man's existence. War was a consequence not of God's will but of man's refusal to obey it; and when the mighty disobeyed the right, their subjects suffered because of the structure of the world and society within it. The king thus shoulders a frightful responsibility, and Henry is agonizedly aware of it. Hence his caution on starting the war and in conducting it, and his appeals to the French to reconsider their disobedience; hence the responsibility for the suffering of the innocent lies on those who refuse, as the devils refused, the right. But if war is a consequence of the disorder caused by human sin, God's providence can nevertheless use it to punish the guilty and redress the disorder of the world into a temporary balance – before the next round of sin caused by man's fallen state. 'War is His beadle' (IV.i.164) – that is, his policeman: the idea is not far from that which Marlowe gives to Tamburlaine, who causes cruel havoc by his conquests, seeing himself with huge pride as 'the scourge of God'. War, however horrible, is thus somehow purging and cleansing; it is also a necessary consequence of human freedom and the love God showed for man in giving him that freedom.

But while Henry accepts his own, and King Charles's, peculiar responsibility, there are limits to it. The issue is discussed acutely in the conversation with Bates and Williams (IV.i). The peasant sense of Williams is sceptical of the disguised Henry's assertion of the 'king's cause being just and his quarrel honourable' (ll. 123–4): 'That's more than we know.' Bates sees, however, that they are not qualified to judge the issue, and that if they as individual soldiers behave as good subjects even in a bad cause, they are guiltless of that cause's guilt. Williams rejoins that if the cause is not good, the king must bear a 'heavy reckoning' (l. 131) for leading men to their deaths before they could put their own souls in order – that is, he must carry not only the responsibility for his own misjudgement but for the damnation of those who might die in sin. With careful logic Henry demonstrates that this cannot be so (ll. 143ff.) and the individual soldiers must be responsible for their own moral conduct as individuals in so far as it is based on their own choice and actions –

this the king cannot take on himself: 'Every subject's duty is the king's; but every subject's soul is his own' (ll. 171–2). War is no excuse for conduct that would be evil and immoral in peace, even in the heat of the sack of a town like Harfleur. The effective argument convinces Williams and Bates,[10] and is yet another demonstration of Henry's power of leadership and his possession of that inspiring common touch that can make a ruler not just obeyed but loved. (When Henry later reveals himself to Williams in IV.viii, he does so with such grace, humour and generosity that the 200-year-old tradition of Henry as an exceptional king of men becomes credible indeed.)

Henry's reaction to this conversation (ll. 218ff.) is his only soliloquy in the play (it is briefly interrupted by Erpingham, recalling Henry to his public duties), and that alone is enough to signal its significance. He reveals as nowhere else in the play the deepest elements in himself; and the speech shows him not only as a philosopher who understands the burden of rule, but also as an honest man. He explores more deeply the attitude to the crown we glimpsed in his reaction to his father's sickness in *2 Henry IV* (and Henry IV himself, in his guilt, observed: 'Uneasy lies the head that wears a crown'; cf. *2 Henry IV*, III.i.4–31 and IV.v.22ff.). He is no longer an observer, though; he wears it himself and knows its cost. He is lonely; the king is separated by his role from his subjects, yet he is a man as they are, and his crown cannot cure his ills. The common labourer knows delights of rest and sleep and simple honest work the king can only envy, and the king must take responsibility, at great personal cost, for providing the conditions in which the peasant can sleep in peace (ll. 272ff.). The king must bear, too, the blame the commons put upon him without thought. In this moment of stillness in the play, before the great clash of Agincourt, Henry has found himself and accepted the full implications of the hard condition of a king, on whose decisions rest both peace and war. As his prayer confirms (ll. 283ff.), he has not only committed his cause to God but also accepted his own sinfulness and his inheritance of guilt. His pious acts cannot undo that primal Fall, be it Richard's murder or the Fall of man. He, like his subjects, is under judgement, dependent on the mercy of God. The Chorus opening this act reminded us of the terrible tension between the

10. In III.vi.104–7 we saw Henry putting it into practice when he condemned Bardolph for behaving as soldiers all too often do: 'We would have all such offenders so cut off: and we give express charge, that in our marches through the country there be nothing compelled from the villages, nothing taken but paid for . . .' Bardolph receives the same impartial justice as the traitors. War is no suspension of the moral imperatives. (See p. 169.)

public face on whose confidence and courage everyone depends, and the pain and fear felt by the inner man. We have seen both in action in this scene.

The depth and thoughtfulness of Henry's understanding of his role and conduct is illuminated by the contrast with the French reactions to his campaign. In III.v, after the quiet delicacy of the scene with Katherine, the French Court – thirty nobles on stage at once, nearly all to be killed at Agincourt – explodes in anger and hurt pride, at once mystified by the success of the enemy and scornful of them. The Dauphin is particularly strident. The French do not pray; they merely swear. Here is no policy, merely folly. The Constable, against all the warnings of the siege of Harfleur, wishes the enemy stronger so that the *personal* glory of defeating them might be the greater.[11] There is strong contrast with the (comic) pride in their mastery of the practical arts of war that Fluellen and Macmorris have shown in III.ii and the quiet dignity and efficiency of Henry. When Henry receives the insulting message insultingly delivered by Montjoy (III.vi.116ff.), his self-control shows in his firm and courteous reply. There is no Dauphin-like bravado; he is aware that his army is small, tired, sick, yet – 'God before' (l. 154) – he will advance. Gloucester's trepidation (l. 166; cf. IV.i.1ff.) only elicits once more Henry's confidence that his cause is 'in God's hand' (l. 167).

In the scene that takes place the night before Agincourt, Shakespeare has shown us the king understanding, in his isolation, the burden he must bear; the same scene also shows us an army tense, serious, yet united by the personality of Henry. Against this is set, in point for point contrast, the other, deliberately parallel, night scene in the French camp (III.vii). While the English are serious, tense, fearful, the French nobles are longing for the night to pass. Henry visits his soldiers and understands them; the Dauphin is insufferable, boastful, praising his horse – it is not even a proper warhorse! – to a ludicrous degree. He is insulting to the Constable, and there is an undertone of mere quarrelsomeness for its own sake that only the Constable's good humour prevents from flaring into open anger. This is not the sensitivity to the real issue of the king's trustworthiness that lies behind the ironic comedy of Williams's quarrel with Henry – just the sort of thing that might happen in moments of such tension – which is rapidly smoothed by Bates. The Dauphin and

11. Henry in his victory gave the glory to God, and was glad his army was so small: the risk to his country was so much less (IV.iii.18ff.).

Rambures are stupidly over-confident, holding their enemy in derision. Yet the Constable, far more sensible and experienced than the others, suggests that the Dauphin's courage and abilities are strictly limited (ll. 89ff.). The picture is not a flattering one, and in the Dauphin we see what royalty should not be. The contrast with Henry's attitude to war could hardly be greater.[12]

We see the same qualities in IV.ii. The Constable's speech (ll. 13ff.), another 'general's address to his soldiers', obviously contrasts with Henry's before Harfleur. Its over-confidence and contempt for the enemy is not simply ironic – for we know that Henry will win the battle; it illustrates a godless tempting of Providence, a regret that the slaughter will not be greater. Set against this the humanity, humour, true honour, generosity and courage of Henry's rallying call to his army in IV.iii, where the idea of the king as leader of a united *country* is brought vividly to life. This is where all the discussions of honour in the Henry IV plays reach their climax; the very tones of Hotspur – a Hotspur who, unlike the Dauphin, has grown up – are heard in

> But if it be a sin to covet honour,
> I am the most offending soul alive.[13]

(ll. 28-9)

Montjoy's second arrival (IV.iii.79) reminds us of Henry's appeal to the Governor of Harfleur to surrender; but the only mention of mercy is ironic – a suggestion that the soldiers make a good confession before their inevitable deaths. Henry's reply is gallant and even manages humour; but underneath, as the hypermetric line (l. 128) musingly reveals, he knows their plight is dangerous.

The success of Henry – beautifully conveyed by the verbal slapstick of IV.iv, where even Pistol, the comic simulacrum of soldierly valour, wins a prisoner – throws the French into angry and horrified confusion (IV.v). Even the Dauphin at last recognizes the real nature of the enemy. The reaction is to lead a counter-attack to retrieve 'honour' by a pointless

12. Shakespeare has neatly avoided a tricky problem here. He has to have an opponent to Henry who will contrast with him in almost every way – in attitude to honour, humility, relations with his fellows, lack of policy, and so on. And we have to dislike him. But he could not portray King Charles like this, as he needed to keep him reasonably credible as a future party to the peace and father-in-law of Henry. So he carefully keeps Charles in the background and pushes the Dauphin forward.

13. The speech looks forward to a future that is the Elizabethan past, where Agincourt is a legend of a monarch and people united in a common and glorious purpose.

death – not the honourable and noble death of York, recounted by Exeter (IV.vi.7ff.), but an attack that is far from noble. Its fruit is the killing of the unarmed boys of the baggage train. Fluellen, from whom we hear of it first, is horrified by this breach of the law of arms (IV. vii.1ff.). Gower's anger leads him to applaud Henry's reported order for an action that would be equally horrific: to cut the throats of the prisoners (ll. 8–10). But Henry, angry and shocked as he is, is no butcher; he is prepared to do this only if the French – the Dauphin and others, who did not take part in the attack – do not join the fight, or leave the battlefield (ll. 56–7). Even here, in the heat of battle, the motive is to limit further slaughter.

Casualty lists are never pretty reading. But the size of the English victory, emphasized by the roll-call of the great names of France fallen in this field (IV.viii.75ff.), had a central place in the Elizabethans' myth of their own history, just as their defeat of the Armada had for later generations. Shakespeare could have shown Henry here simply as the glorious and triumphant king and got away with it. In fact he makes him turn right away from any pride, ascribing the honour and glory to God alone. His first thought is of humble gratitude and of his own littleness in the eye of Providence. The seriousness of the faith of this mirror of all Christian kings has been tested in the furnace, and God has vindicated him. He is a holy monarch. In line 106 he quotes the first verse of what is now Psalm 115 in the English Prayer Book, and later orders it to be sung in thanksgiving (l. 122); it is one of the psalms of celebration of God's deliverance of his chosen people Israel from their enemies, and in the Vulgate Latin text is part of Psalm 114, which begins: 'When Israel came out of Egypt, and the House of Jacob from among a strange people'. The link in Henry's – and the audience's – mind between the English army defended by God from the power of the French and the Israelites' escape across the Red Sea from Pharaoh's army is quite open. Then and in later times, many Englishmen (in particular the Puritans) saw their nation as a holy country in whose affairs Providence frequently took a hand, as God had intervened in the politics of Israel. Such a country needs a monarch who will be both a David and a Solomon.[14] Henry is shown to have been both, and a mirror for future monarchs.

14. This issue is too complex to go into in detail, but the evidence for this assertion is manifold. It can be found in quotations from the Bible, especially the Psalms, in prints like that of the defeat of the Armada, in Christian names (particularly of Puritans), and in the literary use of biblical history as a cover for discussion of English affairs, for example in Dryden's *Absalom and Achitophel* or Milton's *Samson Agonistes*. One specific example of the

So far we have only seen Henry at war, or preparing for it. The arts of peace belong to a monarch too, and Act V concentrates on these. Before taking us on in time (five years) to the final peace, the Chorus to Act V describes the return to London in a triumphal procession quite proper to a conqueror, but here again the emphasis is on Henry being 'free from vainness and self-glorious pride'. Once more there is a heightening comparison – this time to Julius Caesar, another of the Nine Worthies (see p. 150, and below, p. 167).[15]

But a conqueror must be judged not just by the battles he has fought but the peace he concludes, and it is that which constitutes the business of this final act. The complex tableau of the peacemaking is preceded by the lightness of V.i, where Pistol gets his comic come-uppance at the hands of the delightful Fluellen. It is not mere diversion; symbolically it is integral to what follows, for here, in the comic mode, the proper ruler shows up the fake for the deceit and silliness it is. As Henry re-establishes England and the crown, so Fluellen cleanses the English camp of the fakes and the cheats and the rogues. We have had plenty of time to observe both Fluellen and Pistol in the play, and the similarities between them emphasize a deep contrast. Both of them maul the language to the point of occasional incomprehensibility; both are proud to a fault; both love Henry (Pistol may be taken as sincere in IV.i.44ff.); but Fluellen is a real soldier and an honest man, not the mere appearance of both that Pistol has attempted (sometimes with success) to sustain. (In III.vi.12ff. it is clear that he managed to fool Fluellen himself for a time.) The scene is important, since it dramatizes in Fluellen's punishment of Pistol the final rejection and discomfiture of all false honour and pretence. Pistol's grotesque language is a mere extension to nonsense of the hyperbolic posturing that heroes, in and out of plays, are often given to. His connection with the *miles gloriosus* of Roman comedy should not blind us to his connection with the selfish, sterile, hyperbolic honour of Hotspur and the Dauphin, while his capture of Monsieur le Fer must remind us of Falstaff's similar capture – by illusion – of Colevile of the Dale. Real

Puritan vision of England's troubles must suffice: in 1646, John Hancock published a print entitled 'Englands [*sic*] Miraculous Preservation Emblematically Described', where the Civil War is seen in terms of the successful weathering of a storm by an Ark – an Ark, doubtless, of the Solemn League and Covenant! – in which, with unconscious comedy, are the House of Commons, the Lords, and the Assembly of the Church of Scotland. Various royal and royalist figures float in the waves.

15. Lines 29ff. refer to what was hoped of Essex; the topicality might extend a good deal – and dangerously – further.

honour appropriate to his rank is shown by the honest, frank, not frightfully eloquent, touchy Fluellen – who, indeed, in his love for and pride in Henry, signals to us one very important standard of assessment (see below, p. 167).[16]

But the world is not cleansed finally; it will always have its Pistol. He sets off for a new career as bawd, thief and professional Old Soldier. who fakes wounds and scars in order to beg the better. (The number of vagrant old soldiers – genuine or not – begging in this way was one of the scandals of Shakespeare's age, incidentally.) Falstaff, at the end of *1 Henry IV*, merely did the same thing on a larger and more barefaced scale. Eastcheap will always be with us.

The second scene divides into three parts: the full Court scene, the wooing of Katherine by Henry, and the final conclusion of the peace. In the first section the dominating speech is that of Burgundy, the peace-maker, but before he speaks the queen gives a striking reminiscence of Henry's own conceit before Harfleur – of the face distorted by anger into that of 'grim-visaged war' (V.ii.14ff.); now, the 'venom of such looks . . ./have lost their quality'. Burgundy, as I have said above (p. 110), pulls together all the garden/farming images of the four plays in a formal and exhaustive catalogue of the disorder in the kingdom – a disorder caused by the war against her true master. Vines, hedges, fields and meadows all need tending, the weeds must be uprooted, and the tide of blood must be turned back by a proper gardener. The whole catalogue is governed by the personification of peace that introduces it:

> *Why that the naked, poor, and mangled peace,*
> *Dear nurse of arts, plenties, and joyful births,*
> *Should not in this best garden of the world,*
> *Our fertile France, put up her lovely visage?*

(ll. 34–7)

The pathos of this personification of peace as vulnerable, abused femininity focuses the images of rape and sexual violence that have been insistent accompaniments to the war. (Interestingly, the French when invaded saw their honour as somehow sexually connected: cf. III.v.5ff., 27ff.; IV.v.15–16.) As the delegates leave to discuss the treaty, Peace herself puts up her lovely visage. For just as the delicacy of the earlier scene with Katherine – which on the personal level more than

16. Notice how his feelings almost get the better of him in IV.vii.90ff. Henry's replies to him are very gentle, and the little vignette heightens the emotions felt in the moment of success by, as it were, defusing them.

suggested her interest in King Henry – made visible the femininity that war could debauch and destroy, this part of the scene works both as a delicate wooing of the two persons, with all the charm of Henry's soldierly gaucheness, and also uses Katherine as a symbol of that peace that will be restored in the marriage of the two kingdoms. She is, as Henry says, 'our capital demand' (l. 96). But philosophers like Erasmus had stressed that a marriage merely for the sake of an alliance was likely to lead to further strife. Shakespeare is at pains to show us, within the conventions of the stage, that this is a love-match too.

The switch to prose signals a drop to intimacy and privacy after the publicity of the Court. It shows Henry in a most attractive, entirely new, light. He is, we know, witty and fond of word-play, but in the Henry IV plays that wit had been at someone else's expense. Here it is at his own. He is eloquent, yet his long prose speech is uncomfortable in its rhythms, embarrassed and confused in its argument, lacking in any of the devices of the stage wooer. For a moment we are reminded of the curiously attractive clumsiness of Hotspur with Lady Percy. And his conclusion is that 'a good heart, Kate, is the sun and the moon – or rather, the sun, and not the moon; for it shines bright and never changes, but keeps his course truly'. This is what this sun-like king is offering. The scene is completely convincing and suddenly makes the hero entirely human and believable. The 'silken dalliance' the youth of England left in the wardrobe for the war (II, Chorus, l. 2) is worn again. The divorce of king from country symbolized by the separation of Richard from Isabel is healed; these lovers, unlike Glendower's daughter and Mortimer, can understand each other despite the barrier of language (see Chapter 11).

The return of the rest of the Court confirms, as expected, Henry's title to France. Peace is concluded. But before that announcement is made, Shakespeare includes a striking prose passage between Henry and Burgundy, the imagery of which is of the greatest importance. The marriage of Katherine and Henry, the male aggressive and the female receptive, is of course a symbol of the equilibrium of balanced opposites that constitutes the best peace man can hope for; Katherine is France and Henry England. But Shakespeare draws in other ideas through a chain of sexual word-play. 'Conjure up the spirit of love' (ll. 284–5) has an obvious play on 'spirit', and Mercutio uses virtually this phrase to Romeo; 'conjure', though, introduces ideas of *magia* (see p. 19), which Burgundy picks up. The spirit of love, Cupid, will be called up 'naked and blind', which leads into other plays on 'wink', 'yield', 'do', 'stands', 'girdled', 'walls', 'will', and so on. Now this joyous playing with the idea of sexual intercourse transposes into the major key the subtheme in the imagery throughout, of war as *violently* sexual; it has a last echo here (ll. 355–8). This congress is willing and willed without destroying proper feminine modesty. But the aim of the magus was the 'alchemical marriage' of opposites in a balance that would be healing and harmonious, and go some way towards restoring the image of Eden on earth. The imagery delicately suggests this hope for Katherine and Henry, perhaps even suggests the necessity for this in Elizabethan politics. Moreover, the symbolism of Katherine is underlined both by her lover, 'who cannot see many a fair French city for one fair French maid that stands in [his] way', and by her father in his response: 'Yes, my lord, you see them perspectively,[17] the cities turned into a maid; for they are all girdled with maiden walls, that war hath never entered.' The obvious reference to virginity hides from us another neat visual allusion. Cities were often depicted allegorically as women, crowned with a crown of walls. Katherine 'is' these cities of France that she will bring with her as her dowry to her lord.

And so in the mystery of marriage the just war is over, the rebellion quenched, the effects of the fall stayed for an interim. The land can be cultivated once more, and the gardener knows his job. In one sense the ending of *Henry V* is comic *at this point*, for the ideal king has found himself and his role, is married to his kingdom in a harmony that reminds us of that costly harmony at the end of some of Shakespeare's comedies. But the cost, public and private, has been huge, and payment will continue to be exacted till the day of doom. For the play does not end with peace and the marriage; it closes with the Chorus predicting, in a regular Shakespearean sonnet, what the audience knew had actually happened – the loss of all that Henry had won.

The choice of a sonnet is itself of interest. Sonnets, to most of us, are just sonnets; but the Elizabethans recognized several different types which did specific jobs. Shakespeare's choice of the sonnet form (as in the first meeting of Romeo and Juliet) is therefore a signal to the audience, at the very least of a serious and aphoristic overview of the experience of the play. It begins and ends with the difficulties of the medium – a favourite idea, the inadequacy of words or vision to compass reality.

17. The word has changed its meaning. A perspective could mean a distorted picture that, viewed from a different angle, suddenly became lifelike. There are many Renaissance examples – the famous portrait of Edward VI, for example, or the skull in Holbein's 'The Ambassadors', that was designed to be seen from the side and above. (The painting was meant to hang at the foot of a staircase.)

This is, indeed, how the play began. But in the third quatrain, which builds up to the conventional emphatic pause before the final couplet, the Chorus looks forward to the loss of France by Henry VI. 'So many had the managing' of his state that Henry V's achievement was undone, and, in a last and striking return of the images of *Richard II* and the opening of *1 Henry IV*, 'made his England bleed'. This is history, and the material of Shakespeare's own popular *1 Henry VI*; but it is also a deliberate and open warning. If the state is not united in counsel, as in the 1590s England was not, if the wrong counsellors have the prince's ear, then England will bleed again. The ideal monarch is but a man, and men die. Elizabeth had not yet named an heir, and was obviously nearing her end.

We must therefore return briefly to that picture of the monarch Shakespeare has given us. He is a just prince and a good man, who understands his people, be they Pistol who bumps into him (significantly, in the dark), or Fluellen, or Williams; he understands his father too. We have in him a deliberate conflation of the ideal of a Christian man whose every act is felt to be in God's eye, and the classically derived 'Aristotelian mean' – the man in whom passions are felt but controlled, who knows himself for what he is and avoids excess in any particular. Then add to this the ideal of Christian kingship, where king, people and Church act in concert: the play shows Henry harnessing not only the support of the Church and his nobles to the cause, but also that of the common people, down to the very rogues. Finally, Henry is linked to the great conqueror Alexander (see above, p. 150), but surpasses him. Fluellen's delicious attempt to find parallel incidents in the lives of the two men (IV.vii.12–51) is highly comic. Pedant that he is, versed (not very well) in the ancients, he constructs in the proper rhetorical manner a 'comparison' between the two. He compares the places where they were born, seeking similarities between the Monmouth he knows and the Macedon he does not, and then moves on to look for parallel events in the lives of the two. All he can manage is the dissimilarity between Alexander killing Cleitus when drunk and (significant!) a sober Hal turning away Falstaff. Behind the humour is something serious; Henry is actually superior to the great Alexander, for he is a Christian and not a pagan prince.

The true hero knows when to fight and when to seek peace, when to beat the ploughshare into the sword and when to return to the field. Before Harfleur his imagery, particularly his pun on 'metal', kept alive the notion of an England of farmers suddenly and exceptionally called to labour in a different field:

> *And you, good yeomen,*
> *Whose limbs were made in England, show us here*
> *The mettle of your pasture,*

(III.i.25–7)

who sold their pasture to buy their warhorses (II, Chorus, ll. 3–5). But summoning up the blood must have an end and the fields must be ploughed after the blood has been shed for another harvest. Behind the glory of the figure and the reign of Henry, Shakespeare lets us see the shadows. And they will not go away. All flesh is grass, the grass withereth, and the flower thereof fadeth away. Here is no abiding city, and there will never be peace on earth, for man is fallen.

And so man – all men – can only throw themselves on God's mercy. They must work, labour in the vineyard in the heat of the day, for that is a condition of existence, but in the end it is God's mercy that will save or not. The prince, as God's vice-gerent, needs that mercy too, but is also in peculiar need of the quality of mercifulness. This is the attribute of power that validates all the others; it is in this that a king may be called, as with unconscious irony the Duchess of York calls Bolingbroke, 'a god on earth':

> *The quality of mercy is not strain'd,*
> *It droppeth as the gentle rain from heaven*
> *Upon the place beneath: it is twice blest,*
> *It blesseth him that gives and him that takes,*
> *'Tis mightiest in the mightiest; it becomes*
> *The throned monarch better than his crown.*
> *His sceptre shows the force of temporal power,*
> *The attribute to awe and majesty,*
> *Wherein doth sit the dread and fear of kings;*
> *But mercy is above this sceptred sway,*
> *It is enthroned in the hearts of kings,*
> *It is an attribute of God himself;*
> *And earthly power doth then show likest God's*
> *When mercy seasons justice . . .*
> *. . . in the course of justice, none of us*
> *Should see salvation: we do pray for mercy,*
> *And that same prayer doth teach us all to render*
> *The deeds of mercy.*
> (*The Merchant of Venice,* IV.i.180ff.)

## Epilogue: the first version of Henry V

The evidence we have of the Oldcastle scandal, the promise of the Epilogue to *2 Henry IV*, and certain lines still in *Henry V* as we have it, make it probable that there was an earlier version of the play, and some suggestions can be made about its structure and interest.

If the original play did indeed have Falstaff in it, a real and significant pattern seems to emerge of three contrasting 'kingdoms':

### 1. FRANCE
King Charles, supported by various French nobles, among whom the Dauphin and the Constable show the dangers of ill counsel;

### 2. WESTMINSTER
King Henry, supported by various nobles, among whom Scroop, Grey and Cambridge exemplify a kingdom not yet united;

### 3. EASTCHEAP
Falstaff (Lord of Misrule), supported by various quarrelsome lower classes, especially Bardolph, Nym and Pistol.

All the characters are tested and weeded out by the processes of a war in pursuit of Henry's right and duty to rule all three 'kingdoms'. As it happens, the French Court (and King Charles) passes from the bad counsel of the Dauphin to the good counsel of Burgundy; Henry's noble followers are people like Exeter, Erpingham and Westmorland, who are united behind his leadership; and in place of the Eastcheap group Fluellen and Williams represent a purged and faithful breed of subjects. These characters are brought forward for their loyalty and ability, and the qualities they display in the course of the play. War is after all 'God's beadle', which he uses through his intermediary on earth, Henry, to separate wheat from chaff. At the end of the play, Henry is king of all three kingdoms.

However, this structure must break down with the removal of the extreme embodiment of the values of Eastcheap, Falstaff, and in performance the play becomes occasionally very odd to watch. What were presumably Falstaff's comments on his companions are given to the Boy. These direct conversations with the audience (much more direct even than soliloquies) distort the play; and the casual death of the page distracts the audience's attention from the victory Henry has won.

Again, the absence of Falstaff from the night scene before Agincourt means that Shakespeare has no opportunity for what would have been a splendid final conflict between the king and the world he appeared to inhabit as Prince Hal – an encounter that would beautifully have echoed that between Prince Hal and Falstaff at Shrewsbury. Echoing the Gadshill episode of *1 Henry IV*, where he did not know the disguised true prince, a failure by Falstaff, like Pistol, to recognize the king in the dark could have led elegantly to a final and public rejection of Falstaff.

This later charge (if so it be) in *Henry V* makes Henry's provisional rejection of Falstaff at the end of *2 Henry IV* final – which, in fact, the text does not suggest it was, despite the unease many feel at Falstaff's exit. A possibility of Henry's favour being given again is hinted at, if Falstaff reforms. In *Henry V* all the denizens of Eastcheap are given an opportunity to redeem themselves by Henry – the fact that they do not places the full moral responsibility for their actions, and their fates, upon themselves rather than upon Henry.

# 11. A Trim Reckoning: Language, Poetics and Rhetoric

There is no doubting the contemporary and general importance of the issues Shakespeare raises in these four plays. They may be summed up, indeed, as an examination of the predicament of fallen men caught in a world where as moral beings they have to make decisions and choices without knowing all the limits set on them, or the consequences of their choice. Moreover, we are explicitly not watching historical reality, but an illusion created in the theatre by the words the playwright (himself a man in history, caught in the same web) gives his characters to speak. The medium of the plays, language itself, and contemporary attitudes to it, therefore demand our attention.

For along with the discussion of the idea of England and her polity which I have suggested is central to these plays, I would argue that Shakespeare has been exploring the very speech itself that identifies men as English, its resources, its relation to truth and reality, the way the individual creates in it the world he inhabits – and the ironies of the clash of those individual worlds. He is not in the least unusual in this, for at the end of the sixteenth century and throughout the seventeenth, English was being self-consciously 'discovered' as a language, and the analysis of words attracted practically everyone's attention in one way or another. This interest may on the one hand take the form of serious analytical discussion of language theory – as in Bacon's *Advancement of Learning* (1605) or Jonson's *English Grammar* (1640); on the other, it may manifest itself in the dictionaries of thieves' cant or slang which were often included from the end of the sixteenth century in popular catchpenny, sensational 'rogue pamphlets' describing the criminal world which has always been both feared and envied by respectable citizens. The demonstrable interest in language *qua* language of Shakespeare and his contemporaries has profound implications for the styles and utterance Shakespeare gives his creatures. And when we recognize the central metaphor of the Fall and its consequences that dominates these four plays, that issue becomes even more urgent. For how can the Fall be undone when language itself is fallen?[1]

1. The issue does not go away. Most readers of this book will be familiar with Milton's

So we cannot pass from these four plays without at least airing this problem; and we cannot examine it without first glancing at how Shakespeare's predecessors and contemporaries thought about language. The issue is not a small one: how could language and words not be a central and conscious concern, in the front of all thinking men's minds in an age when the crux of the Reformation theological debate lay precisely in the *meaning* and *utterance* of the words in the Gospels and in St Paul's writings? Did the language of the Bible relate to real things existing independently of their description, or was language merely a convention among human beings that, ultimately, could only discuss itself? Armies marched and men were burnt over whether the Greek word *dichaion* meant 'make righteous' (the sense of the Latin *justificare*) or 'pronounce righteous'. The number of books on language, its theories, forms and uses published between 1500 and 1700 is huge, and there is not the slightest doubt that no one of even the most minimal education could have avoided stubbing their toes on the issue. At the heart of the way men thought about these things are the notions of the creating Word of God (Genesis i), uttering all that is into being, the language of Adam and the myth of the Tower of Babel (Genesis xi). It is only when we grasp this fact and its implications that the significance of the vast number of medieval and Renaissance engravings and paintings – for example the one by Breughel – of the Tower of Babel becomes clear (see p. 173).

## i *The problem of language*

The Creation was an act of speech – speech that immediately, without intermediary or hindrance, makes real what is in the will of God. The Trinitarian understanding of the Deity identified the Son with the all-creating Word, and borrowed and modified from the Platonists the concept of the *logos* ('word') as the creating activity of the divine mind. This is more than metaphor; for how does the Platonist or the Christian connect the concept of the eternal deity of whom nothing can be predicated with a world of predicated things, except by means of the will, the Word, of the deity expressing itself eternally *in* that world? So it is the Word itself that gives life to all the ranks of creation.

But this problem, though it fixes for us the crucial idea of speech as action and 'realizing', is too high for human beings. We have problems

problem in *Paradise Lost*, where he has to represent a pre-lapsarian world with post-lapsarian language, and the strategies he chose to cope with it.

enough. In Eden, when Adam was yet unfallen his unclouded eyes saw Truth in all her naked beauty and he walked with Him who is Truth in the cool of the evening, as a man with his friend. One of Adam's first tasks was to give names to all created things over which God had given him absolute rule, and those names expressed and conveyed the inner, real nature of those things without the possibility of confusion – a language that was literally knowledge. As A. Richardson put it long after Shakespeare's death, '*Adam*, by seeing into the nature of every Creature, could see their names, though we cannot do it' (*The Logician's School Master*, London, 1657, p. 13). Milton presents his Adam as doing just this: 'My tongue obeyed and readily could name/What e'er I saw' (*Paradise Lost*, VIII.272–3); 'I named them, as they passed, and understood/Their nature' (VIII.352–3). His language penetrated the surface of things, because the surface, multiform and capable of being seen from different angles as it is, is confusing. It moved directly to inner nature. Adam's language was everywhere comprehensible, not ambiguous like modern speech or writing; and this complete 'knowing in language' was both the means and the mark of Adam's power over nature.

This desirable situation was spoilt first by the Fall. Adam's reason, the faculty he alone of the material creation shared with the angels, was clouded – not extinguished, but newly fallible. Yet for a time his descendants spoke his language, the inheritance of one family. But after the Flood, the first great punishment for sin and the prefigurement of the Last Judgement, their pride led them to seek to build a great tower in the land of Shinar, which would reach up to Heaven itself. The commentators on the passage in Genesis xi emphasize the ease with which they all, whatever their nations and trades, understood each other. They were capable, as man has never been since, of perfect cooperation. Just such perfect understanding is represented in the diligent and total cooperation of all trades in the building of the magnificent structure Breughel depicted, and man's power was unlimited. But God confounded their language so that they did not understand each other's speech. Language itself was now fallen, and ceased to bear an exact communicable correspondence to the nature of things. Dante is neither the first nor the last philosopher to see all the world's languages as ultimately deriving from this mythic moment when, in a second Fall, men were divided by their labours and saw only a part of the whole of reality (*Inferno*, XXXI.76ff.; *De Volgari Eloquentia*, I.4.4.). A quite serious aim in the minds of many men, in the Renaissance and later, is the finding of a true language, isomorphic to reality, which will undo the damage of Babel and once more restore to man the dominion over nature Adam possessed. The linguistic researches of the seventeenth century (see Appendix) which embody this aim are intimately connected with what, with hindsight, we see as the growth of the empirical scientific approach. It is no accident that, among many others, Bacon saw his programme for reform in the arts and sciences as depending a good deal on clearing up the mess language had got itself into, nor that the philosophers of the Port-Royal in France and those who came to form the Royal Society in England were so interested in the understanding of how language worked, and in its reform. For words are power. By the late sixteenth century, no one of any intelligence whose business was writing – including playwrights – could have been unaware of the problem of the relationship between words, language,[2] and the perception or description of the world. The issue is so fundamental to the background of Elizabethan and Jacobean poetry and drama that I have felt compelled to include in a book already long enough (and more) an Appendix (p. 199, below) summarizing the main outline of the discussion.

From Antiquity and throughout the Middle Ages, there had been thorough and serious discussion of the nature of human cognition, the part played by words in it, and the nature of speech, both in itself and in relation to 'reality' and 'the world'. Plato, for example, had suggested that words were not mere labels attached to things for the sake of convenience, but that they were actually related in an organic way to them, containing within themselves the seeds of their own meaning. Aristotle, on the other hand, took the view that nouns (for example) did not have meaning in this way, but gained it by the habitual imposition of meaning on the mere sound. Ancient writers – Varro, Cicero, Quintilian, for instance – had considered these matters deeply and with extraordinary intelligence, and the Middle Ages inherited from late Antiquity[3] a programme of study which continued and developed their ideas. The seven liberal arts, the format of medieval and Renaissance learning, was deliberately divided into the *trivium*, which dealt with those arts that

2. The distinction is important. I am using 'word' and 'language' in the sense of de Saussure's *parole* and *langage* to signify respectively the particular utterances of language and the semiotic discourse into which they are put and which qualifies their individual signification (*Cours de Linguistique Générale*, 1915).

3. St Augustine, as in so many other areas, deeply influenced the discussion both by the way he responded to his classical predecessors and by his own original insights. As a professional teacher of rhetoric, he was necessarily concerned with the nature of language and the modes of signification literature could employ.

studied and exploited words, and the *quadrivium*, which examined number and measure in arithmetic, music, geometry and astronomy. The arts of the *trivium*, grammar, rhetoric and dialectic, were related but separate. Grammar was the scientific study of language and of meaning in language;[4] it could range from examination of syntactical relationships, the cement holding the bricks together, to what we would call linguistic philosophy and the detailed reading of a text – and, in a rather old-fashioned way, at the end of the fifteenth century when other conceptions were already current, this is how Perottus defines it. On a grasp of grammar depended a man's competence in the other verbal arts of rhetoric and dialectic. The distinction between these was old even when Plato, in the *Gorgias*, defined 'rational', i.e. logical, speech as that which deals with what is, while rhetorical speech is that which does not convince by means of rational knowledge but persuades by the pleasing exploitation of metaphor and other means of verbal colouring. He saw the rational as a higher form, but rhetoric as necessary to persuade men to action. An analogy first used by Zeno and often repeated in the Renaissance (for example, in England by Sir Thomas Wilson, Francis Bacon and John Donne) puts this in the form of an easily remembered[5] visual image: logic, the rational ground of the art of dialectic, is the powerful closed fist, while rhetoric is the welcoming and receptive open and extended hand.

The Renaissance, with the great benefits conferred by the recovery and subsequent general availability of so much of the writings of the ancient world, continued this analysis of speech and writing, and explored their social and political functions as well as their philosophical problems. There had been and continued to be an understanding both of the provisional nature of post-Babel human utterance, and of its crucial ability to create meaning (a world, indeed), to impose order, and to interpret the world men inhabit. Inevitably this leads to a consideration of the authority and origin of poetic utterance. Ultimately the recovery of ancient texts and the pressing need to analyse the authority and

4. The main Western tradition down to the Renaissance was to believe that words do, dimly, hint at the nature of things; the great encyclopedia of Isidore of Seville, one of the seminal texts for the Middle Ages, is not called the *Etymologiae* for nothing.

5. The accurate memorizing of quite vast bodies of material was a common skill, with arts all of its own. Here is not the place to go into a discussion of classical, medieval and Renaissance arts of memory; let me just say that many of them use a visual image or sequence of images to 'fix' often very complex abstract ideas, concepts and discussions. (Dramatic spectacle could of course be used in this way.) Those interested can start to dig deeper by looking at F. Yates, *The Art of Memory*, London, 1970.

nature of language and of the Word of Life itself led to a shattering of the old moulds and a redefinition of the accepted arts.

## ii *The nature of rhetoric*

An age like our own that uses the word 'rhetoric' in an almost exclusively pejorative sense – the sort of verbal obfuscation employed by politicians with whom we don't agree – finds it difficult to grasp the great importance of this art in Antiquity and the Renaissance. Originally the art of rhetoric was that skill in writing and speaking to best advantage, in choosing the appropriate style – grand, middle or *genus humile* – to your person, situation, audience and purpose. In its discussion of rules and techniques it was a practical discipline indispensable to life in a community where persuasion, oral or, later, written, had a major political, religious or moral place. Rhetoric became the second of the arts of the *trivium*; in the Middle Ages and the Renaissance no man of even minimal education could be ignorant of it, and fail to recognize the skill (or lack of it) with which a writer or speaker was presenting his case. Indeed, so fundamental is the idea of rhetoric to communication in general that even what we would call 'body-language' is classed within it. Cornelius Agrippa, the sixteenth-century scientist, talks of dancing as a branch of rhetoric, and the handbooks for actors and speakers by John Bulwer, *Chironomia* and *Chirologia* (1624) (see above, p. 46), clearly imply this sort of understanding.

The nuts and bolts of rhetoric are, of course, the some 5,000 'figures', or linguistic or articulative patterns into which words could be put to achieve effectiveness. Many of these are explored and exemplified in the *Rhetorica ad Herennium*, a first-century work attributed to Cicero, frequently and very cheaply printed in the Renaissance. But the art is more than mere decoration; Cicero in the *De Inventione* recognized five rhetorical operations – 'invention' of the subject, its arrangement, its style, the techniques for memorizing it, and its delivery. It is a unified and coherent discipline, a practical social, political and psychological tool, which can train the mind, win over friends, persuade or ridicule enemies. Hardheaded Bacon says: 'It is eloquence that prevaileth in an active life' (*Advancement of Learning*, 1605). It was valued as a supreme art because it mobilized the will, moved affections, affected judgements, made men feel intensely, to will, to act, to understand and to believe. Logical argument appealed solely to the reason in a plain and unadorned style – Bacon saw it as appropriate *only* for a learned audience; but to orate and to persuade demanded a 'coloured' style that – Bacon again – 'can bring the imagination to second reason, and not to oppress it'. Cicero's old definition of rhetoric's aims – to teach, to please, to persuade – is still current, and in the Renaissance, that polemical age, there was increasing stress on persuasion.

As in the case of so much else, Aristotle is the source of basic doctrines of words and their use inherited by the Renaissance: just as the *Organon* taught logic, the literature of the closed fist, so the *Rhetoric* explored that of the open hand. It is very significant indeed that the only place in his entire philosophy where Aristotle discussed the emotions and psychology systematically is in this book, and thus the study of rhetoric became a study not just of words but also of human motivation. In England, the book was well known; it was lectured on to an admiring audience by John Rainold between 1572 and 1578 at Oxford and his notes for these lectures, bound in his copy, demonstrate that the Elizabethan study of rhetoric was a highly sophisticated endeavour, based on classical and contemporary theories as well as continental scholarship. Rainold stresses the utility of rhetoric in the professions of men. Indeed, the trend of rhetorical studies after the work of Ramus (see p. 202) is to concentrate on style and delivery (*elocutio*) for practical, persuasive and polemical reasons.

The very large number of books published on rhetoric in the sixteenth century compels us to recognize that knowledge of the art was very wide indeed. My own copy of the *Rhetorica ad Herennium*, printed by Cesano in Venice in 1550, seems to have been in the possession of the Landi family for at least a hundred years; there are notes in a neat *cancelleresca cursiva* hand, others in a 'secretary' hand, and what look like a child's notes in a seventeenth-century hand; and one of these readers – probably the last – found time to give the cut of Cicero a moustache. Even conservative guesses of the size of editions (where it is not certainly known), plus the fact that few copies would have merely single readers, indicate that we are talking about several million people, reaching well down the social scale, knowing what is what in rhetoric. In the seventeenth century, indeed, it was a major subject in nearly all schools.

Several conclusions follow. No one using words, be he pamphleteer, preacher or poet, is going to be ignorant of the art. Shakespeare, for example, had wide knowledge of it, and well over 200 recognized formal rhetorical figures of the 'grand' style have been counted in his work. Second, the audience of a work is going to be aware of the art with which the words are disposed, and may even be detached enough to watch the effect of those patterns on their own minds. Rhetoric as a consciously perceived dimension of action will affect the viewing of plays, especially when we remember the ubiquity of the idea of the world as a stage and vice versa (see Chapter 3.v). Third, the conscious discussion in the period of language and its relation to truth means that a natural correspondence of words in speech to things cannot be taken for granted, and therefore the danger will be apparent that effective persuasion may, after all, be misleading. Shakespeare makes this very clear in his use of two contrasting formal styles of rhetoric for Brutus and Antony in their speeches after Caesar's murder in *Julius Caesar*. And with special reference to drama, we have the complex situation of two audiences; the one watching the play in the manner I have just described, distanced from the action while moved by it and influenced by their assumptions about language and rhetoric (as well as all the ideas outlined much earlier, in Chapter 3), and the other *in* the play, representing as they must men in the real world, who are also being manipulated by and manipulating language. But this last idea raises the issue of the nature and status of poetic art.

### iii *Poetics*

Rhetoric does not explain poetry any more than manure, soil, sun and water explain a particularly fine turnip. Poetry inevitably uses figures of thought and speech, but that does not imply its identity with rhetoric. What poetry is, and what is the business of the poet, is a different discussion altogether.

The recovery of Aristotle's *Poetics* in the later fifteenth century, which I have already mentioned in Chapter 3.xi, altered the terms of the discussion of the art of poetry for ever. Of course there had been many men before that who had addressed themselves to the peculiar problem of an art which, while known to be not 'true', moved men with true emotions, and in the fourteenth century Dante, Boccaccio and Petrarch had made pretty august claims for the status of the poet as revealing divinely inspired truths that could not be expressed other than through fiction or *fabula*. But Aristotle taught critics to distinguish the generic differences between closely related arts that might all in the Middle Ages have come under the umbrella of poetry: oratory, history and scientific exposition were different from poetry because of a unique element in the latter. Poetics in the Renaissance is no longer a mere branch of rhetoric or grammar; it is thought of as a particularly gifted way of revealing truth through the linguistic form of stories and fictions, while oratory and learned argument work through statements and demonstrations.

Aristotle had said that all art is 'imitation': that is, it is not reality, but represents it. He stressed, too, the conscious control of the poet in selection and use of his materials. It is in these two concepts that the nub of the discussion lies. For in the Renaissance art is commonly seen not only as the presentation of a subject matter about reality, but also as an analysis of the form of reality. And as speech is only just below reason in the order of God's gifts, poetry must be the highest achievement of man in art. Some critics, like Scaliger, had limited the poet to the making of verse – that is, they had seen him primarily as a metrician – but this is not a general view. By the end of the sixteenth century we can discern the development of a distinctively English idea of the poet, which seems to owe something to the humanist Christoforo Landino: in Puttenham's *Art of English Poesie* (1588), in William Webbe's *Discourse of English Poetrie* (1586), in Ben Jonson's *Timber* (1640), the issue is raised of whether for the substance of his art the poet is in fact bound to the reality our senses perceive, or whether he can create by his own invention. One key Renaissance critical idea that keeps cropping up in the discussion of poetry is *fabula* – we might say 'fiction'. Thomas Wilson's *Arte of Rhetorique* (1553) defines poetry quite simply as 'fable', citing the authority of Plutarch and Erasmus. Sidney insists that poetry, unlike other verbal arts, proceeds by fictions, not by direct statement. Sir John Harington, Queen Elizabeth's witty godson, who read the manuscript of Sidney's *Defence of Poesie*, sees poetry and fiction as one and the same thing. In *Timber*, Ben Jonson puts it very strongly: 'Fable and Fiction is (as it were) the forme and Soule of any Poeticall worke, or *Poeme*.' All these ideas synthesize the Aristotelian principles of 'imitation' and 'plot', and when Francis Bacon calls poetry 'feigned' history the semantic contradiction would have been quite unremarked.

So if the poet is free to invent, what seriousness ought we to attach to the invention? In Sidney's *Defence of Poesie* we have the issue stated very clearly. He sees the status of the 'right poet' as something higher and more august than merely clever imitation, and pulls together the main critical strands from Antiquity in a brilliant synthesis:

These third [kind of poets] be they which most properly do imitate [here Aristotle is accommodated] to teach and delight [here Horace and Cicero, with especial emphasis on the moral dimension of poetry]: and to imitate, borrow nothing of what is, hath bin, or shall be, but range, only reined with learned discretion, into the divine consideration of what may be and should be [and here we have the Platonic idea of the poet glimpsing the world of the ultimate ideas from which all life derives].

(Defence of Poesie, ed. Feuillerat, Cambridge, 1962, p. 10)

Poetry, as Sidney says, is not an 'arte of lyes, but of true doctrine': these are high claims indeed. The evidence is that some pretty substantial people accepted them. These poetics are the very ones on which the art of Spenser is based; they are essentially identical to those of Milton; and in the speeches he gives to Theseus and Hippolyta in *A Midsummer Night's Dream*, V.i, Shakespeare is clearly airing the issue. In that play we have witnessed – but not in the manner the lovers have experienced – the happenings in the wood which Theseus thinks are merely false. With irony (for Theseus is himself a poet's creation), Shakespeare makes him link the lunatic, the lover and the poet together in the way their imaginations and preoccupations control their perception of reality; but even Theseus betrays, in the power of his language, that there is something much more serious in the nature of the poet:

> *The lunatic, the lover, and the poet*
> *Are of imagination all compact.*
> *One sees more devils than vast hell can hold.*
> *That is the madman. The lover, all as frantic,*
> *Sees Helen's beauty in a brow of Egypt.*
> *The poet's eye, in a fine frenzy rolling,*
> *Doth glance from heaven to earth, from earth to heaven.*
> *And as imagination bodies forth*
> *The forms of things unknown, the poet's pen*
> *Turns them to shapes, and gives to airy nothing*
> *A local habitation and a name.*
> *Such tricks hath strong imagination . . .*

But this is too easy: Hippolyta confronts him with the hard fact:

> *But all the story of the night told over,*
> *And all their minds transfigured so together,*
> *More witnesseth than fancy's images,*
> *And grows to something of great constancy . . .*

Something real and important has happened, in the play itself and as we watch it; and the only way of connecting to it is through the illusion or 'feigning' of art.

So the assumption of the high status of the poet and the mysterious nature of his art we can take as one Shakespeare shared; certainly the figure of Prospero suggests this. While the emphasis and understanding may be new, it is not without parallel. For rhetoric, and the poet as a practitioner of rhetoric, had been seen in the past as the very foundations of society. Cicero in the *De Inventione* had pointed out the poet's power to create, to give corporate identity to, a community – and we could argue that Virgil's *Aeneid* is premised on this very assumption. Cicero's idea is repeated by the twelfth-century Brunetto Latini in the *Livre dou Tresor*, in which he sees society as originating in the need to work co-operatively, and in the way the poet as orator gives expression to a sense of common purpose:

Politics is the highest science and the loftiest activity of men ... [society] achieves this in two ways: one is through work, the other through words. What it achieves through work occurs through all the occupations ... what man achieves through words occurs through his mouth and tongue.

Salutati, Petrarch's pupil, drew on ancient authorities to prove his contention of the close relationship between poetry and government. This general recognition in the Middle Ages and the Renaissance of the primary importance of rhetorical speech and the figurative discourse of the poet cannot but affect the writing, and the watching, of drama. The discourse within the plays is rhetorical – particularly crucial in political plays like the histories, where so much of the action is persuasion; but the play itself, giving to things unknown a local habitation and a name, is poetic. The dramatist has the highest possible status, and must be taken seriously.

But plays are emphatically not the reality they represent, rather something that interprets it to the real world we live in. They are thus a sort of extended metaphor. And metaphor, of all classes, is something in which the Renaissance took great interest.

Erasmus, writing to Peter Giles in 1514, praised metaphor as the most useful of all rhetorical figures; like Comenius over a century later, he saw it as peculiarly powerful in conveying to the mind what had not been, or could not be, directly experienced. Some of the Italian Humanists had gone even further, and elevated it to a method of knowing. Cristoforo Landino, in his inaugural lecture at the Studio Fiorentino in 1458, said that poetry and metaphor have priority over all the liberal or 'free' arts, for poetry encompasses them all. He sees the poet as what Horace called a *vates*, a prophet, whose 'fantastic' speech, metaphorical in essence, is ultimately 'truer' and superior to the merely rational. But there is metaphor and metaphor; in a universe imagined on neo-Platonic terms, where the ultimate nature of things is only dimly glimpsed by men seeing the shadows on the back wall of the cave, the really valuable metaphor is that which is 'reversible' – that is, the reader must be able to perceive it not as merely illustrating the concrete but as illustrated by the concrete. Meaning must be inherent in metaphor, not casual or arbitrary; it must be a dynamic cosmic correspondence, not a mere transference of meaning. For example, the metaphorical vision of himself that Richard II offers us in his fall will work not just by redefining our perception of what is happening to him; what is happening to him will illuminate the texture of the universe that is the ground of his metaphor. The poem or play, made by the poet, is in fact a little world. Like the world itself, it is an inclusive metaphor. Once we grasp this point, we can of course see that metaphor can be used 'straight', or not. For example, it can be set up and then tested, as *Troilus and Cressida* tests its centrally expressed metaphor in Ulysses' speech in I.iii, or as *Richard II* tests the validity of the correspondences between human and cosmic bodies that the play employs. Art tests the language of art, but then tests itself; and also the nature of the worlds it, and we, assume.

So the language that marks men as English, and what is created in it, is not a thing that can be dismissed simply as 'a newly vigorous mode of expression' which 'delights in its own resources'. There are a number of deeply philosophical issues just under the surface, and there is no doubt in my mind that Shakespeare was aware of them; indeed, he would have had to have been of an unparalleled stupidity and ignorance not to have been. A Dogberry, an Armado, a Pistol or a Falstaff are premised on a consciousness of language and on the nature of theatre as acted language. The very being of his major characters is defined by their language – a particularly celebrated case is Othello – and as their language changes, so we watch them facing their selves and their predicament. Dante believed that a poetic language that would genuinely define the issues of his countrymen and his time could be found only in that used where men daily confront who and what they are – that is, in work, in communication with others, and in the face of their own passion or suffering. The four Ricardian plays seem to be dealing with the finding of just such a high language, a mode of perception and communication 'true' for England – or, at least, a vision of England. That language sets the parameters for the political and moral debate.

iv *A confusion of tongues*

A play that opens with the figure of Rumour 'painted full of tongues' (*2 Henry IV*, Induction) must in some sense be 'about' those tongues. The centrality of word and speech to human community and to the understanding of the nature of things, which we have just glanced at, can hardly not be in question. Rumour is honourably descended from Virgil, *Aeneid* (IV.173–97), and from Chaucer's *House of Fame*; but those personifications in no way equal the dramatic force of this figure. For one thing, it opens the play; the braying command, 'Open your ears' precedes the emphatic main point that Rumour is a liar, 'stuffing the ears of men with false reports' before moving on to the essential exposition we expect.[6] For another, he taps visually, as a sort of *ne plus ultra* in the emblematic mode, the audience's conceptualization of the idea of hypocrisy, commonly depicted in emblem books as a detached tongue with wings. But Rumour's point reaches deeper; implicit in the speech is the problem of how we or anyone else can tell truth from falsehood when there is no independent proof one way or the other, If our ears are 'stuffed' – the imagined passivity of the ears suggests false reports cannot be avoided – we cannot hear truth. Is what our eyes have seen represented in *1 Henry IV* at Shrewsbury, or read in the history books, 'true'? In what sense?

This problem is peculiarly evident in *2 Henry IV*. It is not only that the political scenes are dominated by men, hypocritical or politic – and what is the difference? – using words to say what they don't mean: Northumberland's 'crafty sickness' is coloured by verbal messages, evasions, rationalizations; Prince John wins a bloodless victory by deliberately misleading his adversaries by false appearances and language set up to be *mis*construed. The passion of the Archbishop's case, convincing as it indubitably sounds, is ironically framed by the realization of its fundamental clash with his office – pointed, indeed, by Westmorland – and the fact that he has been pretty slow in arriving at this reaction if it was so self-evident. The 'comic' scenes, too, exploit the gap between statement and reality: Justice Shallow, prompted by Falstaff, is creating in language an illusion about the youth he has lost, and only the past tense keeps him in any sort of touch with the reality Falstaff sees – 'Old, old, Master Shallow.' The selectivity of memory, moreover, means that the illusion bears little relation to the Shallow Falstaff (how accurately?)

6. It is tempting to suggest that Shakespeare is playing with the Cretan paradox . . . 'I met a man from Crete who told me all Cretans are liars.' The play is, after all, not reality but a recreation of it through historical narrative.

remembered. Falstaff himself throughout the play works on the assumption, which we know to be false, that the mad England whose symbol he is will triumph. And when reality breaks in, not only of the political state of affairs but also of *what he is* (no longer 'they hate us *youth*' but 'How ill white hairs become a fool and jester'), he tries to escape the realization through weaving a final fiction that not even he, let alone Shallow (whose £1,000 is real enough), believes. As Rumour's last line has it, 'smooth comforts false [are] worse than true wrongs'. There is more than a glance at the perennial political nuisance of flattery, of using words to give people a version of reality they want to hear.

And yet behind all this confusion of language, where people speak but not to communicate, where the family is broken and members of the body politic cannot unite in common action, there is an England that is real and vital, where headlands have to be sown with red wheat, and where men actually live and grow old and die. For a moment Shakespeare seems to be offering us the notion that there is a world where men are what they seem, where men's names do reflect their inner nature – Wart, Mouldy and Bullcalf, Shallow and Silence and Pistol (with the bawdy pun on 'pizzle'). But this is only to take it back from us, for as the quarrels and disputes among the rebels make quite clear – where no two of them can even agree on the nature of their own situation, let alone the past – reality is more various than that. Moreover, since the fundamental convention of drama is that we accept it as providing a glimpse into a world of cause and effect like our own, it must, in the nature of things, be presumed that the physical appearance of Falstaff's 'food for powder' on stage is a mere incident in a continuum of their lives where their names do not express their totality. Doll Tearsheet was once, and maybe still could be, more than her name indicates, just as in Part 1 Francis the drawer must, *once* we accept the play's illusion, be more than a man who says little more than 'Anon, anon, sir'. This problematical unreliability of language, intended through deceit or hypocrisy or not, seems to me to be a major area of Shakespeare's interest.

But Rumour does not just open *2 Henry IV*; he is the hinge between that play and Part 1, and thus is in a central position in the whole balanced and mirroring structure. His symbolic figure invites our reconsideration of Part 1 and primes our watching of Part 2. He is the physical manifestation – not in any real sense 'in' the plays – of that public opinion which plays so important a role as ground for action and inference in both Parts. The issues he presents of deceit and the gap between words, signification and reality, 'smooth comfort', reach back into the dark abyss of time, back even to the fickleness of opinion glimpsed in *Richard II*. From the very first Boar's Head scene in Part 1 (I.ii), words and what they can mean have been forced on to our attention. Hal's soliloquy casts an ironic light over everything he subsequently says to Falstaff, and over Falstaff's reception of it, and on the reactions of other characters; yet there is no way Falstaff could ever realize the trap in which he is caught. Moreover, the striking feature of the dialogues between Falstaff and Hal is that they depend on two things: the creation and deliberate exploitation of a flight of fancy which is bodied forth into an illusory reality – as when Falstaff plays King Henry in Part 1, II.iv; and on the ambiguities of words exploited in pun, *double entendre*, and the self-conscious lie. The nature of pun is to exploit our understanding of possible but conflicting meaning or reference carried by certain homophones. It draws attention to the gap between what is and what might be, and the humour depends on the mixing of incongruous frames of reference. Few puns in Shakespeare are not, at bottom, highly serious. On the other hand the self-conscious lie, as when Falstaff is challenged about his behaviour during the robbery, amuses us because we are aware of the real nature of the events, of the plausibility of Falstaff's case if we did not, and because at the same time we are aware of Falstaff's awareness of his implausibility. But it is one level of discourse that is carrying all this.

Part 1, therefore, alerts us (at the very least) to the problems of description, interpretation and inference. Its first two political scenes are centred round the interpretation of reports of conduct. But as I have shown above, it also alerts us to the way concepts of abstract qualities determine the conduct of men. Take, for example, honour. Hotspur's Marlovian lines,

> ... *methinks it were an easy leap*
> *To pluck bright honour from the pale-faced moon,*
> *Or dive into the bottom of the deep,*
> *Where fathom-line could never touch the ground,*
> *And pluck up drownèd honour by the locks,*
> *So he that doth redeem her thence might wear*
> *Without corrival all her dignities*

(Part 1, I.iii.199–205)

do more than personify honour as a tangible (possessible?) feminine being. The moral and verbal idea is hypostatized into a fake reality, which takes over Hotspur's own perception of the world. The *woman* becomes more important than the concept. Moreover, the conceit allows him to create a story with himself as hero of the dramatic rescue: it is ultimately self-flattering, and any moral idea is, so to speak, completely submerged. I have already looked at the inadequacies Shakespeare demonstrates in Hotspur's conception of honour; the point here is that he – like the Dauphin might be said to do in *Henry V* – sees the abstract moral quality not as qualifying his own being, but as something extraneously 'real' and self-existent that can be proudly owned – ultimately a matter of public opinion and subject to Falstaff's 'detraction'. Hal, on the other hand, shows a proper balanced understanding of the abstract nature of honour as a moral imperative which exists in so far as it modifies his own being and conduct as a man (see above, p. 134). The ideal becomes real when predicated of a man's moral action. (Mowbray, *Richard II*, I.i.175ff., seems to approach this ideal.) But on the field of Shrewsbury, Falstaff, the archetypal old sweat, puts the other extreme: 'What is honour? A word. What is in that word honour? What is that honour? Air' (*1 Henry IV*, V.i.133–5). By implication Falstaff's catechism reduces all abstract ideals, all the moral values for which men live and die, to mere sound, signifying nothing: the very parameters of moral life are mere illusion, Bacon's Idols of the Market Place (see Appendix, p. 204). And the public opinion that awards the useless label of honour in the first place will not value its own creation for long: 'Detraction will not suffer it.' Yet note the irony; this is said by a man for whom the business of speech throughout the two plays is almost exclusively to lie.[7] Aware himself specifically of the power of language to give new names to things, he uses it to obscure reality, to mislead, to twist facts: 'A good wit will make use of anything; I will turn diseases to commodity' (*2 Henry IV*, I.ii.249–51). But against this 'smooth comfort', against the illusion of words that some of his characters create, Shakespeare sets the hard fact; events were not like that, life is not like that. Hotspur's or Falstaff's reading of reality may be self-consistent, may be syntactically and lexically coherent, but it is a vision which is ultimately solipsistic. The vision defines not so much the world as its holder, and these two visions are mutually exclusive. It is in Hal, whose discourse (uniquely in these plays) straddles the two worlds of Eastcheap and England, that Shakespeare is exploring a comprehensive perception. 'I know you all' (*1 Henry IV*, I.ii.193ff.) would seem to imply, as the plays progress, an

7. Nevertheless he tries to have it both ways. Concepts that do not suit him are mere 'air', but he relies on ideas about Hal's future conduct whose genesis is entirely in his own hopes. He who reduced all meaning to 'air' is hoist by his own petard.

understanding of inner nature that the Gardener of England must have.

The issue of the relation of understanding and speech to the world as it is is never far from these four plays. Later I shall look at the way Richard, initiator of this second fall explored by the four plays, mistakes words and speech for reality and action. But not only Richard is affected. As a simple practical problem for the man writing a play, the utterance Shakespeare gives his people is the only way their selfhood can be established and in which they can be related to each other and to us; they live in their reality unaware of us, but we are doubly aware – through our historical knowledge and our consciousness of watching a play – of what they cannot know. The Choruses of *Henry V* push this issue towards us: they all remind us of the reality of history, the distortion of it through report (or Rumour), and the inadequacy of the words and action that represent it on the stage. They demand that we contribute from our own individual sensibilities and experience to validate the illusion of the play in a non-verbal or supra-verbal way. Only *then* will the 'text' of the play acquire any shadow of what it represents. And even with the audience's imagination working at full stretch, the reality of events is as far away as ever: it is still a play, it is still '*conjecture* of a time' the dramatist and the audience are cooperatively creating. However powerful we may find *Henry V*, this device emphasizes that its very success implies its failure adequately to represent, to delineate, the world as it was. Yet the case is not hopeless. *Something* of value is being communicated, even if it is fuzzy round the edges. Shakespeare would not have written such topical and serious plays had he not believed he could affect the men who watched them to the better actual achievement of a just polity.

The problem he is addressing is basic. Language – the language Shakespeare and his audience shared – is the speech of fallen man, and therefore fundamentally flawed but not totally removed from truth. Something can be communicated, but its reception is problematical. Pistol is the central symbol of this. His noisy and furious verse, signifying little, is an image of the faulty reception and memory of the verbal discourse of other illusions in the theatre (for most of his tags are theatrical in origin) – a neat self-reference. It is also received with some awe by those who only hear noise and do not distinguish words, where the rhetoric of tone and gesture conveys more than the semantics. For those like Monsieur le Fer, whose separation through speaking another of the post-Babel languages allows him to do *only* this, a Pistol unknown from other contexts is indeed formidable. But those with a glimmering of sense and honesty begin to perceive the sham. The one who never does so is Pistol himself, whose attitudinizing discourse gets him into situations he cannot handle – for example when he is soundly beaten by Fluellen. (Fluellen, incidentally, is a man whose bookish discourse, clearly comic in some measure, is focused entirely on right action in real conduct.) The logic of Pistol's rhetorical level takes him willy-nilly into situations beyond his control, and his language prevents him knowing even what he is. And Pistol lives on, a continuing life of deceit, in Henry V's England.

Moreover, the central metaphor of the fallen Garden in these four plays naturally leads us on to seeing the different personal languages – even the different perceptions of reality that lie behind language – that Shakespeare's characters speak as the consequence of a second Babel, when the family of man is broken up and they are no longer of one language. The banished Mowbray (*Richard II*, I.iii.154ff.) sees the hardest part of his banishment as being unable to communicate in his native English – his sentence is 'speechless death'. But as we have seen, even Englishmen do not – intentionally or otherwise – always speak the same language.

In these plays – unusually for Shakespeare – some characters, of course, really do speak a different language, and the scenes where this happens must be taken very seriously. It is easy to contrast Mortimer and Glendower's daughter's failure to understand each other – Babel come again for him who would be king – with Henry V's charming penetration of the barrier of language with Katherine – the just king winning his legitimate second realm. In these two moments, indeed, we do see something important about the idea of kingship and the need for unity in a realm; we also see how meaning *can* transcend verbal discourse. But French is also used as early in the sequence as that terrible scene where a father calls for his son's execution (*Richard II*, V.iii). York exploits the opposite meanings of the English 'pardon' and French '*pardonne-moi*' – the tongues are *willingly* confused as the family is destroyed. Together with this symbol of disorder striking at the root of society is the notion of language being used to mean the opposite from what is expected. A much more light-hearted – but not less important – instance is the scene in *Henry V* (III.iv) between Katherine and Alice. (Shakespeare may well be glancing at contemporary controversies about the teaching of language – the natural sequence was often argued to be letters, syllables, words, sentences.) Katherine, long before a peace treaty, is learning the language of her 'natural' lord; what we have is a sort of 'naming of parts', giving her body its names in the language of her king.

Her innocence in this naming must remind us of that other innocence in Eden. But in the language itself lies a serpent. The chain of English/French puns that runs through this scene are almost without exception bawdy – not at all the sort of thing well-brought-up young princesses in romance are supposed to talk about to their ladies. Katherine professes shock – but repeats her lesson. She is accepting that the language she will speak in her most intimate relationship is provisional in its meaning on the associations of its hearer. Later, when Henry woos her in person (V.ii.98ff.), she elevates her perception into a general statement. First Henry deliberately misapplies her 'like me' to offer the nearest he can ever get to 'love-talking': 'An angel is like you, Kate, and you are like an angel.' The chiasmic structure of the line draws attention both to the vapidity of the simile and its inherent improbability; and the fact that it is a simile necessarily implies that Kate is not an angel. Kate's response could serve for an epigraph to the whole of Shakespeare's discussion of this issue: '*O bon Dieu! Les langues des hommes sont pleines de tromperies.*' The deceits of men's languages are indeed a good part of Shakespeare's subject.

## v *Metaphor in the Ricardian plays*

The four plays work in very different modes (see above, Chapter 6) which it is clear Shakespeare intended his audience to recognize and use as tools with which to interpret the spectacle on the stage – even if, as with *Henry V* (see Chapter 6.iii), the treatment is daringly innovative. But other, more fundamental, ways of approaching them are implicit in the very fact that they are poetic drama. Drama depends not only on the shared experience in the theatre, but also, as we have seen, on the expectations of the symbolic and generalizing nature of the representative action on the symbolic stage. The theatre and the world, as concepts, can each stand for the other (see above, Chapter 3.v). So behind the literal untruth of the play lies the expectation of a deeper truth revealed in and through it; the concepts of the poet's status we looked at a few pages back are obviously determinants in the audience's response too.

The plays cannot but be topical, as we have seen. But they also move beyond the topical to the generic. They offer an anatomy of the political body as it might be presumed or represented to exist in the past, in the present, and, possibly, in the future. They are thus in a very real sense metaphorical as I have described the term above (p. 182), offering, as it were, a lens through which to scrutinize reality, while the reality we live in values the world they offer us. Within their general metaphor, therefore, the detailed use of extended metaphor is of major importance, and is in particular usefully examined in *Richard II.*

How we focus the represented events is heavily affected by the language that surrounds them. (This is of course a general truism; I think it was Marghanita Laski who 'translated' the bland and reassuring advertisement, 'inexpensive gowns for the fuller mature figure' into its 'real' sense, 'Cheap and nasty dresses for fat old ladies'.) We have discussed at length in Chapter 7 the valuing perspective provided by the 'Georgic' imagery that runs through the whole cycle, and there is need for a brief return to that discussion. The ideas of gardens and growth (and husbandry) run through all four plays, and culminate in Burgundy's vision of a desolated France that may at last be properly husbanded. In *Richard II* the repeated use of the verbs to plant, pluck, crop, fall and wither, applied to kings, princes and members of the commonwealth, show how central is the idea of the natural world and its management – the task entrusted to Adam. But the other task entrusted to the first gardener was to know the nature of his subjects.

Particularly, the linking of Richard himself with plants is important: he is several times likened to the prince of flowers, a rose (as Hotspur, *1 Henry IV*, I.iii.173, reminds his father and uncle, who have planted mere wild briar in his place); he is withering when Isabel takes her leave of him (*Richard II*, V.i.8); he is a tree whose branches offered protection and support to the parasitic plants that now cause his fall of leaf (III.iv.50ff.). These images value all the labourers in this vineyard, providing a standard of judgement by which none of them escapes censure. Richard, as a plant in his own badly managed garden, is allowed by the image to be seen not only as guilty, subject to a higher power and a higher Gardener, but also as victim in a process he affects but does not control. Moreover, with the greatest economy this chain of growth and garden images running through all four plays constantly keeps in our minds the idea of time: a seed-time growing to a bitter reaping, a time of judgement under which all men stand, when the sins of the fathers are visited on the children. Even at the triumphant end of *Henry V* the final Chorus does not allow us to forget time: the equilibrium achieved is only momentary, and the primal curse works on. This connects clearly with the idea of the suffering the innocent inherit from their fathers' sin: as Exodus xx.5 puts it, when the honour that should be reserved to God is not paid, 'I the Lord thy God am a jealous God, visiting the iniquity of the fathers upon the children unto the third and fourth generation'. For with time in human affairs is implied the idea of birth and inheritance: another fundamental metaphoric pattern, especially in *Richard II* – though Hal's inheritance of his father's throne (and, as he perceives as king before Agincourt, the possibility of his guilt) is hardly a side issue in *1* and *2 Henry IV*. After all, the question is quite open: who shall, who *should*, inherit England's garden – a Hotspur? the Shallows and the Falstaffs taking their ease in Gloucestershire, or the Davys who do the work? But it is Richard's seizing of Bolingbroke's inheritance (like a fruit – II.i.153ff.) that sparks off the movement to crisis; and York sees the implications of that action (II.i.189ff.) striking at the root of all the laws on which settled society depends – just as Bolingbroke claims (II.iii.117–35). Images of birth, of inheritance, of time itself monstrously fruitful, physically pregnant with portents, are common. In II.ii.10 the queen, in a striking semantic anticipation of Richard's prophecy in III.iii.87ff., sees 'Some unborn sorrow ripe in fortune's womb' coming towards her, whose forefather is grief (l. 35), and whose delivery comes about when Green breaks his news (ll. 58–61). Edward's sons who inherit his royalty are perished like a tree lopped of its branches (I.ii.11ff.), destroyed by their own family (II.i.104–5). Richard, himself the sinner, is valued by the prophecy he himself makes to Northumberland of the children yet unborn who will suffer for their father's sins (III.iii.87–90). The point is that in a play whose narrative deals with the breaking of the family of England the metaphoric lines never allow us to forget the necessity of fruitful growth, the due season for men's actions and the burden of the past on the present. A play about history is built on the premise that 'then' and 'now' are significantly related in the same continuum, that what happened a long time ago matters now. The speech that men do use says more to us than men use it to say, because of our perspective, than they could ever know.

The metaphor that most deeply affects the way we view the issues, and especially the kings, of these plays is Shakespeare's deployment of the standard correspondence between the king of the planets and the kings of men. If we look at the heavens in their great dance we see an example of harmonious order, the very fabric of Creation itself. Linking a king to the sun was a cliché when Edward IV adopted the sun in splendour as his badge, and yet it had still enough life in it for Louis XIV to use it in all seriousness. But in these plays the correspondence quite clearly has a deep ambiguity, and more is in question than just the decorum of the image.

Before Richard's return from Ireland, Salisbury (II.iv.18ff.) sees his falling glory as a meteor – portending trouble – and significantly disjoins him from the sun to which his royalty corresponds: '*thy* sun sets weeping in the lowly west. . .' Implicit in this is the hint that the mystical identification between king and sun is not an automatic or invariable one. But Richard, returning in III.ii, speaking with a nervous grandiloquence he never later uses, deliberately and formally, using the royal 'we', identifies himself with the sun rising in the east and reddening (with shame) the faces of those who look at him (ll. 47ff.). The concept of himself he relies on is one in which there *is* an automatic mechanism of mutual support between the immutable hierarchy of Heaven and the hierarchy of the polity. But the confidence is immediately undercut by its very need to be stated; it may be true that anointed kings cannot be un-anointed, but they can be deposed. By the end of the scene he has accepted, in a final ironic sun image, that Bolingbroke has now won the day. At Flint Castle (III.iii) it is Bolingbroke who applies the image to him:

> *See, see, King Richard doth himself appear,*
> *As doth the blushing, discontented sun*
> *From out the fiery portal of the east*
> *When he perceives the envious clouds are bent*
> *To dim his glory and to stain the track*
> *Of his bright passage to the occident.*

(ll. 62–7)

The simile, of course, states un-identity. But nevertheless Bolingbroke is recognizing a royalty in Richard that cannot be fully removed, and his conceit is not only a clue to how Richard should be played but is also self-valuing: Bolingbroke is the cloud, is envious, storms will follow. And it goes further. Bolingbroke, however ultimately powerful, is not royal. This speech contains a truth that he begins to perceive only when he is king. But the audience already perceive it.

It is at this point that there is a massive leap in Richard's understanding. The next sun image (ll. 178–9) denies the identity with the sun he has so far claimed. He is now like the sun's son, who could not manage his father's job and caused havoc. Implicit in the image is the quite new perception that being successful as a king isn't automatic; it is a job that demands high skill. The penultimate stage in Richard's redefinition of himself through the exploration of metaphor and language is reached when, in IV.i.260, he transfers the king/sun, idea to Bolingbroke melting the snowman, the 'mockery king' that is himself. His face may have been 'like' the sun (l. 283), but it was only a 'brittle glory'. Subtextually his language suggests his winter giving way to Bolingbroke's spring. But we have already seen that Bolingbroke is no true sun. The metaphor thus conveys an irony of some complexity.

This discussion in *Richard II* does reach some sort of conclusion; but it is a conclusion that only the hindsight of history allows. Heads, like Bolingbroke's, that wear crowns do lie uneasy, for the universe, and man in it, are moral. There is a certain royalty of nature that Richard reaches when real kingship is denied him. But, of course, Shakespeare's discussion does not end with this play. It is carried forward to the image of the sun at its zenith used by Vernon of Hal (*1 Henry IV*, IV.i.102) – a striking anticipation of the dazzling and chastening effect that King Henry V will have on France (*Henry V*, I.ii.279–81; cf. IV, Chorus, 43). (Hotspur's reaction is interesting. The sun he thinks of is not at midsummer; Vernon's praise affects him as the fickle and unhealthy sun of March.) It is also noticeable that in the Henry IV plays the sun imagery is conspicuously muted. Henry IV, significantly, compares himself with a comet – a disturbance in nature rather than the pattern of order – and not the sun (Part I, III.ii.47); and implicitly cites 'sunlike majesty' as an attribute Richard ought to have possessed (l. 79). Only Hal uses it with any confidence, and yet even he does not claim an organic relationship, merely imitation:

> *Yet herein will I imitate the sun,*
> *Who doth permit the base contagious clouds*
> *To smother up his beauty from the world,*
> *That when he please again to be himself,*
> *Being wanted, he may be more wondered at*
> *By breaking through the foul and ugly mists*
> *Of vapours that did seem to strangle him.*

> (Part I, I.ii.195–201)

Especially noticeable is his use of Richard's semantics – 'base contagious clouds' – in a reversed way, as a conscious misleading of public opinion. Yet this conceit is, and has to be, entirely memorable and *defining* for the audience.

This sequence is far too important to be classified merely as 'Shakespeare's use of imagery'. It is comprehensive metaphor which opens up questions that are not – could not, in fact – be discussed in the narrative of the play. The inclusive metaphor lies behind the play, like some sort of Platonic idea, and is hinted at, brought to our memory, by the local and special uses of it. We cannot look at the sun directly, but by the sun's light we are able to see. For what is under discussion is the basis for the common correspondence of sun/king. Can this fundamental idea, the very existence of which implies a moral and physical model of the real universe, be seen to contain any truth that matters? Is there more in it than 'air', than the conventional signs of speech? Because of their linguistic treatment, the events we watch in these plays do not ask us to examine only the validity of our model of the universe which provides so much of the basis for an understanding of the world and the predicament of men. They also present the way in which words and images create and define our day-to-day world. The world of the play is a world of words; the characters – Richard and Henry V are the striking examples – grow to perceive their selfhood and their roles through the words by which they apprehend their situations; but as words can be – and we never know when – deceptive, what price their new knowledge?

This ambiguity lies at the root of Richard's last speech (V.v.1–66). His peculiar consciousness of himself, as an individual in a role, that has been his distinguishing mark throughout the play now reaches a much deeper level. Throughout, he has sought to alter the nature of the reality besetting him through the use of words drawing on the central cosmic metaphor of the human polity: at the beginning of the play he thinks his mere fiat will alter the nature of the threat posed to him by Bolingbroke and Mowbray's quarrel; later, his passivity before Bolingbroke's challenge is only understandable when we see that, for him, speech and thought constitute action. He has already seen what is happening to him as 'exemplary': in III.ii.155ff. he is forming his own experience into art, clearly implying that he too will become the subject of one of those 'stories of the death of kings', whose recital is appropriate to that moment of his realization of the fragility of rule; in V.i.40ff. he envisages his own story being told on winter nights – indeed, he gets on the lee side of pathetic towards the sentimental. But here in prison (the old image of the prison of the world) when all is lost, there is a new sinew in his reflections. The very opening directs our attention to the elaborate wit of the conceits that follow. The soliloquy, acting both as a map of Richard's mind and as choric comment on the rest of the play, systematically explores the parallel between the world he has lost, the prison he is in, and the imagination that creates a world. The solitude of this prison vitiates it as a precise metaphor for the world, so Richard conceives thoughts to populate it. But like his subjects, those thoughts are in conflict: he 'plays' in his own mind the man whose mind is properly, in his last extremity, on Heaven – and who finds that Scripture, the Word, is contradictory; he plays the ambitious man, desiring an impossible escape from the prison of situation and dying of pride when the grit of reality makes itself felt; he plays the patient sufferer, whose consolation is that others suffer too – and 'in this thought they find a kind of ease'. Finally, he reaches a desire for mere nonentity. The self-references are obvious, and none of the roles are particularly enviable or even honourable – they are also contradictory. But not one of them really gets to grips with who Richard is – he is still role-playing in the theatre of the world, still diverting his mind by conceits from facing what he is. The playing of the music, however, the reminder of a harmony past events have shredded, catalyses what his mind is moving towards; at last he knows himself:

> But for the concord of my state and time
> Had not an ear to hear my true time broke
> I wasted time, and now doth time waste me.

This is not merely the recognition, forced by the rhetorical thrust of the speech, that the king is after all a man as well as a living office. It is at this moment that his exploration of metaphor finally brings him to an acceptance of his moral nature. He recognizes at last that there is more to kingship than the empty bluff of such public lines as 'We were not born to sue, but to command' (I.i.196) – which, if he was playing his role properly, would not need to be said – and the easy reliance on an automatic order in the universe. The king is 'but a man', not a celestial front-man, and he is judged by his office. Yet it is the celestial harmony echoed in human music that has led him to this self-naming. The concept of order is not, in the end, invalidated, but Shakespeare makes it quite clear that it cannot be taken as read. Each king, each man, has to work out his own place in it, and his own salvation, with diligence.

## vi *A rhetoric of rule*

The king is but a man ... In contrast to Richard, isolated in his own mind even when in company, Henry V both in his play and in the Henry IV plays is constantly in some sort of speech-based *relationship* with other characters, fully aware of their otherness. And language is power: Adam ruled through the word, and rhetoric is the ground of human polity. The first scene of *Henry V* stresses that the king is master of the arts of language and discourse, and the play systematically demonstrates his use of the full range of rhetorical modes and registers. He can handle logic and argument convincingly, and even those he condemns admit his justice; he is so much master of the stirring oration that his speeches before Harfleur and Agincourt have become standard war-horses of anthologies of English poetry since the year dot; he is master, too, of the regal address in the full panoply of power, whether it be in Council, or addressing the besieged of Harfleur, or concluding treaties. We hear him at prayer – a special sort of rhetoric and language – and we see him playing the 'rough soldier's wooing' to perfection (which he could not do if he were not aware of the mode he was using). Though he never reaches the intense image-guided self-absorption of Richard, whose world is self-defined, his linguistic and rhetorical range is far more comprehensive. If we also take in the Henry IV plays, it is shown to subsume all the modes of discourse here – including fooling around with the verbal ambiguities that in Mistress Quickly or Pistol are unintentional.

The setting for his crucial soliloquy before Agincourt is extremely significant. Here is a king who takes the trouble to move among his people as a man among men, whom it is impossible in the darkness to distinguish as a king (calling himself 'Harry le Roy' when challenged by Pistol neatly reminds us of the way language and name control the perception of the object). He has learnt the lessons of Eastcheap as no other monarch in Shakespeare: accepting with good humour the insult of Pistol, smiling approvingly at Fluellen's 'care and valour', engaging in a real and reasoned exchange of views about the moral responsibility of kingship with the lowest of his army. Henry's speech, on all levels, actually communicates. The prose dialogue (reminding us, incidentally, of Prince Hal's necessary mastery of that medium too) recalls to us Henry's concern in the very first scene of the play that he could make claim to France with 'right and justice', and emphasizes the limits to the king's responsibility for his subjects. In the soliloquy (ll. 223ff.) the series of rhetorical questions, the enumeration of the external appearances of kingship closing in an aposiopesis, build up to the climactic recognition of the *loss* a man suffers when he is a king. His father's 'uneasy head' had envied the peasant too, but left matters there: Henry accepts kingship as a tough job – a huge responsibility that even at that moment is preventing him from sleep. He is the physical exemplification, in his appearance incognito and his sleeplessness, of the deepest insights of his speech. The soliloquy with its final prayer is a reminder that the public man we see everywhere else is but a man who has to know himself. Such self-knowledge, indeed, Shakespeare confirms elsewhere as essential: not only does Richard grow into it, but Lear's first fault was that 'he hath ever but slenderly known himself'. Both Lear and Richard realize the dual nature of their kingship only when their original lack of understanding has deprived them of it. But if Richard forgot, Henry V never needs to be told that the king has two bodies, the fallible and mortal man who feels cold and fear like any other, and the immortal kingship, the embodiment of law and majesty, the Vicar of God on earth. Richard's mistake was to act and speak – for him, where is the distinction? – as if the two were glibly coincident. But the king is but a man; so it is his moral nature as a man as well as his kingly office that is crucial to the well-being of the realm. Neither is enough on its own. The three English kings of the four plays are all caught and evaluated in this concept, and in a sense one could say that all four plays have a single generic hero: the king England needs.

The man who is king is the mortal representative of an immortal office in the vast hierarchy of Creation. In state he properly uses the royal plural to indicate that in his utterance the concerted will of the community expresses itself. The king's will, the foundation of law and justice – which is still part of our parliamentary and legal procedure today – can only be manifested through speech and rhetoric, just as the creating Word embodied the divine Will. The king is law embodied, and in his judgement the law itself speaks. But as *lex loquens* the king must be master of the speech of his people, and the rhetoric he uses is the ground of the community he serves. Where Henry V differs crucially from Richard and Henry IV is that his public role fits him properly, and his utterance in it properly subordinates his undeniable humanity to the exigencies of kingship. In Henry IV's public speeches – particularly the speech that opens Part 1 – the rhetoric is all a little too clichéd, too easy, too well rehearsed. The style suggests this man is consciously being a king, aware of his insecurity in the role. On the other hand, Richard before his fall was never free from a vitiating inability to read the real nature and implications of the question before him (*Richard II*, I.i) and an insensitivity to the fact that the law – of arms or of England – is more than a matter of the ruler's whim. The overblown rhetoric Shakespeare gives him at that point is not attractive; he sounds, and is, a tyrant.

Henry V, as the last Chorus reminds us, was not immortal, even if his office is. The interim he has won, with England united, lasts only a few short years before the balance is once more upset and bad counsellors and misgovernment destroy it. The tricksters and deceivers are not expunged from Henry's commonwealth, and his restoration and ordering of the garden, and consciousness of the law, are still subject to time.

There will be other rogues like Pistol who reduce language to the noise of half-remembered tags from the illusory figures of plays, who, for a time, it is impossible to distinguish from the true men – the trap Fluellen and Monsieur le Fer fell into. There will be other women like Mistress Quickly for whom every sentence is an assault course on language and sense, whose world is consequently chaos. There will be other conspirators speaking the English of Henry who glose with graceful speech like Scroop, Grey and Cambridge. The family will again be disunited, and they shall not again be all of one speech. While they were, the Lord wrought great things among them and Astraea returned to the earth.

# Appendix. Language and Meaning: a Summary of the Debate

Self-consciousness about English is common in this age, not only as a language that can in its resources challenge comparison with Latin and Greek, but also as a consciously chosen medium for expression. Shakespeare, man of his time that he was, shows every sign of such self-consciousness, as well as an awareness of the problems I shall outline below. But let us begin by looking at two passages which offer different understandings of the nature of language, whose dates bracket Shakespeare's active period neatly.

In *At a Vacation Exercise in the College* (1628), part Latin, part English, Milton plays with several ideas about language that he must have expected his (admittedly learned) audience to pick up and enjoy. English is complementary to Latin, not inferior, and he expresses his desire to use its full resources for 'some graver subject' (which was, of course, to be *Paradise Lost*). Then Milton makes Language itself appear, followed by his sons, the ten predicaments of Aristotle that Scaliger (see below, pp. 201f.) had demonstrated could be applied to language. Behind the puns and the involved Platonist joke lies a serious understanding and rejection of Scaligerian grammatical theory. For in the Invocation is the clearest possible indication that Milton sees knowledge and thought as not dependent on language. The conceit of clothing 'naked thoughts' before they are made public emphasizes the primacy of thought over language, and the context of this passage implies a view of the poet as passively but directly inspired by Deity.

Now take one of the poems in Sidney's *Arcadia* (1590). At the end of the Second Book, Lamon is given a poem in the hexameters that contemporary fashion admired as an attempt to raise English verse to the solidity and dignity of Latin poetry. It is, again fashionably, an 'echo poem' – that is, the last syllable of each line is repeated by the echo in the Arcadian wood. Now this in itself is significant; the repeated phoneme remains identical, but changes its meaning and acts as an ironic comment on its original. (Thus 'echo poems' implicitly play with the ambiguity of language.) But Sidney links the idea of Lamon's falling in love with the Fall itself (semantically they are in any case forced together), and links both with the deceptiveness of language and art:

> *Eie-sight made me to yeeld: but what first pearst to my eyes? Eyes.*
> *Eyes hurters? eyes hurte? but what from them to me falls? Falls.*
> *But when I first did fall, what brought most fall to my harte? Arte.*
> *Arte? what can be that arte, which thou doost meane by thy speach? Speach.*
> *What be the fruits of speaking arte, what growes by the wordes? Wordes.*

The deceiving art of speech, whose only fruit is words . . . Playful it may be, but the playing will not be recognized as playing if the ideas are not current. Sidney is disturbing; the *Arcadia* is a serious and profound examination of the values and ideals of a society in the process of defining itself politically and morally, yet its medium is words, which it shows to be dependent on the illusion of art. The saving idea is that the poet who makes that illusion is, *ex hypothesi*, outside it. But when Shakespeare makes Polonius ask Hamlet what he is reading, the reply is strictly accurate: 'Words, words, words.' The sign, at this moment, has ceased to signify.

The recognition that language was the ultimate defining human quality spans the whole period under discussion. Thomas Hobbes, one of the most radical English philosophers of the seventeenth century, was saying something with which Dante would have agreed when, in *Leviathan* (1651), he wrote that 'the first author of speech was God himself, that instructed Adam how to name such creatures as presented themselves to his sight', and when he saw speech as the 'most noble and profitable invention of all'. But with Hobbes the discussion moved on to ground neither Dante nor even Shakespeare would have found familiar; for now the assumption was that *all* current human languages were fundamentally flawed. Without a reform of language to eliminate the subjective and emotive colourings that it usually carried [1] – and which led each hearer and each speaker to respond to it in different and unquantifiable ways – no true mastery over the natural world, which was given to Adam by God in Eden, was possible. If the damage of Babel were to be repaired, a new language, universally comprehensible and universally learnable, had to be invented. So in England and abroad extraordinary

---

1. The rejection by many people in the seventeenth century of the 'dress' of language – rhetoric and form – in favour of 'things' is exemplified not only by Bishop Wilkins (see below), or by the Royal Society's preference (recorded in Thomas Sprat's *History of the Royal Society*, 1667) for a 'close, naked, natural way of speaking; positive expressions, clear senses; a natural easiness; bringing all things as near the Mathematical plainness, as they can: and preferring the language of Artizans, Countrymen and Merchants, before that, of Wits and Scholars'. Men of political clout and vision also are on the same track – for example, Cromwell: 'Our business is to speak things.'

systems of phonetics, of grammar, of teaching were devised; languages were constructed that bore no relation to any already existing. Men like Samuel Hartlib, Bishop Wilkins (in his *Essay towards a Philosophical Language*, 1668), and Cave Beck (*Universal Character*, 1657), sought a 'universall character to express things and notions', a 'character' or common writing sufficiently transferable that men of different nations 'might with the same ease both read and write it' (Wilkins, *Mercury*, 1694, XVIII.143–6; XIII.105–10). (This partly explains the vogue for systems of shorthand writing at this time.) Shakespeare's career exactly coincided with the period when the groundwork of this position was being laid.

During the sixteenth century the medieval intellectual inheritance came in for a great deal of serious and sustained criticism, particularly in grammar and rhetoric. There were attempts to reform the study of grammar and to describe accurately the nature of language as a phenomenon, none of which was more powerful than that of Julius Caesar Scaliger whose theories of drama we have glanced at above (Chapter 3.x). In *De Causis Linguae Latinae* (1540) he sets out, with great originality, to apply the Aristotelian method of analytical classification to language.[2] The *causa materialis* of language Scaliger defines as phonetics – the sound; the *causa formalis*, semantics or what it means; the *causa efficiens*, the speaker or word-maker; and the *causa finalis*, what is felt and intended to be felt. Like Aristotle, he sees words as representing concepts in the mind which in turn correspond to phenomena in the world of things, and he is in fact developing the medieval notion of the linguistic sign as having twin facets of form and meaning, significant and significate. But his insistence that grammar is not an art

2. Aristotle, and more especially his methods, lies at the heart of medieval science and philosophy. Now Aristotle's view of the world avoids the dualism inherent in Platonism between 'matter' and 'idea'; matter has the potentiality of assuming form, and form can express itself through matter. An object is the basic matter (*substantia*), with what gives it its particular form (*accidens*). There can be no existence independent of substance. (This is the basis, incidentally, for the grammatical distinction in the Middle Ages between 'substantive' and 'adjective'.) The basic tools of Aristotelian and Scholastic logic are, firstly, that any object can be described through the Categories – the five scholastic predicables of genus, species, difference, property and accident, plus the ten predicaments of substance, quantity, quality, relation, action, undergoing of action (*passio*), time when, place where, position and possession (*habitus*). Secondly, Aristotle's doctrine of the Four Causes: the *causa materialis* which is the underlying matter, the *causa formalis* which imposes form on it, the *causa efficiens*, the imposer of form (God, the artisan, the artist), and the *causa finalis* – the end for which the imposition has been made.

but a 'science of speaking derived from usage' (that is, that its principles are best discerned by careful observation and tabulation), whose object is the nature and mechanisms of the spoken rather than the written word, breaks through a mental and methodological barrier. It allows the study of language to be conducted on terms that are quite new. He also makes a significant separation between the logician whose business is with truth, and the grammarian whose concern is with the language in which that truth can be expressed. Truth can only be arrived at when there is an exact correspondence between speech and things, and therefore though words and names must reflect the nature of things they do not have a natural affinity with it. So, in sum, his theory rejects the Platonic doctrine of language, for he sees whatever meaning words might have acquired as accidental and customary. This position, stated in terms that any medieval philosopher could have used (but didn't), begins that long fashion for seeing language as a convention, not organically rooted in reality.

Scaliger's work was recognized as tackling problems that would not go away. In England at this period attempts were being made to refurbish Scholastic logic, but the Reformation also prompted a search for a method of scientific inquiry independent of Scholasticism and Catholic philosophy – for example in Sir T. Wilson's *Rule of Reason* (1551) and Everard Digby's *Theoria analytica* (1579). Decades before the much better known efforts of Francis Bacon, both attempt a new theory of knowledge; Digby, for instance, based his position on the neo-platonic theory of correspondence between the mind of man and world of nature which, as we have seen above (p. 19), is the foundation of *magia*. But Scaliger's position was very influential, and, it could be argued, was a major factor in the development of the thought of the real philosophical revolutionary, Peter Ramus.

Ramus (Pierre de la Ramée) distinguished himself early by defending, in the University of Paris, a thesis that 'all the opinions of Aristotle were wrong'. He was a radical in religion as well as scholarship; like many of his fellow Huguenots, he perished in the Massacre of St Bartholomew in 1572.[3] His *Dialectique* (1555) was a direct attack on the Aristotelian system as employed in Scholasticism. Like his admirer Bacon later, he blames Aristotelianism and its appeal to precedent and authority for much of the confusion of thought and knowledge, particularly about the

3. It is worth pointing out that in northern Europe, Humanism was increasingly allied to movements for the moral improvement of society, and came to be identified with Protestantism and religious reform; cf. Erasmus, *Praise of Folly* (1509).

world around us. He saw scientific and religious reform as inseparable. No return to the pure Word of God was possible without the recovery of the pristine texts, and no return to what nature really was (and thus a return, it was hoped, to nature) was possible without experiment and looking not at books but at things. The strong practical interest in his thought shows too in his insistence that rhetoric and education ought to reflect the needs of contemporary society, for the religious persuasion and controversy that gobbled so much energy at this period required a new plain rhetoric and a practical and effective logic that would present a case no opponent could answer. Ramus constantly insists on the treatment of all the arts as separate and capable of simplification to a few easily remembered rules. This is the background to his *Scholae in liberales artes* (1559) and *Grammatica* (1559), which had a vast influence, not least among the Puritans in England – in 1640 even the once Catholic Ben Jonson attempted to apply Ramist principles to English grammar. His influence is in considerable measure responsible for the accepted position by the end of the sixteenth century, where there is much less readiness to base thought about the universe on inherited material. Ramus's method of observation and analysis, in linguistic study as elsewhere, is fundamentally descriptive – 'how things are'; he sees the basis of what *can* be studied in language as resting in the details of its structure as a tool rather than in the human reason. Ultimately this is, like Falstaff, to see words as 'air' as agreed symbols, even fictions, and the consequences for our knowledge of ourselves and of things that matter to us deeply are, in the end, alarming.

Ramus's ideas were certainly known to Sir Philip Sidney and his circle, but it is Francis Bacon whom we now see to have been their most influential follower in England. It is in the work of people like Bacon, or Sir Humphrey Gilbert, that we ought to look for the intellectual origins of those groups that formed Gresham College (which became the Royal Society) after the Restoration. Bacon has a lot to say about language and words in *The Advancement of Learning* (1605); it is part of his challenge to the usefulness of Aristotelian and Scholastic learning – the title of the *Novum Organum* (1620) is an open challenge to the authority of what was regarded as Aristotle's most useful book, the *Organon*. The basis of his ideas is fundamentally Ramist and utilitarian, long before the latter word was invented. He sees the 'first distemper of learning' as being 'when men study words and not matter', when the mind works on itself, like a spider, producing only cobwebs of learning 'admirable indeed for the fineness of the thread but of no substance or profit'.

Scholastic philosophy and literary discourse submit the 'shows of things to the desires of the mind'; but the reasoned approach he recommends should 'buckle the mind to the nature of things'. He clearly sees language as conventional, and thinking as linguistic in nature. The content of thought, therefore, is affected by language. But language is full of confusions and imprecisions which must seriously qualify the validity of deduction and communication.

One of Bacon's most famous ideas is that of the idols that prevent men from seeing truth. The Idols of the Tribe are the fallacies inherent in human reason, those of the Cave are peculiar to the individual, and those of the Market Place derive from language and society. (Idols of the Market Place might include, for example, the assigning of words to non-existent things like fortune or chance – or honour – and then assuming their reality.) The Idols of the Theatre are those imposed by constructed systems of philosophy and religion, a 'stage-play world' (see Aphorisms XLIV and LXII of *Novum Organum*), the elegance and neatness and self-consistency of which makes them attractive and memorable without necessarily relating to reality. In Aphorism XLIII he sums up beautifully not only his own stance on words and language but the trend of the entire debate we have been examining:

> Words are imposed according to the apprehension of the vulgar. And therefore the ill and unfit choice of words wonderfully obstructs the understanding ... Words ... throw all into confusion, and lead men away into numberless empty controversies and idle fancies ...

If the damage of our first parents is to be repaired, as Bacon hoped, then a new language has to be created, and with it a new attitude to it and its use.[4]

This fundamental divorce in theory, in some quarters, between words and things can hardly leave poets, whose business is words, untouched. It is no accident that just when the uncertainty and speculation about language were reaching their height, poets came to rely more and more on extra-verbal, visual referents to their poetry (like emblems) and on the shapes and forms of their poems themselves as a control on the verbal meaning and its reception. Just when attempts were being made

---

4. It would be unfair to the profundity of Bacon's mind not to mention that he recognized a fundamental distinction between two types of truth: the truth that can be derived from our experience and perception is what we have been talking about above, but Bacon also recognizes a higher truth that may be directly revealed by God, which is not approachable by reason.

to represent in words the essence of nature, the most notable and notorious poetic endeavours were being made to capture, in visually related conceits and in the shapes of poems, the presence of ideas – for example, George Herbert's 'Altar', Crashaw's 'The Weeper', Quarles's 'Hieroglyphiques', or Donne's 'La Corona'. (There are other reasons for this development as well, of course.) Moreover, a re-examination of words necessarily entails a re-examination of the art of rhetoric and the theory of poetry. No serious poet can be ignorant or neutral about these.

# Further Reading

Primary sources are noted in full in the text, and are indexed.

A. Barton: 'Shakespeare and the Limits of Language', *Shakespeare Survey* 24 (Cambridge, 1971).

D. Bevington: *Shakespeare's Language of Gesture* (Harvard, 1984).

R. H. Blackburn: *Biblical Drama under the Tudors* (The Hague, 1971).

J. Briggs: *This Stage-Play World: English Literature and its Background, 1580–1625* (Oxford, 1983).

P. Burke: *The Renaissance Sense of the Past* (London, 1969).

L. B. Campbell: *Shakespeare's Histories* (London, 1947).

N. Coghill: *Shakespeare's Professional Skills* (Cambridge, 1964).

M. Cohen: *Sensible Words: Linguistic Practice in England 1640–1785* (Baltimore, 1977).

A. C. Dessen: *Elizabethan Drama and the Viewer's Eye* (Cambridge, 1977).

T. Fabini: *Shakespeare and the Emblem* (Szeged, 1984).

R. A. Foakes: *Illustrations of the English Stage, 1580–1642* (London, 1985).

R. Fraser: *The Language of Adam* (New York, 1977)

D. Frey: *The First Tetralogy: Shakespeare's Scrutiny of the Tudor Myth* (The Hague, 1976).

E. Grassi: *Rhetoric as Philosophy* (Pittsburgh, 1980).

A. Gurr: *The Shakespearean Stage, 1574–1642* (Cambridge, 1970).

A. Gurr: *Playgoing in Shakespeare's London* (Cambridge, 1987).

M. Hattaway: *Elizabethan Popular Theatre* (London, 1982).

J. Haynes: 'The Elizabethan Audience on Stage', in *The Theatrical Space: Themes in Drama* 9 (Cambridge, 1987).

S. K. Heninger, jun.: *Touches of Sweet Harmony: Pythagorean Cosmology and Renaissance Poetics* (Huntington Library, San Marino, Calif., 1974).

C. W. Hodges: *The Globe Restored* (London, 1968).

S. Homan: *Shakespeare's Theater of Presence: Language, Spectacle and the Audience* (London, 1987).

T. B. Jones and B. de B. Nicol: *Neo-Classical Dramatic Criticism, 1560–1770*, (Cambridge, 1976).

B. L. Joseph: *Elizabethan Acting* (Oxford, 1951).

B. L. Joseph: *Shakespeare's Eden* (London, 1971).

H. A. Kelly: *Divine Providence and the England of Shakespeare's Histories* (Cambridge, Mass., 1970).

L. C. Knights: *Shakespeare's Politics*, Annual Lecture of the British Academy (London, 1957).

M. M. Mahood: *Shakespeare's Wordplay* (Oxford, 1967).

R. Mandrou: *From Humanism to Science, 1480–1700* (Harmondsworth, 1978).

R. Ornstein: *A Kingdom for a Stage* (Cambridge, Mass., 1972).

C. A. Padley: *Grammatical Theory in Western Europe, 1500–1700* (Cambridge, 1976).

M. E. Prior: *The Dream of Power* (Evanston, Ill., 1973).

R. R. Reed: *Crime and God's Judgement in Shakespeare* (London, 1985).

I. Ribner: *The English History Play* (Princeton, N.J., 1965).

A. Righter: *The Idea of the Play* (London, 1962).

M. Rose: *Shakespearean Design* (Cambridge, Mass., 1972).

A. P. Rossiter: *Angel with Horns* (London, 1961).

P. Saccio: *Shakespeare's English Kings: History, Chronicle and Drama* (Oxford, 1977).

B. Salomon: 'Visual and Aural Signs in the Performed English Renaissance Play', *Renaissance Drama*, New Series V (Evanston, Illinois, 1972).

S. Schoenbaum and K. Muir: *A New Companion to Shakespeare Studies* (Cambridge, 1971).

I. Smith: *Shakespeare's Globe Playhouse: a Modern Reconstruction* (London, 1956).

J. L. Styan: *Shakespeare's Stagecraft* (Cambridge, 1967).

P. Thomson: *Shakespeare's Theatre* (London, 1983).

E. M. W. Tillyard: *The Elizabethan World Picture* (London, 1943).

E. M. W. Tillyard: *Shakespeare's English History Plays* (London, 1944).

H. E. Toliver: 'Falstaff, the Prince, and the History Play', *Shakespeare Quarterly* 16 (1965).

D. Traversi: *Shakespeare from 'Richard II' to 'Henry V'* (London, 1957).

B. Vickers (ed): *The Artistry of Shakespeare's Prose* (Cambridge, 1968).

B. Vickers (ed.): *Rhetoric Revalued* (New York, 1982).

S. Wells (ed.): *Shakespeare Survey* 38 (Cambridge, 1985).

S. Wells: *The Cambridge Companion to Shakespeare Studies* (Cambridge, 1987).

G. Wickham: *Shakespeare's Dramatic Heritage* (London, 1969).

G. Wickham: *Early English Stages, 1300–1660* (London, 1959–80).

M. H. Wikander: *The Play of Truth and State: Historical Drama from Shakespeare to Brecht* (Baltimore, 1986).

J. Winny: *The Player King* (Cambridge, 1968).

K. Wrightson: *English Society, 1580–1680* (London, 1982).

F. Yates: *Astraea* (London, 1970).

# Index

# Index

Borgia, Cesare, 22
*Bowge of Court* (Skelton, *c.*1498), 93
Boy (in *Henry V*), 138, 155
Bradshaw, John, 66
Brahe, Tycho, 19
Breughel, Pieter, 172
*Britannia's Pastorals* (Browne, 1613), 36
Browne, Sir Thomas, 103
Browne, William, 36
Buchelius, Arnoldus, 27, 29
bull-baiting, 26
Bullcalf (in *2 Henry IV*), 184
Bulwer, John, 46, 176
Burbage, James, 25, 26, 48
Burbage, Richard, 25
Burgundy (in *Henry V*), 164, 190
Burton, Robert, 46
Bushy (in *Richard II*), *see* counsellors; condemned to death, 116ff.

Caliban (in *The Tempest*), 40
Cambridge (in *Henry V*), 106, 153, 198
Camillo, Giulio, 30
Canossa, 59
Canterbury (in *Henry V*), 151ff.
Canterbury's image of the bees, 58, 102; speech, importance of his, 81
capacity of theatre, 26
Captain Gower (in *Henry V*), 162
Captain Jamy (in *Henry V*), 156
Captain Macmorris (in *Henry V*), 156, 160
Carlisle, 116, 123, 151; prophecy of, 93, 157
cartoons (political), using Shakespeare, 54
Castelvetro, Lodovico, 51–2
Castiglione, Baldassare, 61, 150
*catastasis*, 84
*catastrophe*, 85
Catherine, Queen (in *Henry VIII*), 101
Catiline, 66
*causa efficiens*, 201
*causa finalis*, 201
*causa formalis*, 201
*causa materialis*, 201
Causes, Four, 201
Cecil, William, Lord Burghley, 22, 75, 78
*Celestial Hierarchies*, 18
cellarage, 28, 33
censorship, 138
Chain of Being, 9ff., 12ff., 23
Chalcedon, Council of, 21
character, concepts of, 34, 41ff.
Charles I, 65, 93
Charles, King of France (in *Henry V*), 155ff., 161

Chaucer, Geoffrey, 14, 82, 183; attitude to pagan gods, 10
Chesterfield, Philip Dormer, Earl of, 43, 104
*chiasmus*, 124
*Chirologia* (Bulwer, 1624), 46, 176
*Chironomia* (Bulwer, 1624), 46, 176
chivalry, 132ff.
*Choice of Emblemes, A* (Whitney, 1586), 39
Chorus, use of, in *Henry V*, 149ff.; 187, 190, 197 and *passim*
chronicle plays, 92
Cicero, 174, 176, 179, 181; his views on poetry, 50, 51
*City of God* (St Augustine), 59f.
civil war, fear of, 77; civil wars in Rome, 107ff.; French war as, 156
*Civil Wars* (Daniel, 1595), 97
Clarence's dream, sources of, 68
Claudius (in *Hamlet*), 30, 41, 47, 77, 85
Coleridge, Samuel Taylor, 60
Colevile, Sir John (in *2 Henry IV*), 136
Combe, Thomas, 33
Comenius, Isaac, 181
Comes, Natalis, 83
'commodity', 67f.
Common Prayer, Book of, 149, 162
companies, theatre, 48f.
*Conference about the Next Succession, A* (Parsons, 1594), 69
*Confessio Amantis* (Gower), 60
Constable (in *Henry V*), 154ff., 160, 161
constellations, 13
*contentio*, 124
convention, 37ff., 41ff.
Copernicus, Nicolaus, *De Revolutionibus* (1543), 17f.
*Copie of a Leter wryten by a Master of Arte of Cambridge* (Parsons, 1584), 77
Cordelia (in *King Lear*), 4
*Coriolanus*, 132
Cornelius Agrippa, 176
correspondences, 14, 182f.
cosmic images, 117, 132, 191f.
counsellors, influence of, 77, 78, 84, 112, 131, 151, 153, 154, 167. *See also* faction; flattery
court scenes, 40, 149ff., 164
Cranmer's speech in *Henry VIII*, 63
Creation as act of speech, 172f.
Crécy, 151
Cretan paradox, 183
Cromwell, Oliver, 200
Cromwell, Thomas, 22
Crown, duty of, 44. *See also* 59ff.

# FOR THE BEST IN PAPERBACKS, LOOK FOR THE

In every corner of the world, on every subject under the sun, Penguin represents quality and variety – the very best in publishing today.

For complete information about books available from Penguin – including Puffins, Penguin Classics and Arkana – and how to order them, write to us at the appropriate address below. Please note that for copyright reasons the selection of books varies from country to country.

**In the United Kingdom:** Please write to *Dept E.P., Penguin Books Ltd, Harmondsworth, Middlesex, UB7 0DA.*

If you have any difficulty in obtaining a title, please send your order with the correct money, plus ten per cent for postage and packaging, to *PO Box No 11, West Drayton, Middlesex*

**In the United States:** Please write to *Dept BA, Penguin, 299 Murray Hill Parkway, East Rutherford, New Jersey 07073*

**In Canada:** Please write to *Penguin Books Canada Ltd, 2801 John Street, Markham, Ontario L3R 1B4*

**In Australia:** Please write to the *Marketing Department, Penguin Books Australia Ltd, P.O. Box 257, Ringwood, Victoria 3134*

**In New Zealand:** Please write to the *Marketing Department, Penguin Books (NZ) Ltd, Private Bag, Takapuna, Auckland 9*

**In India:** Please write to *Penguin Overseas Ltd, 706 Eros Apartments, 56 Nehru Place, New Delhi, 110019*

**In the Netherlands:** Please write to *Penguin Books Netherlands B.V., Postbus 195, NL–1380AD Weesp*

**In West Germany:** Please write to *Penguin Books Ltd, Friedrichstrasse 10–12, D–6000 Frankfurt/Main 1*

**In Spain:** Please write to *Longman Penguin España, Calle San Nicolas 15, E–28013 Madrid*

**In Italy:** Please write to *Penguin Italia s.r.l., Via Como 4, I-20096 Pioltello (Milano)*

**In France:** Please write to *Penguin Books Ltd, 39 Rue de Montmorency, F-75003 Paris*

**In Japan:** Please write to *Longman Penguin Japan Co Ltd, Yamaguchi Building, 2–12–9 Kanda Jimbocho, Chiyoda-Ku, Tokyo 101*

# FOR THE BEST IN PAPERBACKS, LOOK FOR THE

## PENGUIN CLASSICS

# FOR THE BEST IN PAPERBACKS, LOOK FOR THE

## PENGUIN CLASSICS

| | |
|---|---|
| Matthew Arnold | **Selected Prose** |
| Jane Austen | **Emma** |
| | **Lady Susan, The Watsons, Sanditon** |
| | **Mansfield Park** |
| | **Northanger Abbey** |
| | **Persuasion** |
| | **Pride and Prejudice** |
| | **Sense and Sensibility** |
| Anne Brontë | **Agnes Grey** |
| | **The Tenant of Wildfell Hall** |
| Charlotte Brontë | **Jane Eyre** |
| | **Shirley** |
| | **Villette** |
| Emily Brontë | **Wuthering Heights** |
| Samuel Butler | **Erewhon** |
| | **The Way of All Flesh** |
| Thomas Carlyle | **Selected Writings** |
| Wilkie Collins | **The Moonstone** |
| | **The Woman in White** |
| Charles Darwin | **The Origin of Species** |
| | **The Voyage of the Beagle** |
| Benjamin Disraeli | **Sybil** |
| George Eliot | **Adam Bede** |
| | **Daniel Deronda** |
| | **Felix Holt** |
| | **Middlemarch** |
| | **The Mill on the Floss** |
| | **Romola** |
| | **Scenes of Clerical Life** |
| | **Silas Marner** |
| Elizabeth Gaskell | **Cranford and Cousin Phillis** |
| | **The Life of Charlotte Brontë** |
| | **Mary Barton** |
| | **North and South** |
| | **Wives and Daughters** |

# FOR THE BEST IN PAPERBACKS, LOOK FOR THE 🐧

## PENGUIN BOOKS OF POETRY

American Verse
British Poetry Since 1945
Caribbean Verse in English
A Choice of Comic and Curious Verse
Contemporary American Poetry
Contemporary British Poetry
English Christian Verse
English Poetry 1918–60
English Romantic Verse
English Verse
First World War Poetry
Greek Verse
Irish Verse
Light Verse
Love Poetry
The Metaphysical Poets
Modern African Poetry
New Poetry
Poetry of the Thirties
Post-War Russian Poetry
Scottish Verse
Southern African Verse
Spanish Civil War Verse
Spanish Verse
Women Poets

# FOR THE BEST IN PAPERBACKS, LOOK FOR THE 🐧

## PENGUIN POETRY LIBRARY

**Arnold**   Selected by Kenneth Allott
**Blake**   Selected by W. H. Stevenson
**Browning**   Selected by Daniel Karlin
**Burns**   Selected by W. Beattie and H. W. Meikle
**Byron**   Selected by A. S. B. Glover
**Coleridge**   Selected by Kathleen Raine
**Donne**   Selected by John Hayward
**Dryden**   Selected by Douglas Grant
**Hardy**   Selected by David Wright
**Herbert**   Selected by W. H. Auden
**Keats**   Selected by John Barnard
**Kipling**   Selected by James Cochrane
**Lawrence**   Selected by Keith Sagar
**Milton**   Selected by Laurence D. Lerner
**Pope**   Selected by Douglas Grant
**Shelley**   Selected by Isabel Quigley
**Tennyson**   Selected by W. E. Williams
**Wordsworth**   Selected by W. E. Williams

# FOR THE BEST IN PAPERBACKS, LOOK FOR THE 🐧

## PENGUIN PASSNOTES

This comprehensive series, designed to help GCSE students, includes:

**SUBJECTS**
Biology
Chemistry
Economics
English Language
Geography
Human Biology
Mathematics
Nursing
Oral English
Physics

**SHAKESPEARE**
As You Like It
Henry IV Part I
Henry V
Julius Caesar
Macbeth
The Merchant of Venice
A Midsummer Night's Dream
Romeo and Juliet
Twelfth Night

**LITERATURE**
Across the Barricades
The Catcher in the Rye
Cider with Rosie
The Crucible
Death of a Salesman
Far From the Madding Crowd
Great Expectations
Gregory's Girl
I am the Cheese
I'm the King of the Castle
The Importance of Being Earnest
Jane Eyre
Joby
Journey's End
Kes
Lord of the Flies
A Man for All Seasons
The Mayor of Casterbridge
My Family and Other Animals
Oliver Twist
The Pardoner's Tale
Pride and Prejudice
The Prologue to the Canterbury
  Tales
Pygmalion
Roots
The Royal Hunt of the Sun
Silas Marner
A Taste of Honey
To Kill a Mockingbird
Wuthering Heights
Z for Zachariah

# FOR THE BEST IN PAPERBACKS, LOOK FOR THE 🐧

## PENGUIN CRITICAL STUDIES

Described by *The Times Educational Supplement* as 'admirable' and 'superb', Penguin Critical Studies is a specially developed series of critical essays on the major works of literature for use by students in universities, colleges and schools.

*titles published or in preparation include:*

Absalom and Achitophel
The Alchemist
William Blake
The Changeling
Doctor Faustus
Dombey and Son
Don Juan and Other Poems
Emma *and* Persuasion
Great Expectations
The Great Gatsby
Gulliver's Travels
Heart of Darkness
The Poetry of Gerard
   Manley Hopkins
Jane Eyre
Joseph Andrews
Mansfield Park
Middlemarch
The Mill on the Floss
Milton's Shorter Poems
Nostromo

Paradise Lost
A Passage to India
The Poetry of Alexander Pope
Portrait of a Lady
A Portrait of the Artist as a
   Young Man
Return of the Native
Rosenkrantz and Guildenstern
   are Dead
Sons and Lovers
Tennyson
The Waste Land
Tess of the D'Urbervilles
The White Devil/
   The Duchess of Malfi
Wordsworth
Wuthering Heights
Yeats